Business Performance through Lean Six Sigma

Also Available from ASQ Quality Press:

Enterprise Process Mapping: Integrating Systems for Compliance and Business Excellence
Charles G. Cobb

Insights to Performance Excellence 2005: An Inside Look at the 2005 Baldrige Award Criteria
Mark L. Blazey

The Certified Six Sigma Black Belt Handbook
Donald W. Benbow and T.M. Kubiak

Lean Enterprise: A Synergistic Approach to Minimizing Waste
William A. Levinson and Raymond A. Rerick

Lean Strategies for Product Development: Achieving Breakthrough Performance in Bringing Products to Market
Clifford Fiore

Six Sigma Project Management: A Pocket Guide
Jeffrey N. Lowenthal

The Six Sigma Journey from Art to Science
Larry Walters

Lean-Six Sigma for Healthcare: A Senior Leader Guide to Improving Cost and Throughput
Chip Caldwell, Jim Brexler, and Tom Gillem

Stop Rising Healthcare Costs Using Toyota Lean Production Methods: 38 Steps for Improvement
Robert Chalice

To request a complimentary catalog of ASQ Quality Press publications, call 800-248-1946, or visit our Web site at http://qualitypress.asq.org.

Business Performance through Lean Six Sigma

Linking the Knowledge Worker,
the Twelve Pillars, and Baldrige

James T. Schutta

ASQ Quality Press
Milwaukee, Wisconsin

American Society for Quality, Quality Press, Milwaukee 53203
© 2006 by James T. Schutta
All rights reserved. Published 2006
Printed in the United States of America

12 11 10 09 08 07 06   5 4 3 2 1

Library of Congress Cataloging-in-Publication Data

Schutta, James T., 1944–
    Business performance through lean six sigma : linking the knowledge worker,
        the twelve pillars, and Baldrige / by James T. Schutta.
            p. cm.
    Includes bibliographical references and index.
    ISBN 0-87389-658-0 (alk. paper)
    1. Organizational effectiveness.   2. Six sigma (Quality control standard)
    3. Customer relations.   4. Production management—Quality control.
    5. Knowledge workers.   6. Organizational change.   I. Title.

    HD58.9.S3844 2005
    658.48'013—dc22   2005007651

ISBN-13: 978-0-87389-658-0
ISBN-10: 0-87389-658-0

Publisher: William A. Tony
Acquisitions Editor: Annemieke Hytinen
Project Editor: Paul O'Mara
Production Administrator: Randall Benson

ASQ Mission: The American Society for Quality advances individual, organizational, and
community excellence worldwide through learning, quality improvement, and knowledge
exchange.

Attention Bookstores, Wholesalers, Schools, and Corporations: ASQ Quality Press books,
videotapes, audiotapes, and software are available at quantity discounts with bulk
purchases for business, educational, or instructional use. For information, please contact
ASQ Quality Press at 800-248-1946, or write to ASQ Quality Press, P.O. Box 3005,
Milwaukee, WI 53201-3005.

To place orders or to request a free copy of the ASQ Quality Press Publications Catalog,
including ASQ membership information, call 800-248-1946. Visit our Web site at
www.asq.org or http://qualitypress.asq.org.

♾ Printed on acid-free paper

Quality Press
600 N. Plankinton Avenue
Milwaukee, Wisconsin 53203
Call toll free 800-248-1946
Fax 414-272-1734
www.asq.org
http://qualitypress.asq.org
http://standardsgroup.asq.org
E-mail: authors@asq.org

*I would like to dedicate this book to Mary Jane,
my wife, for the loving and caring support
as this book was being composed.*

Contents

Figures and Tables

Preface

Lean Six Sigma is helping vitalize many small and large organizations by paying attention to the customer's needs and providing processes with controlled amounts of variation to consistently meet and even exceed customer's needs. The Six Sigma process provides a focus on the process of doing the right things right the first time with little variation to the customer base selected for the market. The processes become more robust and will work within an environment that will vary over time. The variations will be internal to the organization and external as the customers experience the service or products. The challenge for your organization is to ensure that the process will sustain the environmental changes it will experience over time. This task is completed when the organization understands the process better and controls the inputs and the process variations that will affect the customer's needs the most. The lean concepts help the organization eliminate waste. The Malcolm Baldrige National Quality Award (MBNQA) Criteria provide the systematic approach to develop key business drivers for the organization. This book shows how all these concepts can support your business improvement efforts.

BENEFITS OF THE TWELVE PILLARS OF SIX SIGMA

We will cover the benefits of using the Six Sigma concepts, the Twelve Pillars, to support Lean Six Sigma and the problems that need to be overcome during the implementation process. The MBNQA Criteria are also tied to the business process to link the criteria to your Six Sigma and lean efforts. The author has experienced many total quality management (TQM), continuous improvement, MBNQA Criteria systems, and Lean Six Sigma initiatives. These initiatives helped to point out the need to develop the Twelve Pillars to support the implementation process for specific industries. Although some of the experiences are not discussed because of confidentiality, the issues, steps, and the reasons are generic to all businesses.

The intent of the following chapters is to develop the concepts of the Twelve Pillars, which support the Six Sigma improvement process, and tie this to the MBNQA, lean, and the implementation of the Six Sigma process. The executive management of every organization must read this book to establish the foundation for the MBNQA Criteria and Lean Six Sigma concepts to hold and become part of the operating style of the corporation. The tools discussed in this book are just as applicable to making management decisions based on data as they are for the Black Belts and knowledge workers of the process. It is necessary to tailor the approach to implementation to the present culture of the organization. This means that each organization must look at its internal culture, understand its business process, understand the Six Sigma DMAIC (define, measure, analyze, improve, and control) process and the DMADVIC (define, measure, analyze, design, verify, improve, and control) process, choose an implementation approach that will fit the cultural needs of the organization, and then schedule the implementation process. The soft side, or people side, of the implementation process is probably more important than the statistical knowledge for successful implementation. In the next few years we will see that many companies will be looking for the next new fad and may not have a process for continual improvement built into the culture and permanently in place to achieve growth at a rapid pace. The lack of the people side of the implementation of the Lean Six Sigma process may cause this to occur. Those organizations that have this process built within the culture will continue to improve and establish a hassle-free environment. Upon reading this book, you should be able to consider the necessary items for success and decide how you will approach a successful Lean Six Sigma level of performance with the implementation process developed around the concepts discussed.

COMMUNICATION WITHIN THE ORGANIZATION

Communication within the organization is critical to the support of the MBNQA, the projects, success of the Black Belts, and understanding of the Lean Six Sigma process. The organization has many types and ways of communicating the MBNQA Criteria and Lean Six Sigma process, which starts with awareness training, monthly newsletters, project reviews, Black Belt completion celebrations, and so forth. The management staff must maintain a communication process for a successful start-up. They also need to communicate the projects' status and success to the rest of the organization. The best form of project communication seems to be the storyboard approach for each step of the DMAIC process or the MBNQA Criteria as we complete the steps. The completion of the awareness training as early in the program as possible will help with the understanding of the MBNQA, variation, and the DMAIC process. This will help all the employees understand the process of improvements. Communications will help with the success of any program within the organization.

MALCOLM BALDRIGE NATIONAL QUALITY AWARD

The business process performance should follow the MBNQA Criteria to help link the Twelve Pillars and the Lean Six Sigma activities to the success of the business. The MBNQA Criteria will be discussed in more detail in Chapter 22. Note that the criteria should be in place before or at least during the implementation of the Lean Six Sigma efforts.

PROJECT SELECTION

The next important factor is the project selection process and the planning process for the specific projects selected. The organization needs objectives for each project and should have a good goal-setting process that the organization can use and that will support future projects, the vision, the mission, and the organization. The selection process should have some criteria to judge a project's merit before accepting it. This is especially helpful to maintaining the Six Sigma process.

THE TWELVE PILLARS AND THE KNOWLEDGE WORKER

The Twelve Pillars for the support of the Six Sigma process and the knowledge worker of the future will become integrated into the organization's culture. The first seven pillars are the foundation of the process. The foundation links to the MBNQA Criteria. The knowledge worker will use process knowledge, equipment knowledge, customer knowledge, and statistical thinking to create the processes that will lead to the organization's future success. The Twelve Pillars that support this knowledge worker and the Six Sigma process are: market and customer needs analysis; leadership with business process needs and organizational dashboard measures; strategic planning and project alignment; training and consulting; the DMAIC, DMADVIC, and lean processes; voice of the customer; quality function deployment; the process mapping and key process measurers; process capability; problem solving and improvement process; maintaining the changed process; and financial returns and recognition. If you do not support these pillars or the concept of the knowledge worker, you will not be as successful but you can still improve designs or improve processes. The frustration in meeting the goals set for your improvements is usually due to the lack of support for one of these pillars. Each of these items will be discussed in detail.

The knowledge worker training and use of the tools will be dependent on the projects selected, resources available, and management support provided.

CHAPTER OVERVIEW

The first chapter of *Business Performance through Lean Six Sigma* will introduce the concept of the knowledge worker of this century along with the MBNQA Criteria and Lean Six Sigma. The Six Sigma journey to bottom-line results will be described so the reader will be able to identify the fundamentals of the implementation process and possibly some new approaches. The second chapter will then cover the concepts of the Six Sigma process and the concepts that support implementation within your organization.

Chapter 3 will start the first of the pillars, which describes the need to obtain a knowledge base about the market that the organization will be or is presently addressing. The organization must consider the marketplace it is working in to understand the current and future opportunities and threats that will affect the business. Once this has been verified, the management team must make a commitment to focus on the customers of this market and develop the business needs to service this marketplace. Chapter 4 then covers how the management team must focus on the processes that are key to the organization and the customers. Most books that describe the Six Sigma process fail to address the real need to develop the strategic planning process from the market and customer information base. Without this, the projects selected will show improvements in areas that may not be required to satisfy the customer, thus market share or customer satisfaction will not be improved. Chapter 5 will cover the strategic planning process concepts to try to ensure that the organization is considering the minimum needs of the strategic planning process.

In Chapter 6, the training requirements for the organization will be covered to ensure success, and the items to consider when working with a consulting group during the implementation process will be addressed. In Chapter 6 and Chapter 7, the DMAIC, DMADVIC, and lean processes with Pillar Five will allow the reader to grasp the commitment that will be made to training, consulting, and the process to follow for successful implementation of Six Sigma and bottom-line financial results. These first seven pillars will cover the important management commitments that are required in order to be successful. The remaining pillars cover in more detail some of the tools or steps required for proper problem solving and process improvements.

In Chapter 8, the concept of the voice of the customer is introduced to obtain the customers' needs for the process that is being considered for improvement. The process of getting to know the customer and learning about their needs and expectations is discussed in some detail. These first eight chapters and six pillars address the foundation for the Six Sigma process and link to lean and the MBNQA Criteria. Without these steps, the rest of the process will eventually fail.

Chapter 9, then, takes the customer's needs and expectations and translates them to the processes and the requirements of the key processes that will be improved and controlled to ensure that the organization will satisfy the customer base. This leads to Chapter 10, which focuses on the measurement of the current process and future needs in order for the process to deliver the product or service to the customers.

Once we have determined what to measure and have the data to evaluate the organization's level of performance, we then need to establish process capability. This is covered in Chapter 11, which deals with the determination of short-term and long-term stability and the capability to deliver the product or service to the customer base. Chapters 12 and 13 cover the improvement of the process, using the problem-solving tools of the Six Sigma process. The book covers the tools lightly because they are addressed in many books already in distribution. The intent of this book is to ensure we recognize the tools and know when they should be used. The details concerning the use of each tool are left to the reader to review by making use of the sources, suggested reading materials, and the references provided by this book. Each chapter has a list of questions at the end intended to prod thoughts concerning concepts covered, and to help internalize some of the ideas introduced in the chapter.

Chapter 14 covers ideas for recognition and rewards that are sometimes controversial for the organization but must be considered in order to successfully implement the Lean Six Sigma process. Chapters 15 and 16 cover the paradigms of Six Sigma and the knowledge worker who will develop from this Six Sigma process. Chapter 17 provides an additional detailed listing of the tools of Six Sigma and when they may be used successfully. Chapters 18 and 19 cover the pitfalls and successes of Six Sigma noted from lessons learned during the implementation process. The results of Six Sigma are identified in Chapter 20, as well as how the Six Sigma implementation process should be evaluated to test for success. Chapter 21 covers lean, and Chapter 22 covers the integration of lean, Six Sigma, and MBNQA implementation. Chapter 23 will provide some conclusions. The first eight chapters cover the foundation needed for the Six Sigma process to be successful. The remaining chapters cover the tools used in the Six Sigma processes of DMAIC and DMADVIC and the reasons for success and failure in the process.

In conclusion, the process of developing the knowledge worker in this century requires the organization's business knowledge, knowledge of the MBNQA Criteria, and the tools of Lean Six Sigma process. These linkages will allow you to improve your business performance.

Acknowledgments

The following is an acknowledgement of places and people that may have affected the outcome of this book through my experiences. Many people have supported me throughout my career, and they especially helped me get to this point and led the way to the development of this book's content. My career started at the repair centers of Western Electric Company of AT&T. The electronic assembly and testing process had significant opportunities for failure and required some exact processes to minimize defect rates. After a few years I left for Johnson Service, now Johnson Controls, which became the training ground for a lot of my quality efforts. Two people who were a great influence in the quality arena were John Pozorski and Bill Chapmen, who were involved in the operations side and in the quality programs that affected design and manufacturing. Several general managers at Johnson, including Bill Rotham and Joe Lewis, helped me shape the quality programs that are still in place, although modified. Having developed new quality systems and set the stage for process and customer focus, I left after 23 years to pursue more continuous improvement efforts in the employment of Premark International. This move required building personal relationships to help with the cultural change that needs to take place in order to accept key processes improvements. This position allowed me to broaden my career and to understand what it takes to cause significant change within an organization. This company is now part of Illinois Tool Works. During my seven-year stay with Premark International, George Devin, the vice president of operations, helped significantly with the development of strategies to move the company forward in the design and manufacture of equipment for the food processing and preparation industry. This experience, along with my teaching at Milwaukee School of Engineering and the University of Dayton, helped me understand how diversity in employees and staff supports the transition of a business and its quality systems. At these three companies, I came to understand how to determine the key processes of a business and how the needs of those processes have to be determined and controlled in order to provide the required output.

While at Johnson Controls, I had the opportunity to work with Richard Schroeder from Motorola, using the Malcolm Baldrige National Quality Award Criteria while Motorola won the award in 1998 and after that while participating as an examiner for the award process. I was exposed to the Six Sigma approach during the late 1980s while working with Richard and the Baldrige people at NIST. As an examiner for the Baldrige process, I had met many executives at all levels and learned about the quality processes that helped make a difference for these executives. The training provides a lot of interaction with other organizations. During my 10 years with Baldrige, I developed a deep understanding of the criteria's benefits to the typical organization. The international standards for quality (ISO 9000) program and the associated training also exposed me to various quality systems and the approaches used to meet the requirements.

I have learned from Dr. Edwards Deming, Phil Crosby, and Dr. Stanley Marash in the consulting field; from Dr. Carolyn Fisher, chair of marketing at Loyola University of New Orleans; and from Dr. Thomas Davis from Milwaukee School of Engineering. At the University of Dayton I served on an industry advisory board to develop the curriculum needs for industry and to determine how the University of Dayton should meet those needs. These advisory boards helped the education process by providing the needs of industry as input to the curriculum development of the school. Many of these boards and councils helped me develop contacts in the industry and understand the diverse needs of the different industries. At the University of Dayton I worked with Carol Shaw and many corporate people, such as John Mariotti, then CEO of Huffy Bicycle Company, now president of The Enterprise Group and professor at the University of Tennessee. I experienced the type of leadership required to lead industry and education processes. These councils and advisory boards brought into focus the needs of diverse industries and how they performed. These ties to education and industry helped me broaden my understanding of the needs of business and the various industries.

In 1993 I moved into the consulting field by opening S&S Consulting Associates and starting a relationship with some key automotive company suppliers in the use of the Malcolm Baldrige National Quality Award Criteria. This eventually led to relationships with the electronic, lumber, machining, foundry, textile, hotel, and education fields. We developed a relationship with Dr. Stanley Marash, CEO of Stat-a-Matrix, and Dr. Carolyn Fisher, chair of marketing at Loyola University, New Orleans. These relationships still enhance my knowledge base on consulting and education to help with the ever-changing needs of society. Many of the organization relationships I developed allow me to grow together with them and address the needs of industry and education.

I give a special thank you to Ann Mathny for editing the first draft of this manuscript and Annemieke Hytinen, along with Paul O'Mara and Rachel Burbey at Quality Press, for all their help in publishing this book. I would like to thank the friends at Guilford Mills who have implemented quality and business systems to improve their automotive business. I appreciate the continued support and friendships with Dana Corporation; Motorola; 3M Corporation; Johnson Controls; University of Loyola, New Orleans; University of North Carolina, Wilmington; The Partridge Inn; Ramco Pumps; and Premark International.

Many people have helped us improve American industries, education, and services. S&S Consulting grew with the help of Angela Pagenstacher and Mary Jane Schutta, the CEO. Thank you all for helping me reach this point of my career and level of understanding of the business processes. The learning process was heightened by various industries and people I met along the way.

1

Introduction

This and the next generation of worker will require different tools and methods to support the manufacturing and service industries. The Six Sigma approach to process improvements and the process needs of the worker will change, which will require the development of process experts or subject-matter experts. The industry changes in technology, materials, and communications will allow for the development of the knowledge worker position. Dr. Peter Drucker introduced the knowledge worker concept in his book on management's new paradigms.[1] This book will cover the tie between the knowledge worker that Drucker is considering and the Six Sigma revolution that is upon us, the MBNQA Criteria and Lean Six Sigma. The basic implementation process of Six Sigma will be defined for the manufacturing and the service industries based on practices developed since 1984 from many continuous improvement implementations. These experiences of the author are used to develop the best approach for the Twelve Pillars of Lean Six Sigma to support the implementation process and development of the knowledge worker.

PARADIGM SHIFT

The paradigm of Six Sigma is the use of data and statistics to identify differences, distinctions, and commonality of processes using different methods, materials, people, machines, environments, and measurements. We will continuously improve the important processes of the business until we are the lowest cost producer of the highest quality products or processes and serve the customer better than before. We may not want to call this a paradigm shift, but I feel that it is a new level of running the business. It is a cultural change for most businesses and management levels of the organization. We are focusing on the customer, the key processes, and the steps to continuously deliver a product or service that will satisfy the current customers and, we hope, new customers.

THE SIX SIGMA JOURNEY

The new paradigm for management using the continuous improvement process of Six Sigma is the use of knowledge workers with the proper tool set to design, improve, and control the key processes of the service provided or product manufactured. The art of management is to provide a business process for the specific organizational structure, involving planning and strategic thinking. For the continuous improvement process to succeed, we must focus our efforts on processes and problem areas that will affect the organization's strategic plan and vision of the leadership. This means that a strategic plan should be integrated with the project selection process for the Six Sigma approach. The alignment of Six Sigma projects to the strategic plan will be discussed in detail in Chapters 4 and 5. It is my belief that the processes must start with the strategic reasons for success.

KNOWLEDGE WORKER

The knowledge worker concept we obtained from Dr. Drucker is what will become the future worker's capability to solve process variation problems. In the next few years we will be faced with the new cultural issues that the knowledge worker will encounter based on process know-how, knowledge of problem solving, and knowledge of how to handle the statistical data obtained from the process to solve problems and improve the capability of the process. This new culture will require that we focus on the customer's needs, the process measures, and the dedication to improving the process. We will succeed in the future only if the organization develops the knowledge worker of the future.

The knowledge worker of the future, an idea that was first expressed by Dr. Drucker, fits nicely with the Six Sigma concepts. The Six Sigma Black Belts are becoming these knowledge workers. Tying the knowledge worker with Six Sigma is developing some interesting points, which will be discussed in Chapter 16.

THE MALCOLM BALDRIGE NATIONAL QUALITY AWARD

The Malcolm Baldrige National Quality Award (MBNQA) Criteria were published in 1988 and have been improved every second year since then. The major intent of the award process is to recognize, reward, and share the ideas of companies that are performing well. The first winner was Motorola, the organization that implemented the Six Sigma process concepts in the early 1980s. The criteria are defined in detail in Chapter 22, where we address the connection between the criteria, lean, and Six Sigma. It is important that the organization consider the criteria as well as the implementation of the Lean Six Sigma approach. The criteria will help with the first six pillars discussed in this book and in turn provide the proper way to succeed at the Six Sigma process. The knowledge worker of tomorrow must understand the MBNQA Criteria and be able to implement it within the organization. The MBNQA will help drive the organization in the proper direction, and Lean Six Sigma will provide the tactical tools to achieve the results.

CUSTOMER NEEDS

In present and future process developments, we need to focus on the market, the end users, the customer's expectations, the regulatory environment, and the customer's specific needs. This focus will let the design team develop the process for the service or the product. This concept has been around for a long time, but organizations find it too time consuming to find the end customers and to develop the proper questions to ask the customer base to develop the needs and expectations list. The time required to analyze and prioritize the customers' needs also causes concern in many organizations.

If we do not spend this time up front, customers will be dissatisfied with new services and products until the organization gets the customers' feedback. Most organizations then develop a retrospective problem-solving process to redesign the processes and the products to meet the customers' needs. This is where waste occurs in organizations that develop services and products in a vacuum. In this book the concepts of the voice of the customer and the quality function deployment process (sometimes referred to as the house of quality) will be covered in detail in the retrospective DMAIC process and referenced in the design for Six Sigma (DMADVIC) process to help with the development and design processes for service and manufacturing organizations.

Most organizations define the areas of waste and develop processes to eliminate the waste and provide lean operations to service the customer. Lean and Six Sigma processes are used to create more efficient organizations that will cut internal operating costs, support costs, and sometimes sales costs. The intent of this book is to point out that the future will require us to develop new processes that are lean and cost justified before we release them to the field or for customer use. The knowledge worker of the future will be required to understand the customer base, the technology used to fill the customer's needs, and the materials the organization can use to improve processes and products to exceed the customer's expectations.

MANAGEMENT INVOLVEMENT

The management team of the organization must want change to occur. It must also assemble the dashboard metrics (key business indicators) that monitor performance of the organization and determine the status of the organization's processes, customer satisfaction level, and operational performance measures. Table 1.1 lists categories that an organization must use as dashboard metrics to know where it is performing and where the team

Table 1.1   Categories of dashboard indicators.

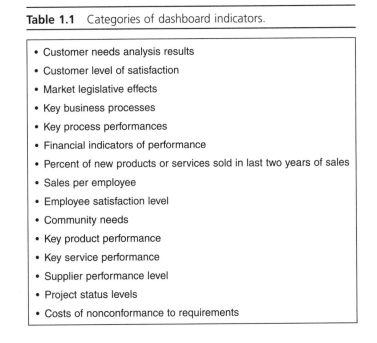

- Customer needs analysis results
- Customer level of satisfaction
- Market legislative effects
- Key business processes
- Key process performances
- Financial indicators of performance
- Percent of new products or services sold in last two years of sales
- Sales per employee
- Employee satisfaction level
- Community needs
- Key product performance
- Key service performance
- Supplier performance level
- Project status levels
- Costs of nonconformance to requirements

needs to pay attention to the future needs of customers and organizational stakeholders. The strategic plan should develop key dashboard measures that can be used to determine progress. The dashboard indicators are those that the management team uses to determine the performance of the business and to provide an idea of which areas of the business require attention. The management team usually makes use of five to ten indicators. These indicators must be important to the key processes and business drivers of the MBNQA Criteria. The indicators will ensure that the organization will improve its performance.

The list in Table 1.1 is in no way intended to include all the items that must be considered, but it is a start in recognizing the key areas for improved performance.

Some of the examples of continuous improvement used in this book are based on actual experiences at organizations, but the data and information for the examples have been changed to protect confidentiality where needed. After reading each section, relate the results and approach to your organization and determine how they may fit your needs. We are now ready for the journey through the Twelve Pillars of Six Sigma and for the knowledge worker of the future.

STRATEGIC PLANNING

There are many good books on strategic planning, so we will not spend a lot of time on this process. More specifics of strategic planning will be covered in Chapters 4 and 5. We do need to cover some key elements of strategic planning and how we will integrate them into the Six Sigma process. This chapter will outline the key elements necessary for us to begin the Six Sigma process. The guidelines for strategic planning follow:

1. Leadership involvement in the strategic planning process is the number one requirement. Sometimes this causes change to occur in the organization or requires a change in the organization's structure.[2]

2. Drivers of change in the organization:
   - We pay the price for failing to take advantage of an opportunity.
   - We will miss a key element in moving from/to "first class" or "leader."
   - We will miss the cornerstone to the overall business strategy.
   - We will miss a major competitive distinction we can gain.
   - We will miss a powerful tactical advantage to overcome a weakness.
   - We will miss something interesting and enjoyable.
   - We will miss our chance to grow the organization.

3. The strategic planning process requires:
   Planning
   - Prepare to plan.
   - Identified customer needs.
   - Environmental scan (internal and external) of the market, operations, and legislation.

- Basic values of the organization are developed and known.

- Does the current company vision and mission support all of these?

- Identify issues that support the mission.

Executing the plan

- Implement the plan, deploy the plan.

- Set goals and objectives.

- Action plans developed.

Checking

- Catch the ball at appropriate steps.

- Assess goals and objectives with those responsible for their implementation.

- Assess action plans with those responsible for their implementation.

- Coordinate changes with those affected by them.

- Implement controls to maintain the changes.

Acting

- Implement the plan and prepare for next cycle of the plan.

- Guide personnel through the changes required.

- Monitor the processes.

- Base decisions on the plan.

- Identify problem areas and potential improvements.

- Identify opportunities (new technology, new strategies).

4. Planning process documentation: Document progress, compare actual results with the plan, and consider updating it if it is out of phase with the problem or opportunity, and the difference is large enough to warrant adjustment.

5. Plan-do-check-act cycle: PDCA for strategic planning is not a cycle, but a Sigmoid curve.

SIX SIGMA PROJECT SELECTIONS

The development of a project selection process will be key to the success of the Lean Six Sigma program. Not only should there be a project selection process, but there should also be a selection process for selecting the Black Belts and Green Belts for training to ensure that we will be successful. After the implementation of the selection processes, we need to create a review process for the selected projects. These are the fundamentals of the building blocks covered in the first six pillars of Six Sigma. We will also need to prepare for the training, consulting, and the customer and market information needs for the first six pillars.

THE TWELVE PILLARS

The methods discussed in this book will cover the Twelve Pillars, which help with an implementation process that Six Sigma and lean needs in order to be the most effective, from the design to the development and implementation of the processes to produce services or products. Because the design of the processes and products comes first, this area will be addressed from a prospective approach and then the manufacturing or implementation process will be covered from a prospective point of view. This prospective approach is covered in Chapter 7, and the rest of the book will cover the retrospective approach to the Lean Six Sigma process in the DMAIC sequence format. The author feels that one of the weaknesses with the existing Six Sigma process is that it is started in the retrospective approach in most organizations and without the proper support, which will make the program die out in three to four years. The design for Six Sigma approach should be started before or shortly after the retrospective process is implemented. This approach will allow for continuous improvement in the development of new services and products.

This book has been written using 40 years of experiences, covering the tools mentioned in this book and the concepts of DMAIC and DMADVIC I used while employed by Western Electric, Johnson Controls, and Premark International, now part of Illinois Tool Works. I have overseen the implementation of total quality management, continuous improvement, lean, Six Sigma, and Lean Six Sigma programs in manufacturing and service organizations. Hopefully, you will find my advice and approaches helpful in your endeavor to improve upon the service and product performances provided to your customer base. I would like to suggest that there is no perfect or best approach for all industries or organizations. The pillars described in this book support the best approach for varied industries and organizations to take to obtain improvements of the key processes.

Table 1.2 Fundamentals to consider for Lean Six Sigma.

1. Top management involvement
2. Top management knowledge of the key processes
3. Strategic plan completed
4. Integration of project selection with the strategic plan
5. Project selection process developed
6. Green Belt and Black Belt selection process developed
7. Adequate training of the senior management team, champions of the process, Green Belts, Black Belts, and Master Black Belts
8. Adequate consulting to support the training and projects
9. Resources for the Black Belt team
10. Sufficient time to solve the complex problems (patience)
11. Problem definition and Six Sigma champions
12. Proper process measures and company dashboard measures
13. Financial results measures
14. Reward system and recognition process in place
15. Promotional path for Green Belts and Black Belts

The implementation approach should be tailored to the organization based on the organization's culture, values, and need to improve.

Before we begin the journey of the review and approach for implementation, please take off the blinders and accept that many approaches to improvement can be modified to your specific areas or organization if you relate the approach to your process and product lines. If you keep an open mind and consider these approaches in your environment, I predict that you will see that these Twelve Pillars can apply to service, not-for-profit, and personal endeavors as well as to the manufacturing sector.

Fundamentals of a good Six Sigma program begin with the need to improve the status quo. When the management team feels the need to improve key business processes, the process of Six Sigma will begin. The fundamentals listed in Table 1.2 are necessary for the Lean Six Sigma program to succeed.

Each of these fundamentals will be explained as we progress through the Twelve Pillars of Six Sigma process and analyze each approach. The following chapters will provide more detail as the implementation process is planned.

The Twelve Pillars are documented in Figure 1.1.

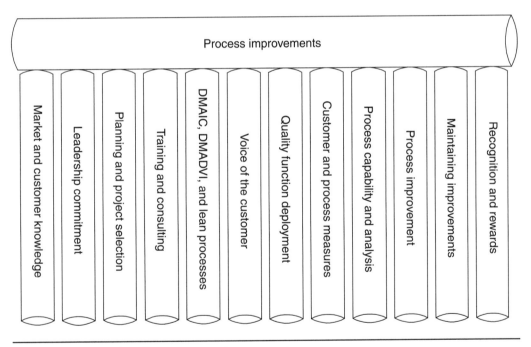

Figure 1.1 The Twelve Pillars to process improvement.

CHAPTER QUESTIONS

1. Why do we need to consider the strategic planning process to implement Six Sigma?

2. Can the Six Sigma process develop the knowledge worker of the future?

3. How does the plan-do-check-act process help in strategic planning?

4. Why must leadership be involved in the strategic plan and Six Sigma?

5. Do we benefit by linking projects selected for Six Sigma to the strategic plan?

6. What paradigm shifts are seen with the Six Sigma process?

7. What are the drivers of change within an organization?

8. Is the strategic planning process cyclic?

9. What are the Twelve Pillars of Six Sigma?

10. What is meant by a lean organization?

SUGGESTIONS FOR FURTHER READING

David, Fred R. *Strategic Management,* 6th ed. Upper Saddle River, NJ: Prentice Hall, 1997.

Drucker, Peter F. *Management Challenges for the 21st Century.* New York: HarperCollins, 1999.

Eckes, George. *The Six Sigma Revolution.* New York: John Wiley and Sons, 2001.

George, Michael L. *Lean Six Sigma.* New York: McGraw-Hill, 2002.

Harry, Mikel, and Richard Schroeder. *Six Sigma.* New York: Doubleday, 2000.

King, Bob. *Hoshin Planning: The Developmental Approach.* Methuen, MA: Goal/QPC, 1989.

Marash, Stanley A. *Fusion Management.* Fairfax, VA: QSU Publishing 2003.

Naumann, Earl, and Steve Hoisington. *Customer Centered Six Sigma.* Milwaukee, WI: ASQ Quality Press, 2001.

Spande, Peter S. *The Six Sigma Way.* New York: McGraw-Hill, 2000.

2

Basic Concepts Required for the Lean Six Sigma Implementation Process

The Twelve Pillars provide the concepts and process necessary for implementation of Lean Six Sigma, which closely follows the fundamentals list from Chapter 1. Each chapter provides more detail concerning the process focus needed for the successful implementation of Six Sigma. This process does not have to be followed in the exact sequence presented. The order may be tailored to your organization's business process. It is important to include all Twelve Pillars in the implementation process. If you miss one pillar, the process may not be as effective in reducing costs, improving efficiencies, and providing increased customer satisfaction. The outline of items to cover in the implementation plan for Lean Six Sigma will be explained briefly in this chapter so you can develop the foundation for its implementation. The concepts of each pillar will be explained in the remaining chapters. This chapter provides the main points that must be considered for the proper implementation process to take place.

Analysis of the market and customer in Pillar One. The process begins with the knowledge we obtain about the marketplace, the different customer needs, and the political climate that may affect the market. This information is obtained from the organization's listening posts, as defined in Chapters 3 and 5.

The management commitment of Pillar Two. The organization's senior management team must recognize a need to improve the present conditions or metrics. The entire management group should be considered a team and be able to work together toward the vision and goals of the organization. The team should have no hidden agendas and must agree to support the vision and mission.

The management group may have to embark on some type of team-building exercise to ensure they will be able to function as a team. Most management teams, if diverse, will have varying viewpoints or approaches to achieving the vision and mission. This is healthy but can be detrimental if the viewpoints and approaches lead to disruption. If this step is not completed, the projects and goals of the organization will be in jeopardy. We do not want a team that is totally in agreement, but we need a team that sees the mission and goals as needed to fulfill the organization's destiny or vision and to ensure that the stakeholders will be properly rewarded for their investments in the organization or processes.

Management training from Pillars Three, Four, and Five. Each senior management team member should attend at least the one-day overview of the Six Sigma process to become familiar with the protocol, tools, and support required for bringing in the results expected of the projects that will be assessed and reviewed for progress. Those executives that will become champions of the Six Sigma process (not only Six Sigma project champions) should be required to attend the three- to four-day champion training program to learn the process and tools to become leaders of the process. In fact, some executives have gone on to become certified Black Belts themselves because the statistical tools help them with making decisions daily.

Vision from Pillar Three. The organization should form a vision that the senior team will support. The vision will let us focus on the projects that will support the strategic plan. The vision represents what we want the organization to be in the near and distant future. It should project the view of the senior management team and be somewhat achievable within a reasonable time frame of 10 years or fewer.

Mission from Pillar Three. The mission of the organization should be established by a group larger than just the senior team and should be something that the personnel in the organization can relate to and help achieve. Each functional area may develop its own mission around the central mission of the management team.

Strategic plan development of Pillar Three. With the management's team vision and mission in place, we are now ready to review the strategic plan for the organization. As mentioned in Chapter 1, many books cover the establishment of a good strategic plan. The planning process is what is really important, because it allows us to focus on the issues at hand. This is why a strategic plan is a dynamic document that should be reviewed frequently. At least once a year we need to evaluate the possible changes that will affect the future of the organization. The planning process starts with the review of the last plan and the market analysis from Pillar One. Then we evaluate the strengths and weaknesses of the organization based on the environmental scans of the internal plants, organizational structure, and the outside changes that have occurred or will be occurring. In this evaluation we also review the competition and legislative issues that could have an impact.

The opportunities and threats for the organization are derived from the external scan of the competition, economy, customer's needs, market needs, and the regulatory environment of the federal, local, or foreign governments that may affect the product or services. We will become customer focused and move from product measures to customer's measures. This process will help develop a SWOT (strengths, weaknesses, opportunities, and threats) or TOWS (threats, opportunities, weaknesses, and strengths) analysis, which will determine the direction of the plan.

Project selection process of Pillars Two and Three. The projects a Black Belt will work on should satisfy the customer's needs, improve the processes that will satisfy the customer, reduce variation and costs, and increase quality and profitability. Project alignment must be reviewed to ensure that the project will fit the strategic plans, objectives, and goals in some direct way. The project selection process should be built from the TOWS analysis in the strategic planning process. All projects that we take on for Six Sigma should point to the key processes, the customer, and the customer's key metrics. They should also encompass the process and the key indicators or dashboard of the organization's operations.

Awareness training of Pillar Four. Six Sigma awareness training must be provided to the entire facility that is embarking on the Six Sigma process to ensure that the personnel will understand the meaning of the DMAIC and DMADVIC process and how they may be affected or be involved in the process. This awareness training can last from one to three hours, depending on the amount of support required from the operational personnel. The personnel should become familiar with the Twelve Pillars of Six Sigma, the tools used, and the project selection process to be used.

Communication plan of Pillars Two and Four. An extensive communication plan is required to ensure that the Lean Six Sigma process will continue to be supported and improved. The communication plans can take on several approaches. The most important point is to use existing communication processes such as internal newsletters, department and plant meetings, Black Belt ceremonies to recognize Black Belt status, successful project completions, project status reports, and storyboard presentations for the plant and office personnel. Sometimes career promotions can be used to support the Six Sigma process.

Champion selection process from Pillars Two and Four. The project champions need to go through a training program that will cover the Six Sigma philosophy, the Twelve Pillars, the meaning of variation within the process, voice of the customer, quality function deployment, measurement systems analysis, use of control charts, process capability, the strategic planning process, and then a quick overview of the advanced tools of hypothesis development, designed experiments, regression analysis, and other needs. The champion covers three levels of the organization. There usually is an executive champion, who understands the Six Sigma process and supports the implementation. The next level of champion is the Six Sigma coordinator, who helps in the Black Belt and Green Belt selection process and the project selection process. The last champion is the individual, who supports the specific project and provides direct help to the Black Belt for the project success.

Black Belt candidate selection of Pillars Two and Four. The Black Belts must be qualified to enter the training program under some established criteria. The first criterion is a willingness and desire to participate in the training and to change from his or her present job. Some companies ask an employee to make a two-year commitment as a Black Belt before going back to another position within the organization. The management team needs to commit to making the candidate available for the training and allowing adequate time to complete the project. Some of the other qualifications might be leadership skills, desire to learn, team player, analytical skills, and process experience within the organization, communication skills, and the capability to achieve within the organization.

Green Belt candidate selection of Pillar Two. This process is basically the same as the Black Belt selection process, with the exception of less need for leadership skills, analytical skills, and the capability to achieve within the organization.

Master Black Belt selection process of Pillar Two. The use of Master Black Belts will help maintain multiple projects when you have 10 or more Black Belts. Master Black Belts need to take two more weeks of Design for Six Sigma training (DFSS) and pass a test on the Design for Six Sigma process. The Black Belts are potential candidates to become Master Black Belts, providing they have the time and ability to complete five to six successful projects and can teach and coach Black Belts on the use of all the tools of the Six Sigma process.

Training requirements for Green Belts from Pillar Five. The Green Belts should have two weeks of Six Sigma training that will cover, at minimum, the curriculum listed in Chapter 6. This curriculum will ensure that they will be able to identify process variation and reduce it.

Black Belts require an additional two weeks of training from Pillar Five. The Black Belt training will provide advanced tools that are especially helpful in the measure, analysis, and improvement phases of the DMAIC process. The following list provides more advanced tools that are different for the Black Belts. A more detailed list appears in Chapter 6. Curriculum additions for Black Belts include:

- Completion of Green Belt training
- Advanced design of experiments
- Advanced hypothesis testing
- Response surface methods
- Evolutionary operational (EVOP) analysis
- Poka-Yoke or mistake-proofing
- Design for manufacturability
- Design tolerancing and reliability
- Synchronized process flow
- Advanced control chart techniques
- Change management skills
- Multiple regression analysis

Master Black Belt requirements of an additional two weeks of DFSS training from Pillar Five. The Master Black belt will require completion of additional projects, the ability to teach the Black Belt curriculum and the additional DFSS curriculum provided below. A more detailed list of DFSS curriculum appears in Chapter 6. Requirements for Master Black Belt qualification are:

- Successful completion of the Black Belt training
- Advanced quality function deployment
- Anticipatory failure determination
- Taguchi analysis
- DFSS

Supporting continual learning from Pillars Two and Four. The management team needs to support continued learning opportunities for existing Black Belts and new Black Belts. It must also support the need for the entire organization to be trained in the concepts of customer focus, process focus, and metrics focus. The need for reduction of variations present in all organizational business processes must be communicated to the employees. This should lead to thoughts of process capabilities and how the capabilities can be refined to deliver the needs of the internal and external customers. The process capability needs must be maintained for the organization to grow and maintain profitability.

Cultural change supported by Pillars Two and Three. To be successful in the Six Sigma process, we need to ensure that an organizational change can take place. It took several years for GE to do this. The initiation process started in 1990 but did not take hold until 1995. The preparation really started with small changes back in the 1980s and was finally implemented when Jack Welch started to show that the path to promotion was through Six Sigma training. He also tied a percentage of bonuses to Six Sigma implementations, and stock options were tied to Six Sigma performance. Black Belts can help this process by becoming change agents. Their training must include the ideas of negotiation, change management, and control of the change process.

Some of the changes that must take place are that the organization becomes focused on customers and process, thinks statistically, and recognizes that the system is a series of work activities tied together by the processes that deliver the service or products to the customers.

Project review in Pillars Two and Twelve. Once the projects are in place with Black Belts and Green Belts, we need to consider a project review process to verify progress and determine whether help is needed on the process or project. This approach should allow for the separate stages of DMAIC to be reviewed as the project progresses through each stage. We must keep in touch with the project and process owners at least once per month. A storyboard approach to the project presentation may be used as long as the different stages and needs of the specific project are covered. At each step we need to check on the financial setting, the progress made to develop root causes of the problem, and the revision to the charter. All projects should point to the key processes within the organization, the key customers, and the metrics of the customers for satisfaction as well as the organization's metrics for survival and improvement.

Most frequently used tools in Black Belt projects covered in Pillars Five, Six, Seven, Eight, Nine, Ten, and Eleven. The most frequently used tools will vary according to whether we are working on a manufacturing, service, or transactional process. The tools are identified for manufacturing use with "M," transactional with a "T," and the service side with an "S." The tools in Table 2.1 are the most frequently used in Lean Six Sigma by Black Belts.

Project gains review from Pillars Eleven and Twelve. The project gains need to be shared with the management team so the positives will be used in other parts of the organization with similar processes. This is like using the lessons learned from the project to show how the result may be applied to other parts of the organization. The process needs to be supported and brought to the management team by the Six Sigma coordinator within the organization. This must be accomplished when the results and the process changes are fresh in our minds and when the impact has been felt by the organization. One approach to the sharing of results would be to invite the appropriate management members to the project reviews during the DMAIC process.

Project recognition in Pillar Twelve. This part of the process allows the team members to celebrate their success and to be recognized by the management team. The way to keep converting employees to the process is to show the benefits of the Six Sigma programs by implementing recognition and reward programs to support the successes. A compensation

Table 2.1 Tools used in the Six Sigma approach to continuous improvement.

• Project selection process methods	M	S	T
• Project management skills	M	S	T
• Voice of the customer	M	S	T
• Quality function deployment	M	S	T
• Measurement systems analysis	M	S	T
• 5S process	M	S	T
• Value stream mapping	M	S	T
• Basic run charts and control charts	M	S	T
• Shewart charts	M	S	
• Process capability analysis	M	S	T
• Total productive maintenance	M	S	
• Single minute exchange of die (SMED)	M	S	
• Hypothesis testing	M	S	T
• Design of experiments	M	S	T
• Process mapping	M	S	T
• Synchronized process	M	S	
• Regression analysis	M	S	T
• Correlation analysis	M	S	T
• Design of processes	M	S	T
• Tolerance analysis	M		
• Cause and effect analysis	M	S	T
• The five whys	M	S	T
• Affinity diagrams	M	S	T
• Process mapping	M	S	T
• Poka-Yoke or mistake-proofing	M	S	T
• Value analysis	M	S	T
• Design for manufacturing	M		
• Design for assembly	M		
• ANOVA (Analysis of Variation)	M	S	T
• ANOM (Analysis of Means)	M	S	
• Chi-square analysis		S	T
• Understanding variation	M	S	T
• Reliability analysis	M		
• Durability analysis	M		

M = manufacturing; S = service side; T = transactional

plan that rewards participants who succeed will continue the process and certainly create a desire to be involved in the process of Six Sigma. Many organizations use differing means of recognizing the Six Sigma team, from a dinner celebration with the management team and family members to monetary rewards based on the savings generated by the project. When the organization publicly recognizes the successful project and the employees who participated, it acknowledges that investing in Six Sigma pays off in results to the organization and the employees who are involved. The following list shares some of the thoughts that have gone into the methods of recognition for the Black Belts and the team members:

- Award recognition by the management team during the final report
- Certification events for the Black Belts
- Promotions after the successful implementation of several projects
- Promotion after a two-year tour as a full-time Black Belt
- Additional challenging projects
- A level of status change within the organization

New product and process development using DFSS, covered in Pillars Two and Five. The major area of improvement not being taken advantage of by many organizations that embrace Lean Six Sigma is the development of new processes and products that are robust to the manufacturing variation and the customer's use variation. I am amazed at the lack of attention to the details of robust designs within many companies. The customers of the next generation will not tolerate product or service process that will not stand up to the swing in variation. Many companies address reliability, durability, testability, and environmental effects during the design, but most do not look at the overall system reliability and the reliability that the customer needs or is willing to pay for in the resulting product or service.

The design processes affect the usability of the product by the customer and the manufacturing ability to produce the product or deliver the service consistently to satisfy the customer. The Six Sigma tools and the advanced Design for Six Sigma tools need to be used by the design team to ensure we will meet the customer's ever-changing needs for our products and services.

Lean enterprise covered in Pillars Four, Five, and Eight. The organization should consider lean concept application as the first step to process improvements. The lean process will help reduce waste in the process from the step's complexity and non-value-added steps. This could be applied during the measure phase of the Six Sigma program, during the mapping activity before leaping into the analyze phase. Lean process steps usually follow the steps and curriculum for training as follows:

- Value stream mapping
- Lead time analysis
- Continuous flow
- 5S process
- Visual management
- SMED
- TPM (Total Productive Maintenance)
- Kanban
- Kaizen
- Error-proofing

Some best practices to consider. Different approaches have supported the successful implementation of continuous improvement for Six Sigma. Some of the best practices are:

- Link project selections to the strategic plan.
- Go for quick results at the beginning, which will pay for the investment within the first six months.
- Match projects and resources.
- Provide for recognition.
- Acknowledge that the soft issues (people skills) are at least as important than the statistical tools.
- Provide leadership commitment to the process and training on the process.
- Assemble a good, knowledgeable steering committee.
- Select a good consultant and consulting company to start and support the process implementation.
- Realize a return on investment of 10 to 15 percent.
- Validate financial returns through finance.
- Verify that improvements in one area do not harm other areas. This means that the teams need to know the key processes of the entire organization and how the process in the project interacts with and resolves all the system problem areas.

Evaluating the Six Sigma Process covered in Pillars Two, Twelve and Chapter 21. The Lean Six Sigma process success depends on the process review and the management follow-up on the results. The following list has some of the items to rate, or evaluate, in order to determine whether the Six Sigma process will sustain itself:

- Evaluate training effectiveness.
- Rate the project's ability to achieve 10 times improvement in performance.
- Rate the savings of at least $100,000 on each project.
- Evaluate the knowledge level of the Six Sigma process within the organization.
- Rate the Master Black Belt status in the organization and projects covered.
- Evaluate project implementation duration.
- Evaluate the continual training plan.
- Evaluate consulting effectiveness.
- Evaluate champions' performance.
- Rate the backlog list of Six Sigma projects.
- Evaluate effectiveness of the project selection process.
- Evaluate management support.
- Evaluate steering council support.
- Rate the dashboard indicator progress.
- Evaluate Black Belt drop-out rate.
- Evaluate use of Six Sigma in the design of products and services.

The process flow for the Six Sigma process and the linkage to the pillars are displayed in Figure 2.1. This flow will be discussed further in subsequent chapters. These concepts or steps do not have to be performed in the exact sequence presented, but all the concepts should be completed to achieve the results that will provide the reductions in process variation and in throughput to deliver the output to the customers. The results will then be tied to the financial improvement of the organization. The Twelve Pillars were discussed in Chapter 1. These pillars support the improvement process that provides increased customer satisfaction. The last pillar considers the financial results expected from the process. It would be difficult to eliminate any of these pillars. The first six pillars on the left side of the flow can be performed in a different sequence, but they must all be completed to ensure that the organization is focusing its Six Sigma efforts in the proper direction to support the needs of the customer, the regulatory environment, and the market. The planning process will ensure that the organization focuses on the competition, the organization's strengths and weaknesses, and the opportunities and threats from the market or the competition. Some of the basic concepts of strategic planning will be covered in Chapter 5.

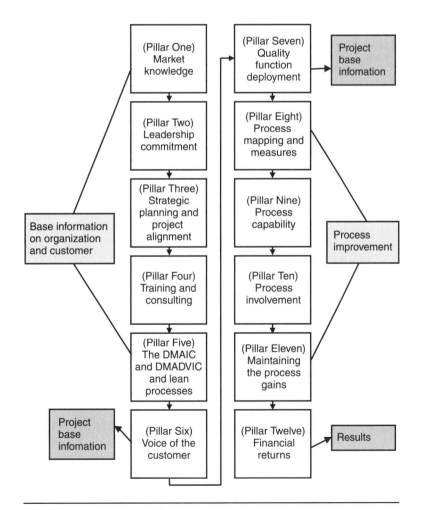

Figure 2.1 The Twelve Pillars to Six Sigma successes.

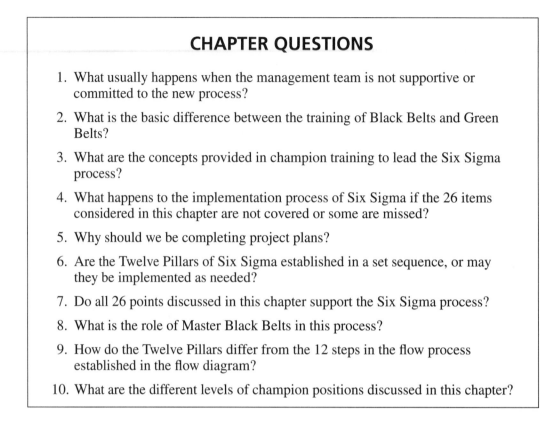

CHAPTER QUESTIONS

1. What usually happens when the management team is not supportive or committed to the new process?

2. What is the basic difference between the training of Black Belts and Green Belts?

3. What are the concepts provided in champion training to lead the Six Sigma process?

4. What happens to the implementation process of Six Sigma if the 26 items considered in this chapter are not covered or some are missed?

5. Why should we be completing project plans?

6. Are the Twelve Pillars of Six Sigma established in a set sequence, or may they be implemented as needed?

7. Do all 26 points discussed in this chapter support the Six Sigma process?

8. What is the role of Master Black Belts in this process?

9. How do the Twelve Pillars differ from the 12 steps in the flow process established in the flow diagram?

10. What are the different levels of champion positions discussed in this chapter?

SUGGESTIONS FOR FURTHER READING

Breyfogle, Forest W., III. *Implementing Six Sigma,* 2nd ed. Hoboken, NJ: John Wiley & Sons, 2003.

Collins, Jim. *Good to Great.* New York: McGraw-Hill, 2001.

Crosby, Philip B. *Quality Is Free.* New York: McGraw-Hill, 1979.

Eckes, George. *The Six Sigma Revolution.* New York: John Wiley & Sons, 2001.

George, Michael L. *Lean Six Sigma.* New York: McGraw-Hill, 2002.

Harry, Mikel, and Richard Schroeder. *Six Sigma.* New York: Doubleday, 2000.

Imai, Masaaki. *Gemba Kaizen.* New York: McGraw-Hill, 1997.

Imai, Masaaki. *Kaizen.* New York: McGraw-Hill, 1986.

Kaplan, Robert S. *Measures for Manufacturing Excellence.* Boston: HBS Press, 1990.

Marash, Stanley A. *Fusion Management.* Fairfax, VA: QSU Publishing, 2003.

Naumann, Earl, and Steve Hoisington. *Customer Centered Six Sigma.* Milwaukee, WI: ASQ Quality Press, 2001.

Spande, Peter S. *The Six Sigma Way.* New York: McGraw-Hill, 2000.

3

Pillar One: Market and Customer Knowledge

The Twelve Pillars for Six Sigma Support and Implementation

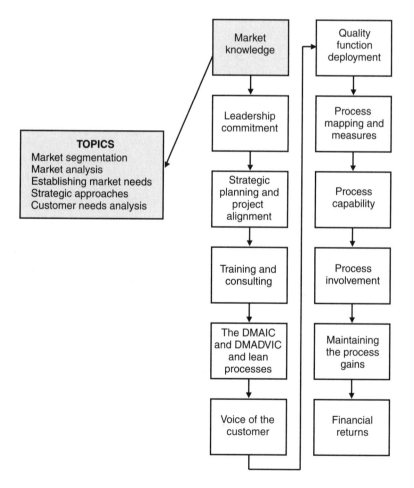

The organization needs to maintain a focus on the market and the customer to ensure that the changing environment, customer needs, and market needs will be addressed by the organization's future service or products. This will require good channels of communication with the front-line scouts of the organization. This communication will help with existing service and product performance issues as well as help drive new development. Most organizations have the marketing and sales departments focus on these issues. In the design for Six Sigma process, as a proactive activity and in the reactive activity of process improvements, the Black Belt and improvement team need to be involved in the transfer of knowledge concerning the customer and market needs to the organization's specifications required to meet those needs. A customer loyalty survey, for example, could be administered at the same time we are trying to obtain the true customer's needs and expectations. This is one of the best ways to learn the customer's needs and loyalty. Responses to loyalty questions may be described as secure, favorable, indifferent, or at risk. The business with the highest customer loyalty realizes some of the highest financial returns, as noted by Robert Ricci.[1]

MARKET SEGMENTATION

Sometimes we need to ensure that we have addressed the proper market segment of the organization's products and services. The following items need to be considered in the market analysis process in order to select the market and segmentation that we will be addressing and before we address the customer's needs based on regional or global markets:

- Determine which market the organization wants to be in and determine the market needs.

- Develop listening posts to gather knowledge about the differences, regionally and globally, in the marketplace.

- Determine whether there are any governmental or political effects on the chosen market. Evaluate the risk.

- Determine the economic and environmental conditions that will affect the marketplace.

- If the market is a niche market, determine the special needs that are being fulfilled.

MARKET ANALYSIS

The information from market analysis will become the input into the strategic plan, using a selection matrix or other planning processes. The organization will need to derive a market needs and expectation analysis from the listening posts or other sources of data and information input. If the organization develops this analysis from a broader marketplace approach, the processes that deliver the product and services will be evaluated against the organization's ability to deliver to those needs and expectations. Some of the approaches were discussed in Chapters 1 and 2; we will cover the major needs of the strategic plan here to relate the market analysis to these needs. Following are several strategic approaches we can take from the market analysis results (these strategic alternatives will be discussed in detail in Chapter 5):

- Market development involves introducing present products or services into new geographic areas.

- Product development is a strategy that seeks to increase sales by improving or modifying present products or services.

- Retrenchment occurs when an organization regroups through cost and asset reduction to reverse declining sales and profits.

- Adding related products or services is widely called concentric diversification.

- Adding unrelated products or services for present customers is called horizontal diversification.

- Adding unrelated products or services for new customers is called conglomerate diversification.

ESTABLISHING MARKET NEEDS

The organization must develop the market needs based on the previously discussed considerations and control the processes that deliver the product or service. Some organizations may start with customer's needs and analysis then develop market needs in response to the customer. This approach can consume a considerable amount of time at the start, but the market analysis can become broader and more complete. The details are developed by approaching the customers, and the market is decided by the organization.

In all aspects of the business unit, the market and customer effects based on needs, environment, laws and regulations, and technology advances must be considered when developing and updating the strategic plan. Figure 3.1 describes the strategic planning process to consider when the organization follows the market selection process to market position.[2]

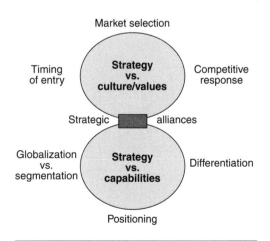

Figure 3.1 The strategic planning process.

The organization has several approaches available for setting the strategy for the future. The strategies listed in Tables 3.1 and 3.2 are discussed in detail in many marketing books[2] on strategic planning referenced at the end of this chapter. Concepts of Fred David and Michael Porter are discussed here.

The marketing information will lead to the strategy, which must also consider cultural issues within the organization and the strategies versus the organization's capabilities to deliver to the market.[2] Using the marketing information, the strategies are developed by some type of selection process such as the matrix analysis. The organization will then prioritize the importance of the issues to address. A generic matrix for selecting high-action items to investigate is depicted in Figure 3.2. This matrix will show how the organizational impact and the probability of the action occurring will be considered in determining which areas need to be addressed. The organization needs to fill in the areas of concern based on the market analysis.

The strategic needs analysis should consider the areas that may concern the organization:[2]

- The global market differences that may require different products or services. This will help determine differences that must be met by the processes developed. If we can develop one process to achieve all market and customer needs, the organization can become the economic producer or service provider to the market.

Table 3.1 Strategies to be considered.

Forward Integration	**Defensive**
• Growth	• Joint venture approach
• Concentration of product	• Turnaround (contraction and consolidation)
• Vertical Integration of manufacturing	• Captive company (to large customer)
• Backward product offering	• Retrenchment of market and product
Horizontal Integration	• Selling out/divestiture
• Intensive product review	• Bankruptcy
• Market penetration with existing product	• Liquidation
• Market development with new products	• Combination of the above
• Product development for the new markets	
Diversification	
• Concentric approach	
• Horizontal movement	
• Conglomerate reduction	
• Stability of product and market	

Table 3.2 Michael Porter's generic strategies.

Strategy	Measures	Outcome
Competitive strategy	Target	Advantage
Cost leadership	Broad	Lower cost
Differentiation	Broad	Differentiation
Cost focus	Narrow	Lower cost
Focused differentiation	Narrow	Differentiation

Probable impact on the corporation ⇓		
Probability of occurrence ⇓	High	Medium	Low
High	High priority	High priority	Medium priority
Medium	High priority	Medium priority	Low priority
Low	Medium priority	Low priority	Low priority

Figure 3.2 The importance matrix.

- The regional and regulatory differences in the country or countries where the product or service is delivered.

- The costs to produce or provide the service for the different markets needs.

- The potential environmental effects on the market, including product or service effects on the natural environment, customer alternatives that are less damaging to the environment, and the governmental laws and regulations that control the environmental effects.

- The value that the product or service provides to the customer.

STRATEGIC APPROACHES

The range of strategic approaches that the organization can take is broad, and this is why we need to understand the market and the customers in the context of the current and future position. This will ensure that when we select the Six Sigma projects they will be aligned with the organization's direction. The next approach is to consider the market conditions in the 21st century where we may need to drive the organization.[3]

The organization must operate on a theory of the business that has a set of assumptions about its business and its objectives and results. The four areas of considerations for strategy in the future, as developed by Drucker, are as follows.

1. Changes in the marketplace.

   - The collapsing birthrate in developed countries.

   - Shifts in the distribution of disposable income by location and age group.

   - Defined performance changes of products and service.

   - Global competitiveness increases in the market.

   - Growing incongruence between economic globalization and political splintering.

   - The aging population.

   - Growth by immigration will outweigh other population growth factors in developed countries.

   - Government instability in developed countries.

   - Retirement may mean two things: trend to early retirement and working part time, not full time.

- Knowledge workers will become a need in the near future.
- The productivity of workers, all workers, will have to increase rapidly in the near future.
- With fewer children, schools will be able to upgrade themselves.
- The consumer market will change with the older workers and spending habits will change.

2. Distribution of income will change.

- Shifts in disposable income and in population will occur.
- The four growth sectors during the 21st century will be:

—Government

—Healthcare

—Education

—Leisure

- Printed books will remain strong.
- Companies will have to be managed for flexibility and rapid change.
- Declining industries will need to reduce costs.
- The pension revolution will come.
- The manual worker will become less important.
- New measures and performance indicators will be needed.
- Low labor costs will not be a cost advantage.
- Governments will not be able to protect labor.

3. The incongruence between economic reality and political reality will grow.

- National boundaries will be an impediment and cost centers will change.
- The first rule will be not to do anything that does not satisfy economic reality.
- Future work in other countries will depend on partnerships and not on mergers or acquisitions.

4. The change leader, the Black Belt, of the future will need to consider that one cannot manage change. One can only be ahead of it. This requires:

- Policies for the future.
- Systematic methods to look for and to anticipate change.
- The right ways to introduce change.
- Policies to balance change and continuity.
- Change policies require the need to change what is being done as well as the new or different changes.

- There must be organized abandonment. The reaction must be "What do we do now?"

- We must be able to abandon old products.

- Organized improvement: This is kaizen and Six Sigma.

- Exploiting success: Focus on opportunities to achieve success.

- Creating change: Systematic innovation. Change is an opportunity.

CHANGE LEADER CONCEPTS FOR THE NEXT CENTURY

The change leaders will have two budgets: the budget to maintain the business, and the future budget. Change leaders are designing for change and yet must maintain continuity.

Change and continuity are poles rather than opposites. They must be balanced. This is one way to make partnership in change the basis of continuity relationships. All of the previous considerations must be aligned with the strategic planning process and the market analysis performed by the organization.

CUSTOMER NEEDS INFORMATION

Once the market strategy is determined, the organization must learn about the customer needs and expectations within the market. The organization can use several methods of obtaining the customer's needs. The purpose of determining customer requirements is to establish a comprehensive list of all the important quality characteristics that describe the service or product. This list will help us focus on customer's measures and will help us develop customer loyalty for the product or service, Some of the areas to search for customer needs and search tools are:

- Involve the people who provide the service or product to the customer in the change process.

- Investigate literature (such as scientific, professional, and trade journals) that discusses specific industries.

- Study the service or product.

The data from the customers will be obtained by:

- Surveys

- Individual interviews

- Focus groups

- Mystery shoppers

- Observe customers

- Field contact

- Employee feedback

- Sales relations

- Direct visits
- Complaints
- Warranty data
- Toll-free hotlines
- Publications

THE CUSTOMER DATA COLLECTION PROCESS

Next, we need to plan for the data collection process to define the voice of the customer needs and expectations. In the planning process we need to consider the following factors:

- What do we need to know?
- Inputs: Customer's wants and needs.
- Matrix format used for recording vital information.
- Permits analysis and determination of priority issues.
- Output: Key action issues to deliver customer's wants and needs.

The typical questions that need to be answered are:

- Analyzing and interpreting the data
  - —Who will edit the data?
  - —Will computer or hand tabulation be used?
  - —What analysis techniques will be used?
- Selecting sample and collecting the data
  - —Who will gather the data?
  - —How much supervision is needed?
  - —What operational procedures will be followed?
  - —What methods will be used to ensure the quality of the data collected?
  - —Who is the target population?
  - —Is a list of population elements available?
  - —Is a sample necessary?
  - —How large should the sample be?
  - —How should the sample be selected?
- Determining data collection method and forms
  - —What specific behaviors should the observers record?
  - —Should structured or unstructured items be used to collect the data?
  - —Should the purpose of the study be made known to the respondents?
  - —Should rating scales be used in the questionnaires?

- Determining research design

  —How much is already known?

  —What types of questions need to be answered?

  —What type of study will best address the research questions?

- Formulating problem

  —What is the purpose of the study . . . to solve a problem?

  —Is additional background information necessary?

  —What information is needed to make the decision?

  —How will the information be used?

  —Should research be conducted?

The types of questions to ask in the interview (and how to develop them) will depend on the knowledge we want to obtain. The following are some items to consider:

- Use simple words and questions.

- Avoid ambiguous words and questions.

- Avoid leading questions.

- Avoid implicit alternatives.

- Avoid implicit assumptions.

- Avoid generalizations and estimates.

Once the customer's market needs and expectations have been determined, we need to prioritize the needs so that we may determine the relative importance of each item. This can be accomplished in several ways. This subject has been covered in many other books, so we will leave it to the readers to determine whether they want to learn more about the process of obtaining the voice of the customer and providing enough information to be able to learn their varying needs and expectations. The author cowrote a book in 2003 on this subject, *Developing New Services* (ASQ).[4] In the book we talk about customer loyalty and correlating the attributes that come from the customers as drivers to increase customer loyalty. A performance map can be created to show where we may have performance gaps compared to the standard for the attributes that will affect customer loyalty. Becoming more focused on customer metrics is an ongoing journey that is accomplished only through lots of effort and research.

One point to consider while trying to learn about the customers is that we do not have to deliver to all the needs of customers if we do not want to sell our services to a certain market or customer segmentation. It is a good idea to establish a customer segmentation base before you obtain the voice of the customer information. This part of the process in the Six Sigma improvement plan is usually the hardest and most time consuming. Some organizations feel that they already know the customer needs and try to skip this step. Unless you are in a niche market, you probably do not know your customer base very well and are missing out on many opportunities to meet new markets or expand on the existing market base. This study needs to be completed before taking on a DFSS (DMADVIC) process and needs to be reviewed in all retrospective Six Sigma improvement efforts using DMAIC. The organizations that successfully implement Six Sigma assure themselves that they are concentrating on the proper customer needs before improving the process. Why should we improve a characteristic that is unimportant to the market and the customer base we are addressing?

FOCUSING ON THE CUSTOMER INFORMATION

The customer focus information helps us drive the projects to achieve higher customer satisfaction, lower processing costs, and increasing market share growth. The data we obtain from the voice of the customer has to be turned into information that will help the organization focus on the customer needs internally and drive the organization in all cross-functional departments to keep the same customer focus. This is accomplished by using tools such as the tree diagram or the house of quality, defined in the quality function deployment process. We will focus on the deployment process for quality function deployment in the following chapters. The MBNQA Criteria also cover the need to focus on the customer and the marketplace and sometimes offer guidance by suggesting items to review in this area. The Baldrige process is an excellent way to drive the business and, if used in conjunction with the Six Sigma improvement process, can lead to the right things to do. Categories 1 through 3 in the Baldrige Criteria will instruct the organization how to obtain the information about the market and customer base, establish the strategic plan, and allow the leadership to drive the organization toward the vision established by the management team. Category 1 considers management's leadership and involvement. Category 2 considers strategic planning. Category 3 covers customer and market analysis.

The knowledge we obtain about customers, the market, and the segmentation of the market will help the organization to exceed their expectations. The parameters that delight the customers will become apparent because customers are made aware of features that had not even been considered available.

Another way of obtaining customer needs and expectations is to observe the customers using the product or service. This can be accomplished at the site of use or in special rooms where the customers use, install, or experience the desired service. We do not even need the customers to provide oral feedback, because the observations speak for themselves. This is sometimes referred to as *contextual inquiry,* which will get to the root of the customer's needs. This is a structured, qualitative market research method consisting of observing and interviewing customers and potential customers. Small teams observe the customers interacting with the product or service provided. The teams note the likes, dislikes, and frustrations that arise from the customers' experience as well as any other interactions. Technical solutions are then developed to overcome the problems noted. Affinity diagrams are used to group the needs of the customer base at this point. Conjoint analysis explores the subjective customer's information through the approaches discussed throughout this chapter. At one point in the 1980s, we used the contextual inquiry method by building special rooms where the products and services were provided to the customer. Looking through two-way mirrors, we observed the customer's experience with the products, instructions, installations, and services. The customers could then share experiences with the designers and note the problems and successes.

Another approach to obtaining the customer knowledge base is to consider a customer internship program. A customer internship occurs when the customer is brought into the design process. We focus on customers who have a lot to offer us in revenue potential, can use our products in their environment, and are knowledgeable about the product or service we are about to offer. This may be considered similar to the focus group process, except it is usually limited to the key customers you need to attract to the marketplace and to your specific product or service.

CHAPTER QUESTIONS

1. What basic strategies can an organization take in developing a strategic plan?

2. Why do we need to review the customer and market needs to develop the organization's strategic plan?

3. What steps must be considered in understanding the marketplace the organization is considering?

4. What are some of the items to consider in the development of the strategic plan?

5. What are some windows of opportunity for the organization to consider in the strategic plan?

6. How does the strategic plan help organize the goals and objectives for the Six Sigma projects?

7. What is accomplished by obtaining market knowledge?

8. Who should be involved in making decisions on the marketplace selection?

9. What are Porter's generic strategies?

10. How do we obtain the customer's input from the marketplaces chosen?

SUGGESTIONS FOR FURTHER READING

Bossidy, Larry, and Ram Charan. *Execution.* New York: Crown Publishing, 2002.

David, Fred R. *Strategic Management,* 6th ed. Upper Saddle River, NJ: Prentice Hall, 1997.

Kotler, Philip. *Marketing Management Analysis, Planning and Control,* 5th ed. Englewood Cliffs, NJ: Prentice Hall, 1984.

Marash, Stanley A. *Fusion Management.* Fairfax, VA: QSU Publishing, 2003.

Schonberger, Richard J. *World Class Manufacturing.* New York: The Free Press, 1986.

Wheelen, Thomas L., and J. David Hunger. *Strategic Management and Business Policy,* 2nd ed. Reading, MA: Addison-Wesley Publishing, 1986.

4

Pillar Two: Leadership Commitment and Business Needs

The Twelve Pillars for Six Sigma Support and Implementation

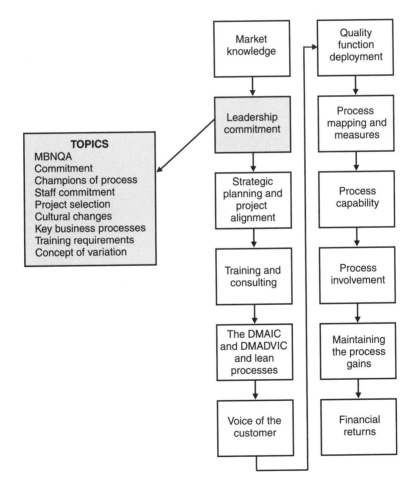

The gurus of quality and improvement processes are right. In order for the improvements to be maintained and established permanently, the top management team must see the need for change and support the change required. This commitment must include an understanding of the MBNQA Criteria and the Lean Six Sigma process through training, experience, and participation.

THE MALCOLM BALDRIGE NATIONAL QUALITY AWARD

The executive management team must let the MBNQA Criteria serve as the business process for the organization. The most critical items to consider in running the business are addressed within the seven criteria. The first three categories will help the leadership understand the market, the customers, and the outside constraints that may affect the business. The first three criteria cover the leadership process, the strategic planning process, and the identification of the key customers, market, and customer satisfaction levels. If the executive team adopts these criteria, some of the key items in the criteria will be linked to the first six pillars addressed in this book. This will make it easier for the organization to obtain the information about the market, the customers, and the strategic issues facing the organization. This then helps the Six Sigma coordinator with the project selection process. The business results should improve because the criteria and the tactical components of Lean Six Sigma are being linked together.

COMMITMENT

Commitment is knowledge and action based upon that knowledge. The management team does not obtain knowledge by delegating the planning, project selection, Black Belt and Green Belt selection, and project reviews and support. The management team must see a need to improve the business processes and take the time to strategically plan for what must be focused on and provide alignment with the project selected. The project activities must support the goals and objectives of the planning process outcomes. Then, to ensure that the projects will succeed, the management team must review each project's status and support the continuous improvement process with resources. The leadership of the organization transforms and motivates followers by making others aware of the importance of the Six Sigma process. Leadership can relate to the vision, and followers trust the leadership. The style of leadership, such as charisma and intellectual stimulation, is important for the process. The higher up in the organization the leader is, the more transformation leadership they need to apply.

Management exists for the sake of the organization's results. It has to start with the intended results from the vision and mission and has to organize the resources of the organization to attain these results. It is the organ to make the institution, whether business, church, university, hospital, or a battered women's shelter, capable of producing results outside of itself. The new assumption on which management, both as a discipline and as a practice, will increasingly have to base itself is that the scope of management is not shortsighted. It has to be operational. It has to embrace the entire process. It has to be focused on results and performance across the entire economic chain. Management's concern and management's responsibility are everything that affects the performance of the organization and its results, whether inside or outside, whether under the institution's control or totally beyond it.[1]

CHAMPIONS OF THE PROCESS

The executive champions of the process and projects must have training and knowledge of the DMAIC, DMADVIC processes, and lean, as well as the projects selected and the key processes within the project's scope. The executive champion training, lean, and the DMAIC and DMADVIC processes are discussed in later chapters, along with the project charter development that champions must focus on. The three to four days of training for the champion must focus on the development of the strategic plan, the organization's dashboard indicators for key processes, the development of the project selection process, and the project reviews. This training must cover the concepts of Lean Six Sigma and the tools that make it successful. The champion must know about the tools and their application to support the Black Belts in the project he or she is reviewing.

The executive staff and the quality council need to ensure that the organization's vision and mission have been stated and that they support the leadership in choosing the proper projects and the Black Belts who will help in the continuous improvement process.

There are three types or levels of champions in most organizations. The executive champion supports the Six Sigma improvement process and knows about the DMAIC and DMADVIC process used. This person has a high level of understanding of the key business drivers, the processes, and the concepts of customer and process focus. This person understands the concept of variation and how it will affect the key processes.

The next level of champion is the organization's Six Sigma coordinator, who understands the Six Sigma concepts, all statistical tools used, and the problem-solving process and who supports the Black Belts by overseeing their projects and helping with the project reports to management. Sometimes the executive champion will handle the Six Sigma coordinator roles, too. This depends on the size of the organization and the products or services offered.

The last level of champion is the project champion, who is usually the sponsor of the project and desires to see the project succeed. This person will select and directly support the Black Belt on the project and provide help obtaining the resources, preparing reports, and selecting Green Belts to help with the project. This person could be the process owner, plant manager, engineer, or executive staff member, depending on the project or the size of the organization.

The project selection criteria will include the assignment of a project champion. The typical span of control and reporting are:

- Executive champion

- Six Sigma coordinator (preferably a Black Belt)

- Master Black Belt

- Black Belt

- Green Belt

- Project workers of the process under consideration

It should be possible to complete the first project selection during the training and consulting period of approximately six months. The project must align with the strategic plan, support operation's key indicators, provide for customer improvements, and generate a savings of at least $100,000 to the bottom line. Projects should be selected very carefully.

The champion course will cover the training needed to support the Black Belt and Green Belt projects. The three- to four-day training process will provide enough information to support the continuous improvement that will take place when using the Six Sigma approach.

To keep this chapter short we will focus on the executive level, not the champion, commitment to the Six Sigma process. The champion for a specific project can come from the executive team and take the champion course. The organization will benefit from having some senior level staff members achieve the champion status in the process. This allows for more understanding and the recognition of the success of the process. The champion must be as committed to the Six Sigma process as the executive staff and follow the executive development process.

STAFF COMMITMENT

The executive staff commitments to the Six Sigma process should include attending at least an overview of the Six Sigma concepts and the DMAIC and DMADVIC process. This must include mastering an understanding of the problem-solving process used to improve the common causes of process variation, which affects the output of the process that the customers will experience. The course covers highlights of the analysis and improvement steps in the Six Sigma problem-solving process. A structured methodology must be followed to ensure that the source of the problem is properly identified and that the solution prevents the problem from returning. This is the step that most organizations miss or cover too quickly, allowing the problem to return later. The more the executive team knows about the process and the tools, the more they will be able to support the team's ability to improve the processes. A good executive training course of one to one-and-a-half days will help.

The next major commitment is for the executive team to develop a strategic planning process and keep it current. This plan should be shared with the employees, as needed, to show the direction the organization needs to take currently and in the near future. The plan should contain the following:

- The TOWS analysis from strategic planning process

- New development needs

- Process improvement needs

- Selection of business dashboard metrics

- Project selections to support the plan

- Selection of champions for the projects

- Project review process

- Black Belt selection for training and the project team selection

- Green Belt training and project needs

- Process measures required

The strategic planning process is discussed in more detail in the next chapter. These inputs into the strategic planning process will help the team recognize which improvement

Table 4.1 The typical musts and wants lists for Black Belt project selection.

Musts:	Wants:
• Improvement in plant and/or customer quality levels.	• Quicker response to customer's changing needs.
• Lower costs to the organization and/or prices to the customer.	• Development of new services.
	• Responsiveness to lead time variation.
• Improved delivery.	• Technical advantage realized.
• A champion who supports the project.	• Continual improvement is obtained.
• The process owner approves the project.	• Will utilize some skills of Green Belts.
• The resources are available to perform the project.	• Reduction in process variation.
• The project affects more than one department.	• Increase in sales.
• The project requires Black Belt skills to be applied.	• Increased customer satisfaction.
• The project will have a financial return of at least $100,000.	• Agility of the process increased.
• The results of the project will support the key business indicators.	

projects need attention and support if they are to drive the organization in the appropriate direction. Sometimes this planning process starts at the corporate level and is passed on through the division levels to ensure alignment within the entire corporation. I am not advocating the major planning departments as seen in the 1960s, but the process of developing the plan will help in understanding the needs for improvement.

PROJECT SELECTION

Once the management team has developed a strategic plan, the Black Belt project selection process must be developed and followed. The project selection should start with inputs from the management team and their direct reports. A decision matrix should be created to help with the selection process. This decision matrix needs to consider most of the items listed in Table 4.1. These items are "musts" for a project to be approved and "wants" that can be weighted by the management team.

The selection process must consider the design and improvements required for processes and products if it is to achieve the needs developed from the planning process and the output of the TOWS (threats, opportunities, weaknesses and strengths) matrix, discussed in Chapter 5. The management team will select the projects, using criteria such as those listed above and the availability of the resources to complete the projects. The executive team should construct its own lists of wants and needs for meeting the strategic planning outcome. The lists will vary based on location of facilities, products or services offered, level of competition, and economic conditions. Items to consider for Black Belt project selection process may include:

- Results will provide a competitive advantage.

- Serves a broader market.

- No new resources are required.

- The project can be completed in a reasonable length of time.

- Has an executive champion.

- Creates a market niche.

- Aligns with current direction.

CULTURAL CHANGE

The next major impact that the executive team will make for the Six Sigma implementation process is to help create a supportive culture. The organization's culture is based on the values and basic beliefs that exist within the building's walls. This subject cannot be given enough emphasis. The people skills of the executive team must be brought forth to promote the use of methods and statistics, along with new technologies, that will support the improvements. Most of the changes will affect the way people work. The team must consider such changes carefully. As with any change process, resistance needs to be overcome. The management team can be helpful during the implementation phase by supporting the changes and understanding the cultural changes that must go along with the physical changes. The Six Sigma executive champion must ensure that the awareness training, project selection and approval process, and reporting systems are followed. The cultural changes should surface during the champion training. The executive team must ensure that the change-management process will support the changes required in order for the Six Sigma process to succeed.

The executive champion should implement awareness training for the Six Sigma process in the entire organization. The reporting process should cover the statistical results as well as the financial returns and the general process variation improvements generated by the projects. The next area to address is the selection of the key indicators, or dashboard gages, that will allow the team to evaluate the performance of the operations. The dashboard indicators are usually in place already; the team needs to determine whether any changes in the indicators are needed. Some dashboard indicators to consider for the executive staff include the following:

- Delivery rating

- Plant inventory dollars

- Inventory turns

- Units produced per person per day

- Daily contribution margin

- Customer quality

- Supplier quality

- Safety rating

- Linearity

- Number of changeovers

- Productivity

- Accidents per worked hour
- Parts per person per day
- Delivery performance
- Amount of scrap
- Outbound premium freight
- Customer delivery performance
- Six Sigma savings
- Plant income
- Closing days
- Employee turnover
- Volume to plan
- Profitability

The list of potential indicators is just a start to allow for the selection of key indicators for your organization. The executive team should usually develop 5 to 10 indicators to monitor for progress. The direct reports to the executive team will include their own 5 to 10 measures that will support or link up to the dashboard indicators of the executive office. The champions of each project should ensure that the charter for the project will contain measures that will support one of the key indicators of the executive staff. The alignment of the indicators and projects to goals of the strategic plan will allow for the desired improvements.

Commitment to the Six Sigma process will mean a cultural change to most organizations. The focus on customer needs is time consuming, and the focus on the process involves understanding the process details and how they affect the output to the customers. Many organizations will find it difficult to focus on the process instead of the product or service. All processes that are key to the organization and the customer outcomes must be measured and controlled. All key processes must be capable of delivering to the output requirements of the process and the customer. This means that all unstable or uncontrolled processes must be worked on before we try to improve the performance consistency. The customers must measure the process output to ensure that we meet their needs. Process variation will be controlled once we achieve Six Sigma levels for the processes that the organization must be good at to satisfy customers. The processes that are not key to our success may not achieve the Six Sigma level. An organization should first improve processes that produce operational gains and satisfy customers.

KEY BUSINESS PROCESSES

Now the executive team should develop the key processes and indicators that will support the operating needs and the strategic plan. This high-level process map will start with inputs and include the key processes that will change the inputs to outputs for the customers. An example of this process is depicted in Figure 4.1.

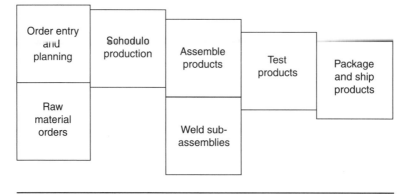

Figure 4.1   Typical high-level process flow of an organization's key processes.

TRAINING REQUIREMENTS

The management team and champions must prepare the Black Belts for their training and project work. I feel that the training should be for four weeks—an intensive five days and nights, at least once per month—with project work taking place between training sessions to practice the skills learned the previous session. It is beneficial for the Black Belt to come to the training with a project selected and a champion already assigned. The Black Belt should come to the first class with any data available about the problem or project that has been selected. A process map of the as-is process will also help during the training. The project champion should make sure that every effort is made to have this information available for the selected project. The Black Belt will use most of the information about the project during the first week to develop the final project charter, scope, and resource needs. The typical items covered in the training for these areas are covered in Chapter 6. The Black Belts should present the project status at the start of every training week, and the champions should be present to observe the status of the project and to support the Black Belt. The organization is ready for the implementation process once the management team has committed to the training, projects, resources for the Black Belt projects, project selection process, and Green Belt training.

The first part of the champion training must address the concepts described earlier. The second part should address the problem-solving process required for achieving the cause-and-effect analysis. The problem-solving training should focus on how the tools can define the causes of the variations and how the Black Belts can locate the reasons or roots of the causes. The tools for the process analysis should be reviewed. The advanced statistical tools should also be covered so that the project champions can be sure the Black Belts are using the proper tools.

The champion must help the Black Belt with the project charter, scope, measurements, and resources. The champion also should use the project review process during the DMAIC improvement process to see whether the Black Belt and team are on track to solving the problem and meeting the project charter. The review process, critical to implementing the project, should occur at the end of each phase in the DMAIC process.

The scope of the first project must be narrow enough to allow the Black Belt to succeed within six months. It should also be within the Black Belt's authority and responsibility to control. The Black Belt may need some good process team members if he or she is not familiar enough with the process or problem areas of the process. The champion must help get the resources.

THE CONCEPT OF VARIATION

The management team must understand the concept of variation. The problem-solving process must be followed to solve problems associated with getting the product or service to the end customer, for example, shipments are not arriving on time. Variances in the key delivery process measures must be understood and reduced. Variances could be in order entry, manufacturing, planning, or shipping. The Black Belt must peel apart the problem areas until he or she understands the real cause of the variances and can resolve the cause, select possible solutions, test for improvement, and incorporate the change into the process permanently.

Let's consider a product that is cut to size for the customer. The customer wants a length of 64 inches, plus 2 inches, minus 0 inches. The width of the product must be 48 inches, plus or minus 1 inch. The length is the critical dimension. If we are capable of delivering plus 3 inches, minus 0 inches, then we know that some of the cut lengths will be too long for the customer's process. If our present process is targeted to 66 inches, plus or minus 1 inch, to achieve a Six Sigma level, we need to shift the process mean to 65 inches and reduce the variation in cut length to about 65 inches, plus or minus .166 inch. A Six Sigma process would allow for a 1.5 standard deviation shift in the level of the process. Now we are at the Six Sigma level of performance for the process. With the typical 1.5 standard deviation shift, the output will supply 3.4 defects per million cuts of product produced. This means that we must improve the process by four times to achieve our goal. The management team should select a Black Belt who is familiar with the process of cutting to length and should announce its support for the improvement process. The process owner should be involved in the changes and controls that will get the process to the Six Sigma level.

A capability study should be run on the process to ensure that we can meet the requirements. We can then determine the Sigma level of performance after the analysis. An example of this data is provided in Figure 4.2. First we show a run chart of the data and then the capability analysis using MINITAB.

The sixpack information in Figure 4.2 provides the individuals and moving range charts for the process data. We can check for stability and any special causes. The histogram will provide a picture of the distribution of the data, and the normality test will check for normalized data. The capability study shows the results of short-term capability of 5.22 and long-term capability of 3.90. This is well above the Six Sigma capability.

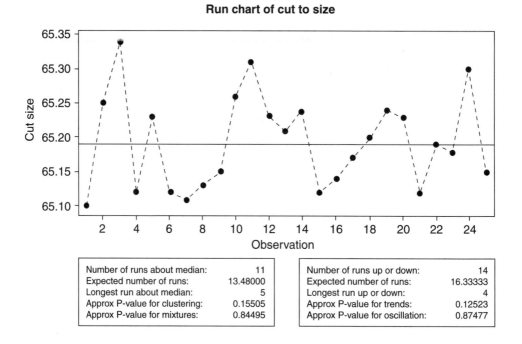

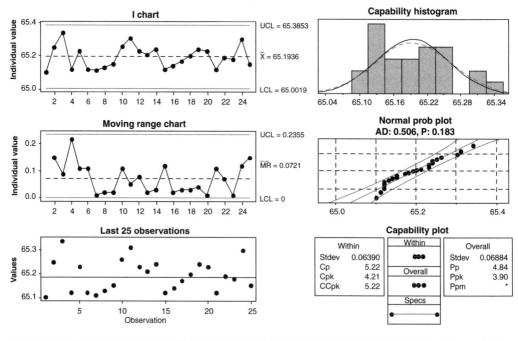

Figure 4.2 Run analysis and capability analysis of cut to size.

CHAPTER QUESTIONS

1. Why should management develop a council to prepare the strategic plan and help with the alignment of projects selected to the goals of the strategy?

2. What are the three types of champions devoted to the Six Sigma process?

3. What should the management team focus on during the planning process?

4. What items should the management team consider in the project selection and alignment process?

5. What kind of culture must the Six Sigma process have if it is to flourish?

6. What should the business dashboard of indicators contain?

7. Why should we develop a high-level map of the organization's key processes?

8. What is the Six Sigma coordinator designated to do for the process?

9. What do we mean by "management commitment"?

10. What are some indicators of management commitment?

SUGGESTIONS FOR FURTHER READING

Collins, Jim. *Good to Great.* New York: McGraw-Hill, 2001.

Crosby, Philip B. *Quality Is Free.* New York: McGraw-Hill, 1979.

Eckes, George. *The Six Sigma Revolution.* New York: John Wiley & Sons, 2001.

Imai, Masaaki. *Kaizen.* New York: McGraw-Hill, 1986.

Kaplan, Robert S. *Measures for Manufacturing Excellence.* Boston: HBS Press, 1990.

Kouzes, James M., and Barry Z. Posner. *Leadership Challenge.* San Francisco: Jossey-Bass, 2002.

Marash, Stanley A. *Fusion Management.* Fairfax, VA: QSU Publishing, 2003.

Spandle, Peter S. *The Six Sigma Way.* New York: McGraw-Hill, 2000.

5

Pillar Three: The Strategic Planning Process and Project Alignment

The Twelve Pillars for Six Sigma Support and Implementation

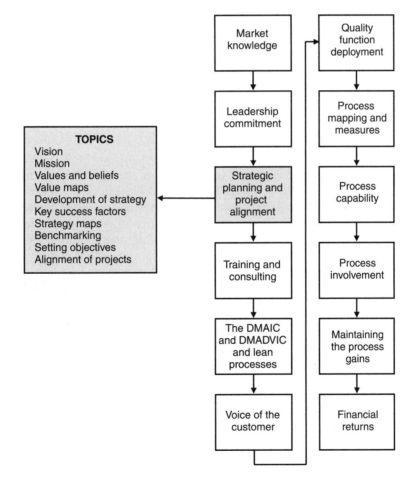

Market knowledge	Quality function deployment
Leadership commitment	Process mapping and measures
TOPICS Vision Mission Values and beliefs Value maps Development of strategy Key success factors Strategy maps Benchmarking Setting objectives Alignment of projects	Strategic planning and project alignment	Process capability
Training and consulting	Process involvement
The DMAIC and DMADVIC and lean processes	Maintaining the process gains
Voice of the customer	Financial returns

In Chapter 3, we covered the main ideas of developing a strategic plan by using the marketplace and customer information that the organization obtains from its listening posts. Now the organization needs to focus on the strategic planning process and levels of strategy to ensure that the projects selected align with the goals and objectives, which, in turn, should align with the mission and the vision. In this chapter, we will cover the concepts of vision, mission, and the objectives with goals that are arrived at through this process. This will ensure that the project selection process for Six Sigma will align with the measures and the direction of the organization from the top down. This is not easy, but if done properly will allow the organization to succeed. This is the time for the leadership to articulate the vision and demonstrate commitment as noted in Chapter 4. The following information can be found in many of the sources mentioned in Chapter 3 and this chapter. In this chapter we will discuss in more detail the points outlined in Chapter 3. I have used Fred R. David's *Strategic Management*[1] in many courses that I have taught to management-level personnel pursuing a master's in quality management at Loyola University in New Orleans. Some of the principles are developed using David's concepts.

This process and the need for it are covered in the MBNQA program. We need to develop, change, or improve the values and critical success factors of the organization in light of the nature of change to be made within the organization. Strategic planning will be used to accomplish this change. The first point is to ensure that the vision meets the present needs of the organization.

VISION

The purpose of vision is to determine the future needs of the organization from the organization's product, or future market. Good leaders have a vision that will be supported by the staff and organization. The vision shows what we perceive to be achievable based on a review of the current market. It also answers the question of what do we want to become as the organization develops? The vision is based on a rock-solid foundation of information about the organization's capability, the marketplace conditions, and the customer base needs.

Today, *vision* is a familiar concept in corporate leadership. However, when you look carefully you find that most "visions" are one person's (or one group's) vision imposed upon an organization. Such visions, at best, command compliance—not commitment. A shared vision is a vision that many people are truly committed to because it reflects their personal vision. What is most important is that these individuals' visions become genuinely shared among people on all levels—focusing the energy of thousands and creating a common identity among enormously diverse people.What is the vision of your company? If you do not know, your company is just starting this process. How will you know whether you have arrived if the future is not in the scope of the vision? The leadership must have a good idea of what is feasible and what has to be accomplished in order to fulfill the vision. The vision should challenge the organization to obtain new levels of performance to fulfill the needs of the marketplace and the customer. Innovation and change will be required if the organization is to achieve new heights and overcome resistance to new challenges. Following are some corporate visions obtained from different organizations.[1]

Core Ideas of Selected Visionary Organizations

- Aerospace
  - —Being on the leading edge of aeronautics.
  - —Being pioneers.
  - —Tackling huge challenges and risks.
  - —Product safety and quality.
- Banking
  - —Being out front, the biggest, best, most innovative, most profitable.
  - —Autonomy and entrepreneurship (via decentralization).
  - —Aggressiveness and self-confidence.
- Manufacturing
  - —Improvement of the quality of life through technology and innovation.
  - —Interdependence of responsibility to customers, employees, society, and shareholders (no clear hierarchy).
  - —Individual responsibility and opportunity.
  - —Honesty and integrity.
- Medical
  - —The company exists "to alleviate pain and disease."
  - —"We have a hierarchy of responsibilities: customers first, employees second, society at large third, and shareholders fourth" (from Johnson and Johnson).
  - —Individual opportunity and reward based on merit.

MISSION

The next task facing the organization is to establish a mission that will support the vision. The following items must be considered during the mission development phase:

- Enduring statements of purpose that distinguish businesses and functions
- Objectives of the business unit with goals
- The plan to achieve the vision
- Direction to achieve the vision
- The scope of a firm's operation in product, service, and market terms
- Identification of what business the company is in for the selected market

What is the mission of your company? If your organization does not have a mission, are you planning for its future needs?

Components of a Mission Statement

The components of a mission statement include:

1. Customers

2. Products or services

3. Markets

4. Technology and materials

5. Concern for survival, growth, and profitability

6. Philosophy of the organization

7. Self-concept of the organization

8. Concern for public image

9. Concern for employees

A mission is the organization's purpose for being; it is why the organization exists and what propels it to endure. For an individual, a mission is the inner calling that demands fulfillment and motivates behavior. Successful organizations align individual missions with the organization's mission. Following are examples from two companies that illustrate visions and missions:[1]

To provide worldwide responsiveness to our customers by offering the highest quality, lowest total cost, customized integrated manufacturing services.

An organization that knows exactly what it wants to be: The leader in serving customers by making things that make communications work.

VALUES AND BELIEFS

Now the organization must consider the values, beliefs, and artifacts for the strategic planning process. This will help determine whether the change process needs to be considered in order to implement the strategies that may counter present values or beliefs.

Core values are basic, unchanging principles. *Value* is simply defined as: "Worth in usefulness or importance to the professor; utility or merit." Fred David indicates that value always comes at a price and therefore can be defined in terms of Value Metrics.[1]

Corporate beliefs provide a set of ideals and sense of purpose, which compose the organization's essential and enduring tenets. Guiding principles are not to be compromised or confused with specific cultural or operating practices.

Consider the 3M Corporation's corporate values:

• Innovation: "Thou shalt not kill a new product idea."

• Absolute integrity.

• Respect for individual initiative and personal growth.

• Tolerance for honest mistakes.

• Product quality and reliability.

• "Our real business is solving problems."

STRATEGIC PLANNING VALUE CHAIN ANALYSIS

Once a strategic plan is in development, the strategic planning value chain should be reviewed. A value chain is a set of activities involved in the production and sales of a product or service. Each activity adds some part of the total economic value that is created by the chain. The chain may involve different companies. An organization can develop distinctive competencies in any one, or in any combination, of these activities. These activities, and how they are linked to one another, are potential sources of distinctive competencies and competitive advantages. Some processes to consider are McKinsey & Company's Generic Value Chain and Porter's Generic Value Chain.

Value Maps

Value is the trade-off between the benefits of a product and the price paid for the product. Value maps are based on how consumers try to allocate money for a number of products within a limited budget. Economic utility suggests that consumers will first choose the product with the most utility per dollar, then the product with the next most utility per dollar, and so on until the budget is exhausted.[1]

In a value map, trade-offs are made between benefits of a product. The scales on the perceptual map are the level of the benefit per dollar of each price. Each brand is placed on the map according to the level of benefit it offers, relative to the other brands, divided by its unit cost. The value chain and map are interesting tools you can use in the planning process. Use the sources provided if you are interested in performing this analysis and the details of the processes.

THE DEVELOPMENT OF STRATEGY

Now, with the vision, mission, values, and beliefs in place, we can look at the strategic planning process. Refer back to Chapter 3 to review the business strategies that an organization may consider after the SWOT matrix is developed. The following are some of the discussed strategies:

- Types of integration strategies
  - —Forward integration
  - —Backward integration
  - —Horizontal integration
- Intensive forward-looking strategies
  - —Market penetration
  - —Market development
  - —Product development
- Defensive or competitive strategies
  - —Joint venture
  - —Retrenchment

—Divestiture

—Liquidation

—Combination

- Diversification strategies

—Concentric diversification

—Horizontal diversification

The first step in strategic planning is to use market listening posts to develop the external issues that may present the organization with opportunities and threats. Following is a discussion of what must be considered.

External Forces

Economic conditions, both current and expected in the near future, must be considered in the strategic planning process. These conditions include social, cultural, demographic, world market, and environmental conditions. The political, governmental, and legal actions that have or will occur could affect the organization's market. We must consider the effects of wars on the market and buying patterns. Technological advances anticipated in the short and long term are major considerations as well. We need to consider the competitive market and the effects of competitors on products and services. International regulations and standards must also be considered.

Economic Factors

Economic factors and conditions might be considered first in the planning process. Economic factors directly affect the potential attractiveness of various strategies. For example, if interest rates rise, capital expansion becomes more costly. Also, as interest rates rise, discretionary income declines and the demand for discretionary purchases falls. As stock prices increase, the desirability of equity as a source of capital for market development increases. Also, as the market rises, consumer and business wealth expands.[1] We should also consider the effects of environmental issues on economics. Some economic variables that often represent opportunities and threats to organizations are in Table 5.1.

Social, Cultural, Environmental, and Demographic Factors

Social, cultural, demographic, and environmental forces should be considered next. These factors have had a major impact on virtually all products, services, markets, and customers. Small, large, for-profit, and nonprofit organizations in all industries are being challenged by the opportunities and threats arising from changes in social, cultural, demographic, and environmental variables.[1] In every way, the United States was markedly different in 1994 than it was in 1984, and 2004 brought even greater changes with the effects of September 11, 2001, and the war in Iraq. More change is inevitable by 2010.

Significant trends to consider for the 2000s include the population becoming older and more educated, early retirement, and self-expression replacing the Protestant work ethic.[1] A partial listing of important social, cultural, demographic, and environmental variables that represent opportunities or threats for virtually all organizations appears in Table 5.2.

Table 5.1 Economic variables to consider for the strategy.

Shift to a service economy in the United States	Consumption patterns
	Price fluctuations
Level of disposable income	Unemployment trends
Propensity of people to spend	Worker productivity levels
Interest rates in the United States	Value of the dollar in world markets
Inflation rates	Stock market trends
Economics of scale	Foreign country economics
Money market rates	Import/export factors
Federal budget deficits	International standards
Gross national product trends	Environmental regulations
Local standards	

Table 5.2 Key social, cultural, demographic, and environmental variables to consider in your strategy.

Birth rates	Water pollution requirements
Immigration and emigration rates	Retirement rates shifts
Marriage rates	Age-group differences
Divorce rate	Changes in product quality requirements
Health care availability	Customer service needs
Social security changes	Energy conservation
Life expectancy	Changes in savings rates
Per-capita income	Changes in customs
Racial equality issues	Increase in landfill pollution
Energy usage changes and prices	Environmental changes
Ozone depletion	Death rates
Amount of leisure time	Changing Medicare needs
Levels of investing	Regional changes in tastes and preferences
Women and minority workers changes	Effect of storm water runoff
Changes in buying habits	Recycling requirements
Changes in average education levels	Waste management

Your organization's listening posts must consider political, governmental, and legal forces. Federal, state, local, and foreign governments are regulators, deregulators, subsidizers, employers, and customers of organizations. Political, governmental, and legal factors can therefore represent key opportunities or threats for both small and large organizations. For industries and firms that depend heavily on government contracts or subsidies, political forecasts can be the most important part of an external audit. Changes in patent laws, antitrust legislation, tax rates, and lobbying activities can also affect firms significantly.[1] The typical areas to consider are listed in Table 5.3.

Table 5.3 Important political, government, and legal variables.

Government regulations or deregulations	Foreign relationships changes
Tariff changes on products	Lobbying group changes
Political action trends	International standard changes
Export requirements	Import-export regulation changes
Changes in corporate profits	Government fiscal/monetary changes
Changes in patent laws	Local, state, and federal changes
Defense budget changes	World oil, currency, and labor markets
Government subsidies	Location and severity of terrorist activities
Antitrust legislation	Risk of wars

Technological Changes

Now the organization should consider the technological forces that may affect future products or services. Revolutionary changes and discoveries such as superconductivity, computer engineering, "thinking" computers, robotics, unmanned factories, miracle drugs, space communications, space manufacturing, lasers, cloning, satellite networks, fiber optics, biometrics, and electronic funds transfer are having a dramatic effect on the world.[1] Some points to consider for the technological areas are presented in Table 5.4.

The analysis process must also consider the competitive forces that act against the organization. The top five competitors in four industries should be identified. An important part of an exceptional review is to identify rival firms and to determine their strengths, weaknesses, capabilities, opportunities, threats, objectives, and strategies.[1]

Some key questions about competitors include:

1. Who are the major competitors?

2. What are the competitors' strengths?

3. What are the competitors' weaknesses?

4. What are the competitors' objectives and strategies?

5. How will the competitors respond to current economic, social, cultural, demographic, geographic, political, governmental, technological, and competitive trends affecting our industry?

6. How vulnerable are the competitors to our alternative strategies?

7. How vulnerable are our alternative strategies to responsive counterattack by our major competitors?

8. How are our products or services positioned relative to those of the competitors?

9. To what extent are firms entering and leaving this industry?

10. What key factors influence our present competitive position in this industry?

Table 5.4 Key points to consider in assessing the technological environment.

Current technologies within the organization.
Technologies utilized in the organization's products or services components and parts.
Criticality of each technology to each of these products or services.
External technologies that might become critical and why. Will they remain available outside the organization?
The organization's investments in critical technologies over time.
The investments and investment patterns of its leading technological competitors. Historical investments? Planned future investments?
The investment in the product and in the process of these technologies. For the organization and its competitors. Design of new products with new technology? Production with new technology?
Subjective ranking of different organizations in each of these technologies.
The applications of the organization's current and future technologies.
In which technology does the organization currently participate and why? In which does the organization not participate and why?
Attractiveness of each of these applications as an investment opportunity in terms of its market growth, its potential for profit improvement, and/or potential for increasing technological leadership?
Growth characteristics of the technology.
Technologies that are critical to the external applications of the product.
What are the competing technologies in each area to address?

11. How have the sales and profit rankings of major competitors changed over recent years? What has caused these rankings to change?

12. What is the nature of supplier and distributor relationships in this industry?

13. To what extent could substitute products or services be a threat to compliance in this industry?

14. How easy is it to enter our industry?

External Information

The selection of external information sources can vary by organization. Some sources are:

1. Customer surveys

2. Market research

3. Professional and shareholders meetings

4. Interviews with stakeholders

5. Periodicals, journals, and reports

In the information age, every organization is flooded with data. Data, in raw form, has little value. It is only through the analysis and understanding of data that it becomes valuable. Probably the most valuable information any organization can acquire is the knowledge of their customers' basic needs in relationship to their products and services along with how well they meet those needs compared to other providers.

When it comes to competitive analysis, an organization can use Michael Porter's five forces. Porter's five forces model of competitive analysis is used to develop strategies in many industries. The five forces are:

1. Rivalry among competitive firms

2. Potential entry of new competitors

3. Potential development of substitute

4. Bargaining power of suppliers

5. Bargaining power of consumers

External information sources are used to develop the organization's strategic plan. An external factor evaluation (EFE) matrix allows strategists to summarize and evaluate economic, social, cultural, demographic, environmental, political, governmental, legal, technological, and competitive information. Another step is to conduct an internal strategic-management audit by constructing an internal factor evaluation (IFE) matrix.[1]

An EFE rating system to set up the matrix is:

1. List critical success factors as identified in the internal audit.

2. Assign a weight that ranges from 0.0 (not important) to 1.0 (all-important) to each factor.

3. Assign a rating of 1 to 4 to each factor to indicate whether that factor represents a major weakness (rating = 1), a minor weakness (rating = 2), a minor strength (rating = 3), or a major strength (rating = 4).

4. Multiply each factor's weight by its rating to determine a weighted score for each variable.

5. Total the weighted scores for each variable.

An example of an external factor evaluation for a lumber company is shown in Table 5.5.

Once we understand our strengths, weaknesses, opportunities, and threats, we can form a SWOT analysis. Key internal and external factors that relate to strengths and weaknesses are:

1. Corporate structure

2. Corporate resources

3. Marketing

4. Finance

5. Research and development

6. Manufacturing and service

7. Human resources

8. Management information systems

9. Societal environment

10. Task environment

Table 5.5 An external evaluation matrix for the wood industry.

Critical success factors	Weight	Rating	Weighted score
Opportunities			
1. The U.S./Mexican and Canadian Free Trade Agreement creating growth	.11	3	.33
2. Building markets are better	.06	2	.12
3. Disposable income is increasing	.15	1	.15
4. Consumers will pay for recycled products	.04	4	.16
5. New mill equipment can shorten product cycle time	.10	4	.40
Threats			
1. Chinese markets are closed to many U.S. wood products	.10	2	.20
2. The European Community has imposed new tariffs on wood	.15	4	.60
3. The Middle East is unstable politically	.06	3	.18
4. Federal and state regulations for building are improving	.13	2	.26
5. Unemployment rates are increasing	.10	1	.10
Total	1.00		2.50

STRATEGIC PLANNING TOOLS SWOT AND TOWS

Now we are ready for SWOT analysis techniques. The SWOT analysis uses key internal and external factors that strongly affect the corporation's present and future performance. An example of the layout of the SWOT matrix is provided in Figure 5.1, with inputs for a lumber company in Figure 5.3.

The TOWS analysis is in my opinion a better analysis to work from, even though both analyses will produce the same results. All that changes is the perspective with which we address the issues. The strategies will all be the same. An example of the layout of the TOWS matrix is provided in Figure 5.2, with inputs for a lumber company in Figure 5.4.

There are eight steps in constructing a matrix:[1]

1. List the firm's key opportunities.

2. List the firm's key external threats.

3. List the firm's key internal strengths.

4. List the firm's key internal weaknesses.

5. Match internal strengths with external opportunities and record the resultant SO strategies in the appropriate cell.

6. Match internal weaknesses with external opportunities and record the resultant WO strategies.

7. Match internal strengths with external threats and record the resultant ST strategies.

8. Match internal weaknesses with external threats and record the resultant WT strategies.

	Strengths—S List strengths 1. 2. 3. 4. 5. 6. 7. 8. 9. 10.	**Weaknesses—W** List weaknesses 1. 2. 3. 4. 5. 6. 7. 8. 9. 10.
Always leave blank		
Opportunities—O List opportunities 1. 2. 3. 4. 5. 6. 7. 8. 9. 10.	**SO Strategies** Use strengths to take advantage of opportunities 1. 2. 3. 4. 5. 6. 7. 8. 9. 10.	**WO Strategies** Overcome weaknesses by taking advantage of opportunities 1. 2. 3. 4. 5. 6. 7. 8. 9. 10.
Threats—T List threats 1. 2. 3. 4. 5. 6. 7. 8. 9. 10.	**ST Strategies** Use strengths to avoid threats 1. 2. 3. 4. 5. 6. 7. 8. 9. 10.	**WT Strategies** Minimize weaknesses and avoid threats 1. 2. 3. 4. 5. 6. 7. 8. 9. 10.

Figure 5.1 Example of the SWOT matrix layout.

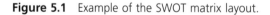

Strategy formulation requires a concerted effort from the management team; it also requires a series of interrelated activities that perform the following:

- Evaluation of results

- Evaluation of strategic managers and issues

- Scanning of the external environment

- Analysis of strategic factors from the previously listed activities

Selection of the best alternative is achieved with the TOWS matrix evaluation. Once the TOWS matrix is completed, we need to develop the objectives. The objectives must

Always leave blank	Threats—T List threats 1. 2. 3. 4. 5. 6. 7. 8. 9. 10.	Opportunities—O List opportunities 1. 2. 3. 4. 5. 6. 7. 8. 9. 10.
Weaknesses—W List weaknesses 1. 2. 3. 4. 5. 6. 7. 8. 9. 10.	**WT Strategies** Minimize weaknesses to avoid threats 1. 2. 3. 4. 5. 6. 7. 8. 9. 10.	**WO Strategies** Overcome weaknesses by taking advantage of opportunities 1. 2. 3. 4. 5. 6. 7. 8. 9. 10.
Strengths—S List strengths 1. 2. 3. 4. 5. 6. 7. 8. 9. 10.	**ST Strategies** Use strengths to avoid threats 1. 2. 3. 4. 5. 6. 7. 8. 9. 10.	**SO Strategies** Use strengths to take advantage of opportunities 1. 2. 3. 4. 5. 6. 7. 8. 9. 10.

Figure 5.2 Example of TOWS matrix layout.

deal with the way the company recognizes the stakeholders, its evaluation of strategies, and its policies. The strategic planning process must be a formal system to ensure that a hierarchy of objectives and strategies exists.

We also need to evaluate the strategic managers involved in the planning process.[1] We will accomplish this evaluation in the following areas:

1. The interaction of the board with top management can have basic styles of chaos, entrepreneurship, or partnership.

2. The entrepreneurial approach focuses on one powerful individual, who focuses on opportunities.

The SWOT Matrix for a Lumber Company

	Strengths—S	Weaknesses—W
	1. Current ratio increased to 3.0 2. Profit margin increased to 7.0 percent 3. Employee morale is good 4. New planning system 5. Market share increased to 10%	1. Legal issues exist 2. Plant capacity has fallen to 50% 3. Lack of a strategic system 4. R & D expenses have increased 30% 5. Dealer incentives not effective
Opportunities—O 1. European unification 2. Rising environmental consciousness in selecting woods 3. Free market economics arising in China 4. Demand for specific wood increasing 15% annually 5. U.S./Mexico/Canadian Free Trade Agreement	**SO Strategies** 1. Acquire lumber company in Europe (S1, S5, O1) 2. Build a manufacturing plant in Mexico (S2, S5, O5) 3. Develop new lumber needs (S3, O2) 4. Form a joint venture to distribute wood in China (S1, S5, T2)	**WO Strategies** 1. Form joint venture to distribute wood in Europe (W3, O1) 2. Develop new packaged products (W1, O2, O4) 3. Develop new wood products (W1, O2, O4)
Threats—T 1. Wood revenues not increasing 2. Other products lead market with 10% share 3. Unstable economics in China 4. Some products are not recyclable 5. Low dollar value	**ST Strategies** 1. Develop new wood needs (S1, S5, T2) 2. Find new niche markets (T4, S5, T2) 3. Develop new markets (T4, T5, S5) 4. New recyclable products (S1, T4)	**WT Strategies** 1. Close unprofitable plants (W3, T3, T5) 2. Develop new margin wood products (W5, T1)

Figure 5.3 Example of a completed SWOT matrix.

3. When problems are secondary, the adaptive approach has reactive solutions to existing problems and is usually called "muddling through the forest" for solutions.

Strategic planning involves proactive searches for new opportunities and reactive solutions for existing problems. We evaluate issues in light of the probability that they will occur and the probable impact they will have on the corporation. We then evaluate strengths and weaknesses of the functional areas. Internal variables to consider include structure, culture, and resources.

When considering strategic approaches, we recognize that organizations with a high rate of return have the following characteristics:

- Low investment intensity

- High market share

- High relative product quality

The TOWS matrix for a Lumber Company

	Threats—T	Opportunities—O
Always leave blank	1. Wood revenues not increasing 2. Other products lead market with 10% share 3. Unstable economics in China 4. Some products are not recyclable 5. Low dollar value	1. European unification 2. Rising environmental consciousness in selecting woods 3. Free market economics arising in China 4. Demand for specific wood increasing 15% annually 5. U.S./Mexico/Canadian Free Trade Agreement
Weaknesses—W 1. Legal issues exist 2. Plant capacity has fallen to 50% 3. Lack of a strategic system 4. R & D expenses have increased 30% 5. Dealer incentives not effective	**WT Strategies** 1. Close unprofitable plants (W3, T3, T5) 2. Develop new higher margin wood products (W5, T1)	**WO Strategies** 1. Form joint venture to distribute wood in Europe (W3, O1) 2. Develop new packaged products (W1, O2, O4) 3. Develop new wood products (W1, O2, O4)
Strengths—S 1. Current ratio increased to 3.0 2. Profit margin increased to 7.0 percent 3. Employee morale is good 4. New planning system 5. Market share increased to 10%	**ST Strategies** 1. Develop new wood needs (S1, S5, T2) 2. Find new niche markets (T4, S5, T2) 3. Develop new markets (T4, T5, S5) 4. New packaging (S1, T4)	**SO Strategies** 1. Acquire lumber company in Europe (S1, S5, O1) 2. Build a manufacturing plant in Mexico (S2, S5, O5) 3. Develop new lumber needs (S3, O2) 4. Form a joint venture to distribute wood in China (S1, S5, T2)

Figure 5.4 Example of a completed TOWS matrix.

- High operating effectiveness
- Low direct costs per unit relative to the competition

The analysis of the strategic factors should include:

- SWOT analysis
- TOWS analysis
- Seeking a niche
- Innovation as a way of life
- Competing on value, not price
- Achieving leadership in a market
- Building on strengths

Key Success Factors

Once we have developed the strategic plan, we need to consider the key success factors for the organization. The MBNQA Criteria will be helpful in constructing the factors. Methods for determining key success factors are:

- Identify major determinants of financial and competitive success in an industry.

- Highlight the outcomes crucial to success in the marketplace and the corresponding competencies and capabilities that have the most bearing on profitability.

- Have a broad scope. A factor can be a skill or talent, a competitive capability, or a condition a company must achieve.

- Keep in mind that a factor can relate to technology, manufacturing, distribution, marketing, or organizational resources.

- Recognize that factors vary from industry to industry and even over time as industry conditions change.

STRATEGY MAPPING

The last strategic issue to consider is the ideas on strategic mapping to help select the issues and support required to overcome the issues for implementation of the strategic plan. The strategy of the organization describes how it will create value for the stakeholders and customers. The mapping process helps the departments involved in the strategic planning process align their actions to meet the plan. The organization must measure the critical few processes and its parameters that will provide for the long-term value creation. The strategy is developed from the items and actions considered previously and then the mapping process helps direct the specific actions required for the department to properly support the strategy.

The strategic plan needs to be executed to achieve the desired results for the organization. The balanced scorecard and the strategy map tie the financial performance with targets for the customers and internal processes to the defined results. This subject is covered in more detail in a book by Kaplan and Norton, *Strategy Maps.*[2] Each department will go through the steps of developing a strategic map for its processes. This will help define specific projects that will tie to the financial result.

Benchmarking Overview

With the strategy in place and analyzed, we can focus on benchmarking the organization's key processes compared to similar processes in order to become the best in the key process. This may become part of the strategic planning process. This process should become part of the normal Six Sigma program, and if implemented at the strategic planning phase it may open up other areas of key process performance. Therefore, we will take some time here to explain the benchmarking process. Benchmarking the organization's key success factors or key process parameters will help the organization understand its ability to meet the needs of its customer base. Benchmarking is not a fad or a quick fix, but a way of managing change. It is, in fact, often a kind of painful group therapy for businesses that provides a reality check at least and a new lease on life at best.[3] Like any therapy, the effectiveness of benchmarking has a lot to do with the level of receptiveness to challenge and change. Benchmarking is a process in which our organization partners with another part of the organization or with another business to understand the other's methods and approaches used in processes key to our organization. The benchmarked organization is usually the best at the process or a similar process that we want to improve. The goal is to learn something from the other organization that will help us improve our process.

Some types of benchmarking processes are:

- Internal benchmarking

- Competitive benchmarking

- Functional benchmarking

- Generic benchmarking

The benchmarking process can:

- Prove a need for (ability to achieve) paradigm change.

- Support strategic planning.

- Support continuous improvement.

The stages of the benchmarking process that an organization must consider before taking on the task are:

1. Provide a benchmarking overview to the key people involved in supporting the process.

2. Develop questions that may indicate a need for benchmarking a specific process:

   - What subjects are most critical to business success?

   - What areas are causing the most trouble?

   - What are the major deliverables of this area?

   - What products are provided to customers?

   - What factors are responsible for customer satisfaction?

3. Evaluate the following questions:

   - What problems have been identified in the operation?

   - Where are competitive pressures being felt?

   - What performance measures are being tackled?

   - What are the major cost components?

4. Include the following data gathering methods:

   - Internal research

   - External research

- Customer research

- Site-visit data gathering

The site visit, where we visit the best-in-class organization, is the most critical and most expensive stage of the benchmarking process. You probably have only one chance, so you must set up a well-planned visit. In the early stages of the process, you should exchange questionnaires with the company to be benchmarked. Then establish a previsit schedule with the organization and create an agenda for the visit. A quid pro quo process, in which the other organization visits your organization, should be considered during the negotiations. From the site visit you will establish a gap analysis with the performance gap(s) defined. Some items to consider on the site visit are:

- Are you using the same measurement?

- Are you using the same criteria?

- Go into the process with a clean-sheet approach.

- Look for the practice gap between your process and the benchmark.

- What do they do differently?

- Why is it a better practice?

The implementation of actions to be taken must be monitored for progress and process improvements. A champion must be assigned to the activity and a mission statement should be developed with measures, goals, and a schedule. These should be agreed upon before the visit. We must then follow up on the progress of the benchmarking process.

For the benchmarking to be successful, we must have a look at the following key items:

- Focus on "top-10," "front-burner" issues.

- Senior management's commitment and participation.

- Availability of resources to support the benchmarking effort.

- Adequate time to integrate benchmarking activity into work schedule (don't drive start or completion dates).

After the site visit and gap analysis are completed, we need to plan the implementation of the new steps into the organization's process and to consider the process for the implementation.

Now we can review the overall planning process, using the internal and external information obtained from the listening posts of the organization and the benchmarking process. The process of generating and selecting strategies requires the following steps:

- Formulate a plan using EFE and IFE matrices and the competitive profile matrix.

- The matching stage focuses on generating feasible alternative strategies by aligning key external and internal factors.

- TOWS matrix, strategic position, and action evaluation are used to evaluate the alternatives. The decision stage uses a planning matrix for final implementation.

- The formulation process.

Now we need to create objectives to support the strategy. These objectives should include managing the forces during the implementation of the action plans and focusing on efficiency and the operational process. This requires motivational and leadership skills as well as coordination.

SETTING OBJECTIVES AROUND THE STRATEGY

Annual objectives are generally decentralized and involve all managers in the organization. They serve as guidelines for action and for channeling efforts to meet strategic plans. Annual objectives should be measurable, consistent, and reasonable, and they should challenge the status quo. They should be clearly stated and communicated throughout the organization. Annual objectives are attained when supported by periodic review and accompanied by commensurate rewards and sanctions. Some policies to consider for the strategy and objectives are:

- Policies concerning how the strategy work will take place.

- Policies to facilitate solving recurring problems and guide the implementation of strategy.

- Policies to provide management control and allow coordination across its processes. These policies reduce management time on decisions.

ALIGNMENT OF BLACK BELT PROJECTS TO THE STRATEGY

Now the organization must align the Black Belt projects with the strategic plan. A process for the selection of projects needs to be developed by the senior management group. This plan should begin with the analysis of the TOWS matrix developed during the strategic planning process. The TOWS matrix should indicate which areas to address. Objectives are then developed around these areas to define the needs of the planning process. The project selection process must ensure that we will meet one of those objective needs or support an operations need. The best way to achieve this is to create another matrix, having the strategic planning objectives on the left, or input side, of the matrix and the selected projects for review across the top of the matrix. This matrix is shown in Table 5.6. The management team's task is to verify that the projects will meet one or more of the needs of the strategic objectives listed on the input side of the matrix. If the matrix is not easy to relate to, then a weighted relationship may be helpful in the selection process.

Table 5.6   A typical matrix layout for checking strategic issues against the project.

Project strategy	Process cycle time	Defect rate reduction	Capacity to deliver	Process capability
Increased profit				
Delivery to customer needs				
Improved throughput				

The selection of DFSS projects must also align and support the strategic plan as well as the key processes or technology. Before we go forward with any project, we need to evaluate the probability of success and be able to measure the value of the project to the organization. Douglas P. Mader, a certified Master Black Belt, derived a net present value method of analysis for projects.[4] This method of value analysis takes into consideration the probability of commercial success, the commercialization or launch costs, and the probability of technical success. A strong voice of the customer and quality function deployment process is necessary for a development project to succeed.

This approach selects a project for development and then segments the projects into high to low impacts. For the high-impact designs, a Black Belt team is assigned to the project. The executive management team and council need to be active in this selection process.

CHAPTER QUESTIONS

1. When should the strategic planning process be performed, and how often should it be updated?

2. What kind of strategic plan should be used if you are losing market share to the competition?

3. What should a good mission statement contain?

4. What is meant by "corporate values and beliefs," and why is it important to know what they are in your organization?

5. What does a value map provide?

6. What are some of the external factors that can affect an organization?

7. What is the difference between the TOWS matrix and the SWOT matrix?

8. What are some of the external factors that can affect an organization?

9. On which areas should your organization's listing posts focus in order to enhance your strategic planning process?

10. How should competitive analysis for the strategic plan be performed?

SUGGESTIONS FOR FURTHER READING

David, Fred R. *Strategic Management,* 6th ed. Upper Saddle River, NJ: Prentice Hall, 1997.

Kaplan, Robert S., and David P. Norton. *Strategy Maps.* Boston: HBS Press, 2004.

Kotler, Philip. *Marketing Management Analysis, Planning and Control,* 5th ed. Englewood Cliffs, NJ: Prentice-Hall, 1984.

Wheelen, Thomas L., and J. David Hunger. *Strategic Management and Business Policy.* Reading, MA: Addison-Wesley Publishing, 1986.

6

Pillar Four: The Training and Consulting Requirements

The Twelve Pillars for Six Sigma Support and Implementation

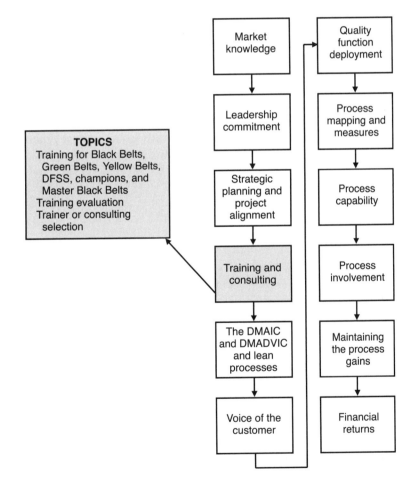

This chapter will cover the types and amount of training required to support the implementation of the Lean Six Sigma process. An overview of the training requirements was presented in Chapter 1. The intent of this chapter is to specify the sequence of the training and discuss the training curriculum that will help develop Master Black Belts, Black Belts, Green Belts, Yellow Belts, and the champions of the process. The Master Black Belts are the most experienced with the tools, project management, and implementation of successful projects. Their training must continue in order for them to become leaders of the process and the most skilled users of the tools that are crucial to the continuous improvement of process- and customer-focused measures. For the Six Sigma improvement process to succeed, the "people issue" needs to be considered in the training process. Most organizations are continually training employees to become team members and team leaders (to lead people). However, it is important that Black Belts also become good negotiators, understand change management strategies, and be skilled in the methods of obtaining consensus on issues that will be addressed by Black Belt projects. With this in mind, it is crucial that the trainer consider the organization's culture and emphasize teamwork, leadership, and facilitation skills that will be required of the Black Belts. This means that the training must be developed in modular or step form so that the individuals will receive the important aspects of the people skills required for leading and implementing changes.

Black Belts must learn more skills in order to become leaders: leadership, open mindedness, statistical thinking, problem solving, process thinking, customer focus, and project management. The Master Black Belt adds the ability to teach these skills and to lead several projects at one time while maintaining open communication with executives. These skills are learned through a training process that will expose the students to the theory, accompanied by the immediate application of the skills to theoretical processes and then to actual organization experiences with the company's processes. It is also beneficial for the Master Black Belt to have training and skills in DFSS, DMADVIC, and the MBNQA Criteria.

A list of specific topics to be covered in the training is presented here and in Chapter 7, but it is not intended to be the specific course structure for any one organization. The list, or subject criteria, of training activities must be tailored to the individual needs of an organization based upon a review of the strategic planning process, the culture of the organization, and an executive staff audit of the understanding and support of the key processes needed for implementing Six Sigma.

The design team needs to consider the Design for Six Sigma approaches to ensure that the products and processes released in the future are capable of attaining the Six Sigma level of performance after a short start-up process. The Design for Six Sigma training basically addresses the philosophy of Six Sigma, process and statistical thinking, and the tools of good design practices. The tentative list of training needs will be provided here and flowcharted in Chapter 7 but, as with the Black Belt training, it is tailored to the organization's specific needs.

TRAINING FOR BLACK BELTS, GREEN BELTS, DFSS, CHAMPIONS, AND YELLOW BELTS

The champion, Green Belt, Yellow Belt, and Black Belt trainings differ from each other only in the amount and level of training devoted to team skills, management skills, negotiation skills, statistical thinking, and the problem-solving process. Most of the training

Table 6.1 Typical topics of Black Belt and Green Belt training.

• The Six Sigma philosophy*	• Single minute exchange of die (SMED)
• The pillars of Six Sigma*	• 5S process*
• The DMAIC process*	• Process capability analysis*
• The DMADVIC process	• Project management*
• Teams and teamwork requirements	• Hypothesis analysis and comparison testing*
• Change management	• Regression analysis
• The art of negotiation	• Designed experiments
• The ability to audit or evaluate differences in processes and the ability to act accordingly*	• Chi-square analysis
	• Multi-vari analysis
• Obtaining the voice of the customer*	• Multiple regression analysis
• Using the quality function deployment process to change the customer's voice to the process needs or critical to quality (CTQs) to critical to process (CTPs)*	• Response surface analysis
	• Evolutionary operational (EVOP) analysis
• Using the four phases of QFD	• Failure modes and effects analysis
• Understanding process controls*	• Control plans*
• Understanding process variation*	• Benchmarking process
• The difference between continuous and discrete data*	• Problem-solving process*
	• Design for manufacturability
• Measurement system analysis*	• Sampling plans*
• Projects planning*	• Mistake-proofing*
• Problem definition*	• The synchronized process*
• Project charter development*	• Strategic planning process
• Shewart charts *	• Coaching skills
• Lean concepts*	• Leadership skills
• Process costing and cost of quality*	• Measures development
• Value stream mapping and process mapping*	• Process improvements analysis*
• Lead time analysis*	
• Total productive maintenance	

*Usually covered in Green Belt training.

requirements were discussed in Chapter 2, and the items that should be in the curriculum are listed in Table 6.1 to make sure that you have at least considered these topics before selecting a consulting group or assigning the training department with the development process to design and construct the training. Appendix B contains a grouping of the tools for the DMAIC process.

DESIGN FOR SIX SIGMA

The next part of the training to consider is the design and development needs required to achieve the Six Sigma level of performance on future products and processes. These products will be developed with the needs of new markets, existing market, and new customers in mind. This will be the Design for Six Sigma (DFSS) process. The topics to consider in this training are listed in Table 6.2.

Table 6.2   Training curriculum for DFSS.

• Advanced voice of the customer and market knowledge	• Tolerance analysis
• Advanced quality function deployment	• Monte Carlo simulation
• Successful completion of Black Belt curriculum	• Design for assembly
• Statistical thinking	• Design for manufacturability
• Process focus	• Design for reliability
• The DMADVIC process	• Design for durability
• New project planning	• Design for testability
• New project management	• Design for maintenance
• Advanced process control	• Design for the environment
• Pugh concepts	• Implementing the design
• Anticipatory failure determination	• Design verification
• Taguchi analysis	

CHAMPION TRAINING

The champion training approach may cover the curriculum listed in Table 6.3, but in less detail than in Black Belt training. The basic knowledge of the Black Belt curriculum items is required in order for the champion to be able to support the Black Belt during the course of the project. This is why the curriculum is so vast and almost identical to the Black Belt training. This training is more from the conceptual approach than from the ability to apply all the tools. The items marked with an asterisk are covered only conceptually.

YELLOW BELT TRAINING

The training that is not talked about too much is Yellow Belt training within an organization. This training need is the same as most awareness training but provides more specific information to enable the employee to participate in the Six Sigma approach within his or her normal job. Yellow Belts are made aware of the Six Sigma philosophies and will support the reduction in variation in the processes they are familiar with in their daily work activities. Sometimes basic knowledge of flowcharting, lean concepts of process flow, and the ideas of process variation help the Yellow Belt. Yellow Belts go back into their daily activities but apply the principles of process improvements to their area. Some subjects to consider for the curriculum of Yellow Belt one-day training classes include the following curriculum:

- The Twelve Pillars of Six Sigma
- Six Sigma philosophy
- Process mapping
- Process improvement opportunities
- Concepts of variation
- Lean improvements

Table 6.3   Curriculum for champion training.

• Strategic planning process	• Project charter development
• Key organization success factors	• Process and quality costing
• Coaching skills	• Shewart charts*
• Project selection	• Value stream mapping and process mapping*
• The DMAIC process*	• Process capability analysis*
• Six Sigma philosophy	• Project management
• Operations measures development	• Hypothesis analysis and comparison testing*
• The Twelve Pillars of Six Sigma	• Regression analysis*
• Process improvement analysis	• Designed experiments*
• Change management	• Chi-square analysis*
• Lead time analysis*	• Multi-vari analysis*
• SMED*	• Multiple regression analysis*
• 5S process	• Response surface analysis*
• Leadership skills	• Failure modes and effects analysis*
• Training on the tools of Six Sigma DMAIC process*	• Control plans*
• Obtaining the voice of the customer	• Benchmarking process*
• Using the quality function deployment process to change the customer's voice to the process needs or CTQ's to CTP's*	• Problem-solving process*
	• Design for manufacturability*
• Understanding process controls	• Sampling plans*
• Understanding process variation	• Mistake-proofing*
• The difference between continuous and discrete data	• Project selection process
• Measurement system analysis*	• Lessons learned process
• Projects planning*	• Black Belt selection process
• Problem definition	

TRAINING APPLICATION AND EVALUATION

The training for the organization must be performed by a Master Black Belt and must be evaluated to ensure the success of the training. The evaluation will be in the form of a formal test on the subject matter and then a hands-on application of the theory on a practical project that the organization has picked for the Black Belt. The challenge for the trainer is to monitor and evaluate the project application properly to verify that the material learning took place. Consulting on the projects and processes improvement required is used to achieve the target for the project. We must link the tools usage to the problem-solving process for the project and ensure the specific goals can be met. It would be beneficial if the trainer for your organization had the following characteristics to work with in the classroom:

- Leadership skills

- Good facilitator

- Broad engineering background unless you are only working with transactional processes

- Ability to question the status of the organization
- Good analogy skills
- Mechanical and electrical aptitude
- Process analysis ability
- Good materials understanding
- Practical application of skills in your type of business
- Process flow technology knowledge
- Situational skills
- Builds confidence in the process being taught
- Good process mapping skills
- Works well with the executive council and the staff

CONSULTING SELECTION

The next item to address is the selection of a consultant and consultation company who will be able to support your process, address your issues, and provide the "train the trainer" teaching process, which will allow your organization to succeed by itself. An excellent consultant will train, coach, mentor, and develop the how-to strategy that will enable your personnel to handle the process without the consultant by their side. Remember, if you catch the fish for your customers they will be able to eat for the day, but if you teach them to fish they can sustain themselves for a lifetime. Good consultants will show you what is required and how to apply the "what," and they will guide you through the results. After the training, application, and retraining, you will be able to apply the process for yourself. This book is not intended to present a formula for selecting the best consulting company nor the best consultant because there isn't one prescription that will fit all. The best approach is to check references, test drive the car, and determine whether it fits your needs. If the answer is yes, then you may have the consultant that is the best choice for your organization. The following list provides items to consider in your selection process:

- Experience level of the consultant
- Number of successful projects completed
- Number of people trained
- Certification as a Black Belt or Master Black Belt
- Experience level with your industry
- Training material available
- Resources available
- Commitment to your success
- Ability to provide a learning environment

- Communication skills

- Leadership skills

The best advice is to assure yourself that the consultant, training material, and references will help the organization succeed at implementing the Six Sigma process. The consulting and training process should provide your organization with information that will allow you to improve the operation.

The continuous improvement process within the Six Sigma approach requires that the people involved can provide process knowledge, data on the process, and a problem-solving methodology to find causes of variation within the process. A good consultant will be able to help identify process opportunities, teach a useful problem-solving process for the organization, and develop the statistical tools that will find the causes of variation. I do not intend to describe the specific characteristics of a good consultant. The organization may want to use one of the problem-solving tools of the DMAIC process as a means to evaluate the consultant or the consulting organization. This tool is a decision matrix to select the best solutions for a project. The decision matrix can easily be used to identify musts and wants in an organization or consultant. In Figure 6.1, let's look at one of the examples we will see again in Chapter 15 for selection of an office PC.

Computer brand	HP	Dell	IBM	Local
Must cost less than $2000	$1895	$1595	$2000	$1780
Must weigh less than 4 lbs.	3.5	3.1	3.9	4.0
Must be 2.2GHZ	1.9	2.3	2.1	2.5
Must have modem	Yes	Yes	Yes	No
Must have CD writer	Yes	Yes	Yes	Yes
Highest RAM Score 10	532 Score = 10	532 Score = 10	256 Score = 5	256 Score = 5
UBS port Score 8	Yes Score = 8	Yes Score = 10	Yes Score = 10	Yes Score = 10
Fast modem Score 5	56K Score = 5	56K Score = 5	56K Score = 5	56K Score = 5
Maximize HD Score 10	10G Score = 5	30G Score = 10	6G Score = 4	10G Score = 5
Totals	28	35 Winner	24	0

Figure 6.1 An example of the selection process matrix for an office PC purchase.

CHAPTER QUESTIONS

1. How does the champion training program differ from the Green Belt training?

2. What are the major types of subjects covered in the DFSS process?

3. What are some of the items to consider in the DFSS course structure?

4. What criteria might be used in the selection process for Black Belts and the Black Belt training?

5. What requirements will prepare people to help support the Six Sigma continuous improvement process?

6. What are the training requirements of a Master Black Belt?

7. What additional training does a Master Black Belt have?

8. Are all the subjects presented in the detailed checklist necessary for the organizational training requirements?

9. On what would you base the training needs for your organization?

10. How should the training be provided to the employees?

SUGGESTIONS FOR FURTHER READING

Brue, Greg. *Design for Six Sigma.* New York: McGraw-Hill, 2003.

Eckes, George. *Making Six Sigma Last.* New York: John Wiley & Sons, 2001.

————. *The Six Sigma Revolution.* New York: John Wiley & Sons, 2001.

George, Michael L. *Lean Six Sigma.* New York: McGraw-Hill, 2002.

Naumann, Earl, and Steve Hoisington. *Customer Centered Six Sigma.* Milwaukee, WI: ASQ Quality Press, 2001.

Spande, Peter S. *The Six Sigma Way.* New York: McGraw-Hill, 2000.

Welch, Jack. *Jack: Straight from the Gut.* New York: Warner Business Books, 2001.

7

Pillar Five: The DMAIC, DMADVIC, and Lean Processes

The Twelve Pillars for Six Sigma Support and Implementation

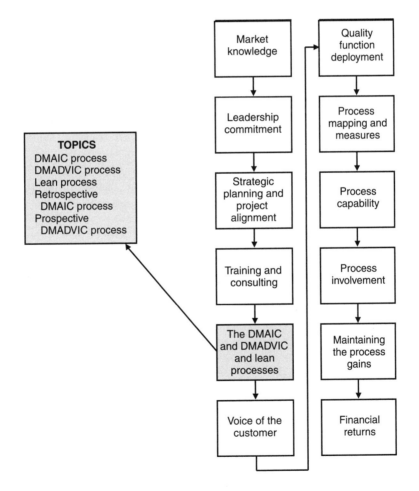

The intent of this chapter is to provide a brief overview of the content of DMAIC, DMADVIC, and lean because they support the improvement of processes.

DMAIC PROCESS

The DMAIC process (define, measure, analyze, improve, and control) must be followed in all retrospective projects selected by the Black Belt or Green Belt personnel. It is important that the DMAIC process be followed in the sequential order, yet each step may require returning to the previous step if we have not provided the answer for the step the Black Belt is presently addressing. The flow in Figure 7.1 shows the split in the DMAIC and DMADVIC processes.

Define

The define stage focuses the organization on the customer and measures of the customer needs as well as the process, with its measures, that must deliver the product or service to the customer. This step sets the stage for the project. From this customer knowledge, the organization or team can select the project charter, scope, and problem definition. This is the time to map the process and complete the as-is map. These maps should provide the actual current operation and all activities necessary to complete the entire process that involves the problem area to be addressed. The voice of the customer is used to obtain the customer focus and viewpoint of the critical to quality (CTQ) characteristics of the product or service. The affinity diagram is helpful in the voice of the customer analysis and the Kano model in understanding the items that may delight the customer. These tools are discussed in Chapters 8 and 9 and in more detail in the previously mentioned book, *Developing New Services.*[1] This will guide the Black Belt in determining key areas to address in order to satisfy the customer.

A good communication plan for the team, as well as between management and the employees, will help the proper personnel understand the project and goals. This helps

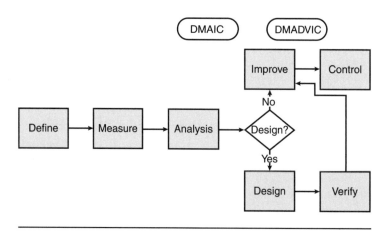

Figure 7.1 High-level flow of the DMAIC and the DMADVIC process for Six Sigma improvements.

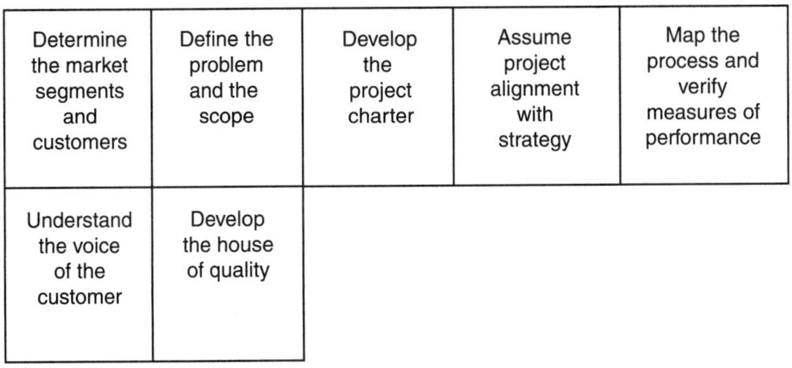

Determine the market segments and customers	Define the problem and the scope	Develop the project charter	Assume project alignment with strategy	Map the process and verify measures of performance
Understand the voice of the customer	Develop the house of quality			

Figure 7.2 Typical flow of the define stage.

support the project and makes it easier to obtain the resources to complete the project. The flowchart in Figure 7.2 illustrates how the project will go through the development of customer and market information collection; it also lists key factors to consider.

Once the project is defined, the organization can establish the process and process owner so the process can be measured for performance of the requirements. The measurements do not necessarily come from the customers themselves but from the output delivered to the customer. Internally, this may be the next operation. The completed charter must have a refined scope that is achievable by the Black Belt team.

Measure

In phase 2, the measure phase, the organization will measure the current process and decide what to improve. At this point, we are also collecting data about defects and their possible causes. The process map may need further detail, and defects analysis is used to determine whether the process contains any special causes and is stable. The establishment of an issues list can be helpful in the future. The special causes or stability issues need to be resolved before we proceed to calculate the sigma level of the process. The use of frequency plots, tree diagrams, cause-and-effect diagrams, Pareto charts, control charts, stratified frequency plots, and histograms will allow the measure phase to provide data about the existing process levels and areas of opportunities. The flow of the measure phase is depicted in Figure 7.3.

The measure phase can provide clues as to whether causes are of a special or common nature. This will help in the next phase.

Analysis

The analysis portion of the process provides the tools for collecting data to determine the causes of the problem that was defined in the first phase. It allows the team to eventually find the root cause of the problem, which is verified in this phase and used during the improvement phase. The analysis phase is usually the longest because we need to determine the cause of the problem and verify that it is the right one of many possible ties to the effect defined as the problem. During this phase, the problem may become more focused and the charter and

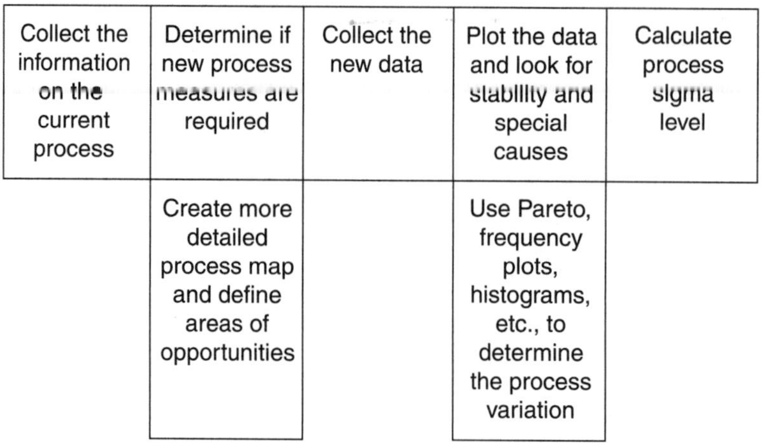

Collect the information on the current process	Determine if new process measures are required	Collect the new data	Plot the data and look for stability and special causes	Calculate process sigma level
	Create more detailed process map and define areas of opportunities		Use Pareto, frequency plots, histograms, etc., to determine the process variation	

Figure 7.3 Measure flow for obtaining data and information on the process.

scope of the problem definition may have to be changed. In essence, the potential causes are defined and analyzed further to determine the root cause of the problem. We may need to collect more data about the process and continue to use the statistical tools employed in the measure stage, as well as designed experiments, comparison tests, and setting hypothesis theory in place. We may want to consider the use of ANOVA (analysis of variances), ANOM (analysis of means), and chi-square. These advanced tools allow the Black Belt to learn more about the differences in the process as well as other processes, or steps, within the process. We must spend as much time as we need to determine the most important causes that affect the problem definition. The flow of the analysis phase is shown in Figure 7.4.

The analysis phase will provide the answers about the cause(s) of variation within the steps of the process. It will also provide more detailed data for assessing the amount of variation and should lead to reasons for the variation. Some of the reasons for variation will be special causes that must be taken care of before we can improve upon the common

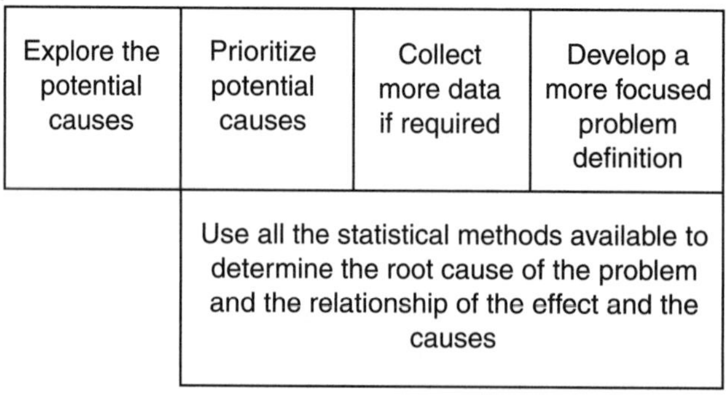

Explore the potential causes	Prioritize potential causes	Collect more data if required	Develop a more focused problem definition
	Use all the statistical methods available to determine the root cause of the problem and the relationship of the effect and the causes		

Figure 7.4 Flow of the analysis phase.

causes of the process. The process is usually looked at as an unstable process until the special causes are resolved. Once the process is stabilized, we can look at the common cause or natural variation for finer improvements. The analyze phase is usually the most time consuming of all phases because the root cause is elusive and the team must analyze all the data in search of the potential causes of variation. We must make sure that the team has taken enough time to collect and analyze all the data to determine when, where, what, and how the variation affects the process performance.

Improvement

The improvement phase determines which of the many available solutions should be used to solve the root cause, or causes, of the problem. This phase requires the use of similar tools that are available in the define and analyze phases. With them, we can determine the proper solution and then implement the solution after verifying that it resolves the problem. The possible solutions are identified at this stage, and the best solution is selected for implementation. A selection matrix rates musts and wants against the potential solutions in order to select the best solution. Once the solution is selected, we need to develop implementation plans, conduct a pilot run of the changed process, and develop the best levels for the process to maintain a consistent output. The results are verified and measured at this point to ensure that the selected solution will work. We must finalize the solution and the approach to be taken for the improvement to occur. The benefits are evaluated and the bottom-line financial results are determined. The flowchart in Figure 7.5 details some of the steps to be taken in the improvement phase.

Control

The last phase is the control phase, which is used to prevent the improvements made from slipping back to the original level. This is accomplished by using some proven tools to ensure that the process stays in a controlled state. Our choices can vary from statistical control charts to audit plans that will be used to control the process parameters. This will

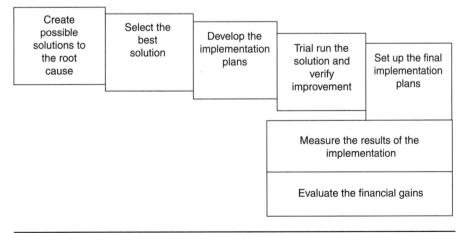

Figure 7.5 Process flow for the implementation process.

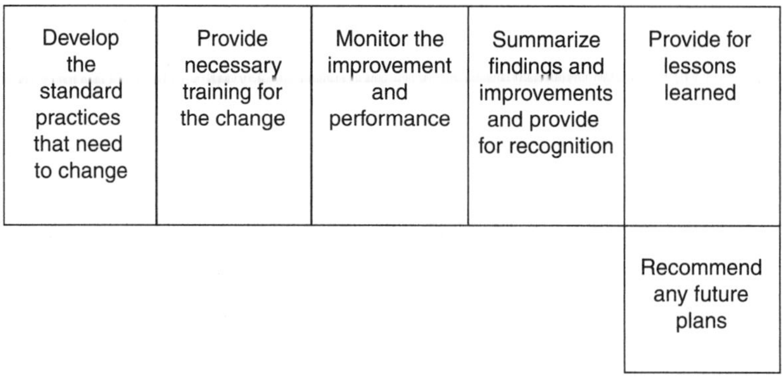

Develop the standard practices that need to change	Provide necessary training for the change	Monitor the improvement and performance	Summarize findings and improvements and provide for recognition	Provide for lessons learned
				Recommend any future plans

Figure 7.6   Flow of the control process.

allow the organization to consistently meet or exceed the customer's requirements. The final documentation changes, training, and methods of monitoring the process are determined and implemented. At this time, the Black Belt should recommend any other actions that may need to be taken concerning the process or other problems relating to customer needs, critical process parameters, and process activities. Plans for future improvement and lessons learned are considered at the end of the project. Figure 7.6 shows the flow of the control phase.

Figure 7.7 is a tools flowchart created to help some clients understand the availability of the tools and the possible sequence of their use. Note that Appendix B lists the tools used for each phase by the phase type.

DMADVIC PROCESS

The next process to consider is the DMADVIC (define, measure, analyze, design, verify, implement, control) process, which is used to design products and processes. It uses phases similar to the DMAIC process until we get to the design phase. At that phase we start considering design tools to ensure that the design will meet the customer's expectations. Emphasis is placed on the design process, which defines both the marketplace, or segments, that we will address, and the customers, or users of the product or service. It will involve collecting and analyzing additional data to complete a design concept. The design concept leads to the design process. This DMADVIC process should be followed by all organizations when developing new products or services.

Define

In the DMADVIC process, the define stage defines the customer, market, process, process owner, design concepts, and customer needs that are to be solved. This stage can be very time consuming, depending upon the amount of information needed. The tools available to select the market and the customer are varied and are covered in many books. The other sources provided will help in the definition of the marketplace and the customer needs analysis.

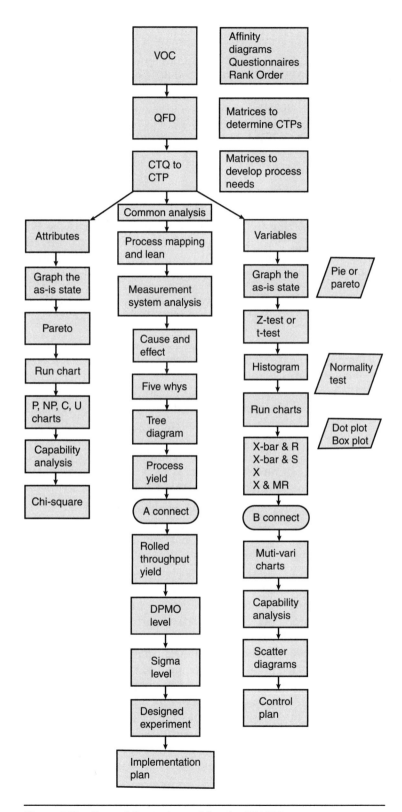

Figure 7.7 Flow of the tools used for the DMAIC process.

Measure

The measure phase ensures that we have chosen proper measures that will reflect the customer's needs and that the process parameters are tied to the output requirements linked to the customer. This should ensure that a linkage exists between the customer and the process parameters. The information derived from the customer base through the voice of the customer should be measured to determine whether we can meet the requirements on either the product performance or the service provided.

Analyze

The analysis phase is used to analyze the data captured from the customer needs and the measures provided to ensure that the proper specifications exist and the feasibility of the design concepts can be achieved. This phase will initially ask what the customer needs, wants, expects, and will be delighted by. To ensure that we have identified the proper parameters and processes, the data analyzed in the first pass is the customer and quality house information.

Design

This leads us to the design phase, where we use the tools of design tolerance, worst-case analysis, finite element analysis, reliability analysis, and testability (to name a few) to test the design of the product or process and our capability to deliver the product or service. The basic design function is performed in this step. The design and development function is usually very detailed in most organizations, but the sequence of tasks is not always followed in the design process. The tools of define, measure, and analyze are very important and must be used in the design and development process. The voice of the customer and quality function deployment, as well as measurement system analysis, become critical in the define and measure phases. During the analysis phase we establish the product and process (CTQ and CTP) characteristics and understand the real needs of the customers.

Verify

The verify phase ensures that testing and design analysis techniques verify that the design will be capable of delivering the product or service and that the process will meet or exceed the customer requirements. The important part of this phase is learning which methods and types of tests will verify that we will meet the customer's and engineering department's needs. The design analysis techniques become critical for the team. We may simply produce pilot lots in a simulated environment or run experimental tests on the factors that may affect output performance. Finite element analysis, prototype development, and simulation techniques all prove out the design in a laboratory environment. We may even perform stress testing of certain functions to determine any weakness of the design. We will discuss these different approaches to verifying the design in future chapters on the DFSS process, and other sources will be provided for study. It has been my experience that the verification process will depend more on product complexity and the availability of realistic testing programs.

Implementation

The implementation phase is the same for the DMADVIC process as the DMAIC process. We set out to plan the implementation of the new designed product or process to deliver the item or service with consistent output. In the DMADVIC process, we ensure that the production process will be capable of building the product to the requirements. Therefore, some form of manufacturing process verification should be performed before we release the product to manufacturing for implementation. The implementation phase should verify that the manufacturing process (including tooling, process set-up, and process performance characteristics) would be held during the build process.

Control

The control phase of the DMADVIC process ensures that the controls to maintain the process consistency are established and will do what the process and customers require. This phase is similar to the DMAIC process, with the exception that the controls are established before the pilot run and refined during the introduction to the manufacturing floor or at the service site. The output of this phase should be a finished and approved control plan for new developments. The important part of the control phase of the DMADVIC process is to verify that the process controls are noted and that the reaction plan is in place in case the controlled items drift out of the controlled zone. The design team needs to be aware of the critical points in the process of manufacture and make sure that the proper tests or checks are developed before releasing the product for manufacture. This task is made easier if the define, measure, and analysis phases were performed properly. A design review process is the best way to evaluate the tasks and ensure they have been completed before the control phase.

Let's now look at the additional tools used in the DMADVIC process by developing a process tools flowchart, shown in Figure 7.8.

LEAN PROCESS

The lean process uses its own set of tools to help eliminate waste and improve processing time. The lean process applies methods and techniques that sometimes parallel those of the Six Sigma DMAIC process. The goal of lean is to improve quality, eliminate waste, reduce lead time, and reduce costs. The quality goals and improvements begin with the voice of the customer, just as in the Six Sigma process. Errors causing failure to meet the customer's expectations are documented and problems are solved by using the tools of Six Sigma. The cause of waste is identified, and we try to eliminate the waste. This is achieved by reviewing the process for non-value-added steps and opportunities to reduce errors. The seven areas of waste considered by the lean process are listed below:

- Overproduction caused by poor planning, forecasting, and response to errors as well as the lack of understanding the customer's needs.

- Waiting to produce, held up by downstream process problems.

- Transportation that wastes effort and sometimes causes more errors and problems because of process queuing.

- Extra processing to compensate for errors that occurred in some of the processes within the operation.

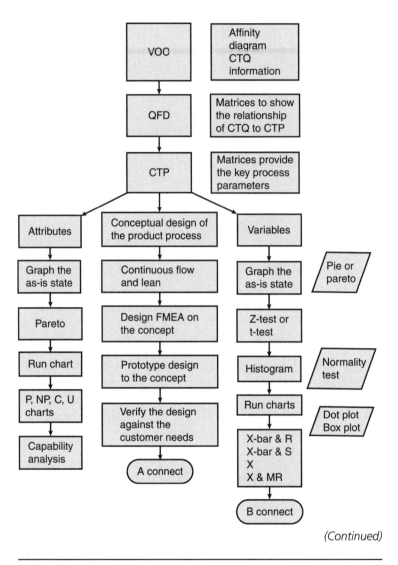

Figure 7.8 Flow of the tools used for the DMADVIC process.

- Poor inventory management resulting from inaccurate forecasts, errors in processes, and overproduction caused by problems within the processes. Excess levels of inventory occur when problems in delivery, manufacturing, and supply are anticipated.

- Unnecessary motions that do not add value to the process or product. These may be in the form of extra steps, improper handling of materials, or back-and-forth movement of parts.

- Defects in the product caused by errors within the process, including supplier or previous processes.

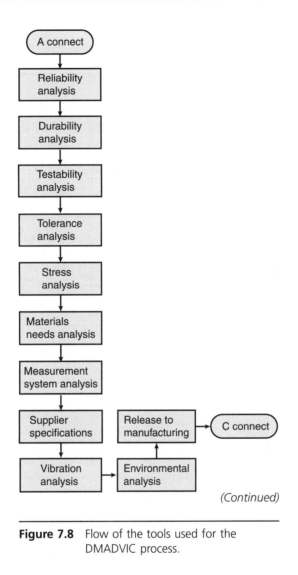

Figure 7.8 Flow of the tools used for the DMADVIC process.

LEAD TIME

Reduction of lead time within the process is achieved by improving the cycle time of the value-added steps and eliminating non-value-added steps in the process, which can also eliminate batch processing of materials, products, and supplier batches. Sequencing parts for the next operation as needed eliminates the process delay times. Kanban operations might be used to improve the sequencing.

VALUE STREAM MAP

A value stream process map is created to show the flow of materials as they move from supplier to the organization, through the manufacturing process and ultimately to the end customer. The transformation of raw materials into finished goods and the flow of information

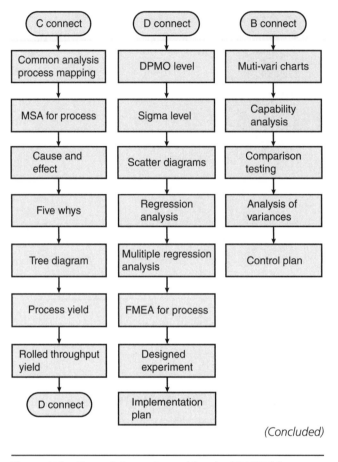

(Concluded)

Figure 7.8 Flow of the tools used for the DMADVIC process.

that supports and directs the movement of materials and the finished goods that have been produced is documented for the organization. This should help the organization understand how the separate parts of the value stream combine to create products or provide services. The goal of this value stream map is to highlight how activities, information, and material flow are interconnected. This provides many benefits. Employees come to understand the entire value process of the organization. The organization can make better decisions by understanding the current processes and related activities and how the process works before implementing any changes. A common understanding and language can develop as a result of understanding of the current process. This map will allow for the detecting of value-added and non-value-added steps that affect lead time of the process. The final benefit of this mapping process is that it will help the employees understand how they can identify and eliminate waste. This value stream mapping process focuses on the following:

- The flow of operational production activities used to produce product.
- The receipt, storage, and process flow of raw and production material.

- The value-added flow of the product or service.

- The push system of material moved from one operation to another.

- The waste involved within the system.

- The pull of materials and product in one operation to the next operation.

- The lead time of the entire process.

- The takt time of the process, which is the total available work time per day divided by the customer demand requirements for the day. The takt time will set production pace.

The process in Figure 7.9 depicts some of the items that can be obtained from the mapping process.

Table 7.1 contains the information for a demand flow analysis showing value-added steps and the amount of labor and machine time used for the assembly of a disposal unit. This is a typical analysis for a manufacturing operation. The value stream shows that 6.7 minutes of the time to assemble the disposal is non-value-added time, versus the 23 minutes of value-added steps.

5S PROCESS

Lean depends on visual management to expose waste, to set and display standards and key measures, and to organize the workplace to become efficient. This leads to a program called 5S, which stands for: sort out the workplace, shine the workplace, set the tools of the workplace in order, standardize the workplace, and sustain the process workplace. This concept provides for more efficient use of the tools and materials and allows for a more productive, mistake-proof process.

ERROR-PROOFING

The error-proofing concepts of Dr. Shigeo Shingo are practiced to prevent errors from recurring. The reader can find out a lot about this process from Dr. Shingo's book on the concepts.[2] Some of the concepts are: zero defects, inspection at the source of manufacture, kanban, Poka-Yoke systems and devices, zero quality control, and continuous flow processes.

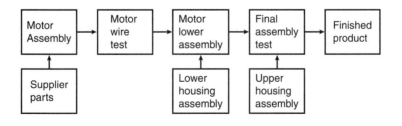

Figure 7.9 Relationship process of the value mapping process.

Table 7.1 Value map of an assembly showing value-added and non-value-added steps for a disposal unit.

Sequence number	Task	VA	Set-up	Machine	Labor	Move	TQC
010	Locate lower housing					.2	Verify housing
020	Check threads		3.5				TQC threads
030	Measure upper bore		1.5				TQC 1.375
040	Press bearing	*		3.9			Press seal
050	Attach spring	*			2.1		Check in groove
060	Apply grease	*			1.5		
070	Press oil seal	*		3.0			Even with hub
080	Attach gasket	*			3.6		No tears
090	Fit flange on gasket	*			3.0		No tears
100	Spread oil on seal	*			.5		10W30
110	Attach spout	*			1.2		Hand tighten
120	Repeat 110	*			1.2		Hand tighten
130	Torque screw	*			1.0		14 ft. lbs.
140	Repeat 130	*			1.0		14 ft. lbs.
150	Verify screw torque	*			.5		14 ft. lbs.
160	Repeat 150	*			.5		14 ft. lbs.
170	Check bore		1.5				Gage C2718
Total			6.5	6.9	16.1	.2	29.7 Minutes

SMED

The next approach is to reduce lead time in the process by SMED (single minute exchange of die) or quick changeover of tooling within a process as the parts or assembly change. One concept used is the one-piece flow design of the process to reduce time that elapses between the customer order and shipment of the finished product. Another approach is the kanban systems, controlling the flow of material in the pull system and building only what is needed at the time and place of the activity in the operation.

TOTAL PRODUCTIVE MAINTENANCE

TPM (total productive maintenance) is used as part of the process to ensure that every piece of production equipment will be able to perform to its requirements when needed. This will allow the organization to focus on improving equipment to maintain consistent production.

Figure 7.10 contains the flowchart of the lean approach to process improvements for any process that will have non-value-added steps. This waste is usually in the range of 30 percent to 40 percent.

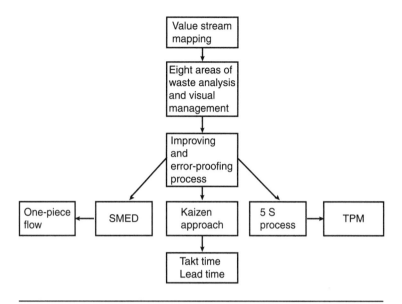

Figure 7.10   Lean process flowchart.

PROCESS DIFFERENCES OF DMAIC AND DMADVIC

Retrospective Improvement

Retrospective improvement of processes uses the DMAIC process. Here we still must consider the customer and the marketplace but, usually, it is to reassure ourselves that they were studied in light of the existing product or service process. This will ensure that the true requirements of the processes are identified. In many improvement projects, when we are working with the team of Black Belts, we reconsider the specifications and ask that the specifications concerning the customer be verified. In some cases we find that the process specifications were arbitrarily established by the sales and design personnel based on their knowledge of the market and customer, which are derived from experience. This can lead to unneeded or overspecified characteristics that the customer did not want. It can also lead to a loss of market share caused by not meeting the unspoken specifications that are basic needs of the customers. Therefore, review of the define phase of the DMAIC process is mainly aimed at verifying changes have been based on the voice of the customer and data from the quality house, using quality function deployment. The other point to make is that the voice of the customer and the quality function deployment process will help the team understand the needs and expectations of the customer base and, most importantly, what will delight the customers.

Prospective Improvement

The prospective improvement process uses the DMADVIC process, which must address the voice of the customer and the quality function deployment processes in as much detail as is needed to obtain the true needs and expectations of the market and the customer base. The product or service we will be selling in the future will require the definition of key parameters. The next major difference is that this process will focus on the design and development processes in detail to develop a robust product or service process. The next additional step is the verification of the design, which is similar to the analysis verification and the improvement verification steps in the DMAIC process. Here the design team must verify that the product or service will consistently meet customer and process needs. The improvement phase will cover the changes required after the verify phase as well as the items or steps required to control the process while it is released for production or service delivery. The control phase requires that specific process controls for the new process have been established and maintain the output of the process to meet or exceed the customer's requirements.

The design phase of the DMADVIC process includes many design and development programs that will help create products and processes that provide consistency to the customer. Without getting into all the steps in a good design process, some of the key development processes used to achieve customer satisfaction and meet or exceed expectations follow:

- Material selection process
- Supplier selection process
- Production requirements to achieve product or service needs
- Design principles of:
  —Tolerance(s) of the components
  —Key parameter identification
  —Measurement system requirements and analysis
  —Testing requirements
  —Stress analysis, such as full load and overload testing
  —Process finite element testing
  —Process tolerance analysis
  —Material needs analysis
  —Supplier specifications
  —Packaging requirements
  —Vibration analysis
  —Marginal specification limits
  —Reliability analysis
  —Environmental effects analysis
  —Testability analysis
  —Failure mode effects analysis

The Implementation Process

Let's cover the typical approach that might be used within an organization. The lean process can be considered the first step in the retrospective approach to problem solving and process improvements. In this step we are considering the process needs and the parameters of the process. We verify that all the steps in the process to build the product or provide the service to the customers actually do add value to the direct customer. The non-value-added processes are eliminated or controlled to ensure that we provide effective and efficient processes. The non-value-added processes sometimes consume 50 to 60 percent of the entire process steps. These non-value-added steps are sometimes necessary if the organization is to produce a product or provide a service. We will also consider waste when evaluating a process for improvements. We must consider the organization's needs for information and technology in the value-added analysis. The value analysis process is another tool for process improvement. The idea of causing change in the organization requires us to use many Six Sigma tools during the DMAIC and DMADVIC processes.

This is a good point in this book at which to stop and consider some of the tools we already talked about and those that need to be considered in order to be successful in this process. The voice of the customer requires that we use the affinity diagram to understand the areas that the customer considers important relating to delivery of the product or service. The value mapping process will allow us to determine our value to the customer. The consequences matrix from the voice of the customer will obtain the key needs. The tree diagram, cause-and-effect chart, and general matrix of the quality house will be used by the design team to develop the key processes or activities. Once we have developed the key processes we are ready to use the mapping process to map out the as-is process steps. At this stage we should be considering the defects, cycle time, and any issues with the steps of the process. Sometimes it might be wise to consider value-added analysis of the process before we go forward in the Six Sigma process. The finished process map will contain the total cycle time of the process, an issues list for the process, and the defect rate of the process. From these steps we can determine the sigma level of the process and the yield of the process. Now we are ready for the stability and capability analysis of the process. This analysis will provide C_p, C_{pk} and P_{pk} figures for the process. The tools used at this stage are:

- Pareto chart

- Histogram

- Dot plot

- Box plot

- Run chart

- Individuals chart

- X-bar and R

- X-bar and S

- Individuals and moving range

- Evolutionary weighted moving average (EWMA)

- Cumulative sum control charts (CUSUM)

- Percent or proportion defective (P)

- Number of defectives in process (NP)

- Number of defects in process (C)

- Defects per unit (U)

- Five whys
- Tree diagram
- Changes and distinctions concepts
- Six points of view of the process
- Six factors of the process.

After performing all this analysis, we are ready to test the final stability and capability of the process. Once we are assured of its stability and capability, we are ready to improve the sigma level of the process. At this stage the advanced tools of Six Sigma come in to play. We must consider comparison testing, ANOVA, ANOM, chi-square, and design of experiments. With stability, capability, and improvement secured, we turn to the tools of implementation of change management, solutions selection matrix, and process controls.

CHAPTER QUESTIONS

1. What is the difference between the uses of DMAIC and DMADVIC processes?

2. What are the key points of the lean process?

3. Does the flow of DMAIC have to follow a set sequence?

4. Why is it better to start with the DMADVIC process for new products or services?

5. What is the difference between the lean and DMAIC processes and their tools?

6. What is SMED, and how does it apply to Six Sigma?

7. Why do we need to error-proof a process activity step?

8. What is the difference between retrospective and prospective improvements?

9. What is total productive maintenance?

10. Why do we need the control phase in the DMAIC process?

SUGGESTIONS FOR FURTHER READING

Bossidy, Larry, and Ram Charan. *Execution.* New York: Crown Publishing, 2002.

Brue, Greg. *Design for Six Sigma.* New York: McGraw-Hill, 2003.

Eckes, George. *Making Six Sigma Last.* New York: John Wiley & Sons, 2001.

———. *The Six Sigma Revolution.* New York: John Wiley & Sons, 2001.

George, Michael L. *Lean Six Sigma.* New York: McGraw-Hill, 2002.

Naumann, Earl, and Steve Hoisington. *Customer Centered Six Sigma.* Milwaukee, WI: ASQ Quality Press, 2001.

Spande, Peter S. *The Six Sigma Way.* New York: McGraw-Hill, 2000.

8

Pillar Six: Voice of the Customer

The Twelve Pillars for Six Sigma Support and Implementation

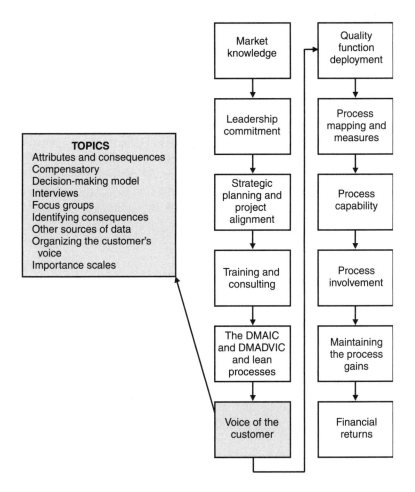

TOPICS
Attributes and consequences
Compensatory
Decision-making model
Interviews
Focus groups
Identifying consequences
Other sources of data
Organizing the customer's
  voice
Importance scales

Market knowledge

Quality function deployment

Leadership commitment

Process mapping and measures

Strategic planning and project alignment

Process capability

Training and consulting

Process involvement

The DMAIC and DMADVIC and lean processes

Maintaining the process gains

Voice of the customer

Financial returns

This chapter will cover the requirements and highlights of the voice of the customer process. The process has been explained in many texts, which will be referred to in this chapter and the reference section of this book. The subject will be covered in enough depth using material from this author's *Developing New Services*[1] so that you can decide what kind of skills will be required to meet your specific needs in the training outline. This chapter should also convince you that obtaining the voice of the customer is crucial in ensuring that your organization's Black Belt projects focus on the specific items that will affect the customer and the operation's bottom line. Most projects start out by selecting a problem area from a list of projects. The Black Belt must determine the need for the project from a business sense and ensure that the customer needs are understood for the output of the process that covers the problem area. The voice of the customer must be applied to DFSS projects by using DMADVIC. In the reactive DMAIC projects, using the voice of the customer information will ensure that we focus on the proper CTQs.

This chapter will cover the highlights of the VOC process, which are: identify the market and customer base, determine the questions that need to be answered by the customer to obtain the needs and the expectations, gather the customer data verbatim, analyze the data, and prioritize or rank the information after grouping the data. There are two reasons for identifying the needs. The first reason is to ensure that the process can meet those needs consistently. This should enable you to verify that you are running at the Six Sigma level. The other reason is that sometimes we make decisions about requirements of the process that may not affect the customer. Customer loyalty is also evaluated during this search for data. The quality function deployment (QFD) process (covered in Chapter 9) will drive the CTQs throughout the organization to develop the key process characteristics that we must concentrate on to be successful. In defining the customer base, we may need to segment the market into areas by geography, customer types, or product types. Segmentation is important if the parameters of the product or service are different based on needs.

Now we will cover the process of obtaining the voice of the customer for a specific project. Some of these concepts come from the book the author cowrote on VOC/QFD for service organizations. The attributes and consequences theory comes from Dr. Caroline Fisher of Loyola University, coauthor of *Developing New Services*.[1]

ATTRIBUTES AND CONSEQUENCES

As service providers, we tend to think of our services in terms of their attributes or features. But consumers are not so interested in service features or attributes, or even the services themselves. What they are really interested in are the consequences of using our services. Customers buy services for their benefits, or positive consequences, not their attributes.

Attributes are the physical or abstract characteristics of the service or product. Consequences, on the other hand, are the results of using the service or product. Attributes are generally objective and measurable. For example, we can objectively measure the length of time a person stands in line (attribute: short waiting times) by using a stopwatch. On the other hand, what one feels about not having to wait a long time is subjective, and we cannot measure it except through the perception of the person waiting. Indeed, what seems like a short wait on one occasion may seem like an interminable wait on another, even to the same person, because of different reasons for waiting or different conflicting time requirements leading to a need to save time.

As the following example points out, consequences are subjective; they exist in the eye of the consumer and are very individual. Consequences include customer perceptions of convenience. A consumer values an attribute only because of its perceived capacity to create a desired consequence through use of the service. One consumer may perceive one consequence for using a service, while another consumer may perceive a very different consequence from using the same service. Consequences exist only if the user perceives them. Consequences are strictly from the viewpoint of the user, not from the viewpoint of the service provider, who may have a very different opinion about the appropriateness of the waiting time.[2]

Because of the number of attributes and consequences and their many relationships, we often use an attribute/consequence grid to visually display the relationships. Table 8.1 shows an attribute consequence grid for a package delivery service. The attributes are in the first column, and the consequences are in the first row. When a positive relationship exists between a consequence and an attribute, we place an "+" in the cell where the two intersect. When a negative relationship exists, we place a "−" in that cell. The number of pluses or minuses indicates the strength of the relationship. If no relationship exists, we leave the cell blank. In Table 8.1, we see a strong positive relationship between careful and no damage; we see a negative relationship between careful and within budget.

So, now we know that consumers select services based on the consequences they expect to receive. However, we still do not know how they select one brand of service out of the many available. Consumers select the service provider that offers the greatest value overall, when all the consumers' needs and wants are considered. The compensatory decision-making model illustrates how this decision is made.

Compensatory Decision-Making Model

Compensatory decision making is a highly logical process that involves rating competing service brands on relevant criteria, weighting them by an importance factor, and then summing these weighted ratings. The consumer selects the brand with the highest sum. For a specific brand, strength on one criterion can compensate for a weakness on another criterion, leading to the term *compensatory* in the title of the model.

Let us look at an example comparing three hypothetical brands of delivery services. We call the delivery companies or brands Acme, Bell, and Class. First, we need a list of important consequences for using delivery services (Table 8.2). We add the consumer's ratings of the importance of each of these consequences. Let us say that our consumer rates them on a scale of zero to 10, zero being the least important and 10 being the most important.

Table 8.1 Attribute/consequence grid for a package delivery service.

	Consequences			
Attributes	**Overnight**	**Delivered the day I want**	**No damage**	**Within budget**
Speedy	+++	+		−
Exact time	+	+++		−
Careful			+++	−
Low cost	-	−	−	+++
Accurate				−

Table 8.2 Importance ratings for a package delivery service.

Consequence	Importance Rating
Delivered overnight	5
Delivered the day I want	10
No damage	9
Within budget	10

Table 8.3 Brand ratings for a package delivery service.

Consequences	Importance Rating	Brand Rating		
		Acme	Bell	Class
Delivered overnight	5	10	2	7
Delivered the day I want	10	4	6	4
No damage	9	10	8	4
Within budget	10	5	8	10

Next, we add the consumer's ratings of each brand on each consequence. Again, we use a 10-point scale. The ratings for each brand appear under the brand name. For example, Bell was rated a 6 on "Delivered the day I want," as shown in Table 8.3.

Now we use the model to calculate the brand of delivery service that this particular consumer will select. The brand rating on a consequence multiplied by the importance rating of that consequence yields a weighted rating, one where we weight the brand rating by the importance. We repeat this calculation for each brand on each consequence. Then we sum these weighted ratings for each of the service brands. These sums are displayed in the bottom row of Table 8.4.

The calculations show us that this consumer would choose the Acme brand despite its low rating on "Delivered the day I want." Its strength on other consequences, especially on "no damage," more than compensates for that weakness.

The emphasis on "this consumer" is critical. As stated in the "Attributes and Consequences" section above, consequences are subjective and individual. We cannot assume that two consumers will want the same consequences, nor that they will rate the

Table 8.4 Full compensatory model of decision making for a package delivery service.

Consequences	Importance rating	Acme		Bell		Class	
		Rating	Weighted rating	Rating	Weighted rating	Rating	Weighted rating
Delivered overnight	5	10	50	2	10	7	35
Delivered the day I want	10	4	40	6	60	4	40
No damage	9	10	90	8	72	4	36
Within budget	10	5	50	8	80	10	100
Sum of weighted ratings			230		222		211

importance of a consequence or the brand ratings on that consequence the same, even when they do want the same consequence. We have to make these measurements and calculations for each individual in order to predict purchase behavior.

Another method we use when we have a large number of consumers is to divide them into groups or segments based on their ratings of the importance of a list of consequences. We want to determine consumer segments that desire very similar consequences, and we want each segment to be as different from the other segments as possible on desired consequences.

The only way to determine consequences is to ask the consumer, to obtain the voice of the customer. Two primary ways to obtain the voice of the customer are through interviews or focus groups. In both cases, we ask the customers what is important to them when selecting our service. Most often, customers give us service attributes, such as speedy service. Because we are looking for the consequences explained previously, we ask "why" or probe for the underlying consequences tied to any attribute a customer gives in response to our questions.

INTERVIEWS

Interviews consist of one-on-one conversations, which are kept in focus by the interviewer. This is probably the best way to obtain the voice of the customer. The interviewer leads the discussion through questions, which have been prepared to collect the desired information. Typical questions used in interviews to obtain customer consequences for pizza delivery are:

- What comes to mind when you think of pizza delivery?
- What brands of pizza can you name?
- Which brand do you normally select?
- Why do you choose that brand?
- Have you ever received bad pizza delivery? Tell me about it.
- What would your ideal pizza delivery be like?
- What is important to you in selecting a pizza delivery service?
- Walk me through the process of deciding to order a pizza through eating the pizza and getting rid of the trash.

The interviewer does not use every question with each consumer. One question is used to get the consumer talking. When the consumer stops responding to one question, the interviewer asks another question.

To elicit consequences from consumers, we use a technique called probing. The interviewer takes each attribute mentioned by the consumer and asks "why." We vary the wording of the question, using some of the following forms:

- Why is that important to you?
- Why do you say that?
- What do you mean by that?
- Why do you want _____?
- What would happen if you didn't get _____?

FOCUS GROUPS

We use focus groups to gain the same information that interviews do, but we are dealing with a group of people instead of individuals. This is the next best approach to the interview. The biggest advantage of a focus group is that the members of the group tend to stimulate ideas from one another, much like brainstorming. A trained moderator usually runs the focus groups because working with groups is more difficult than working with individuals. Someone who has training as a facilitator probably has the skills necessary to run a focus group for purposes of acquiring the voice of the customer.

Each focus group consists of 7 to 12 consumers who are similar in demographics. The reason that we bring similar people together is that they tend to communicate with one another more readily than people who vary significantly. In addition, the similarity in the consequences they desire helps them stimulate additional ideas from other members of the group.

The moderator of the focus group develops a series of questions in preparation for running the session. The questions are the same as those asked in interviews; the main difference is that we give all participants an opportunity to answer each question. Again, the moderator asks one question and then gives all the participants an opportunity to answer it fully. We use probing in much the same way in the focus group as in the individual interviews. When the group has finished answering the question and its probes, the moderator asks another question.

Like the interviewer, the moderator cannot conduct the group, listen and probe, and write down the responses. Using a second person to write down responses is common during focus group sessions. The sessions may be audiotaped, but more often, we videotape them. We also use special rooms with two-way mirrors for some focus groups; people who have a stake in hearing what the consumers have to say may listen and watch from the other side of the mirror.

One of the difficulties of using interviews or focus groups is getting the customers to tell you all the consequences that are important to them. The problem is that customers do not always think about all the important consequences. Indeed, sometimes they are not even aware of important consequences.

The Kano model helps us understand why consumers do not recognize all the consequences that are important to them. The graphical depiction of the Kano model uses two axes, the degree of providing desired consequences and the level of customer satisfaction, ranging from dissatisfaction to loyalty. Figure 8.1 shows these axes, along with the relationship between these two dimensions for the type of consequences generally known and expressed by customers: performance consequences.

Figure 8.1 shows three lines for basic consequences: performance consequences and excitement consequences. It illustrates the relationship between degree of achieving excitement consequences and level of customer satisfaction. Again, this line is not straight and the relationship is not linear. When a brand does not provide these excitement consequences, customers are not dissatisfied. Their level of satisfaction is neutral; they are neither satisfied nor dissatisfied. However, when a brand provides these excitement consequences, customers exhibit very high levels of satisfaction and loyalty.

These excitement consequences are those that no service brand currently provides, at least as far as the customer is aware. They represent cutting-edge consequences that can lead to a tremendous competitive advantage in the marketplace. Examples from the past may include telephone call-forwarding options or color printers.

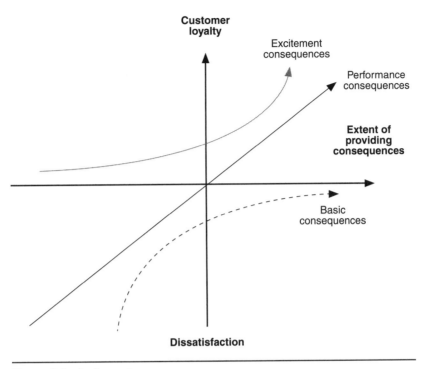

Figure 8.1 Excitement consequences.

We really want to learn about potential excitement consequences, but this is difficult because consumers are not even aware of them themselves. We have to be creative in coming up with these potential competitive advantages based on existing consequences and underlying needs and values of our consumers. One question we use during interviews to try to obtain some of these consequences is, "What would your ideal service be like?" Another is, "What else could this service do for you?" A third is, "Tell me how you use this service." All of these elicit hints of additional consequences. We combine these hints with our knowledge of the services and new technologies to develop new attributes that result in consequences never provided by this type of service in the past.

IDENTIFYING THE CONSEQUENCES FROM THE INTERVIEW TRANSCRIPTS

To get all the desired consequences from the tapes or transcripts of the interviews, we have three individuals review them separately and write down every attribute and consequence they detect. Three individuals working independently seem to detect most of the consequences and attributes mentioned, with diminishing returns provided from using a fourth individual.[3] For best results, these individuals need to understand the differences between attributes and consequences, to understand the Kano model, and to understand the importance of obtaining all the consequences.

OTHER SOURCES OF DATA

Using interviews and focus groups to obtain desired consequences is an important and necessary process. Other sources of consequences are available, however, and we do not ignore them. These sources include industry literature, trade shows, and the knowledge of our in-house experts. You ask employees who have direct contact with your customers and your operations experts to provide their ideas on consequences desired by your customers. Add these to your list before proceeding to the next step, organizing the customer voice. Other approaches to gathering information on desired consequences are to observe customers using our services or to use mystery shoppers, who anonymously use our services and report on their experiences.

ORGANIZING THE CUSTOMER VOICE

We use two approaches to organize the voice of the customer. In the first, the affinity diagram, the team members sort the consequences desired by the customer. The other approach, the customer sort, has a sample of customers do the sorting. Their descriptions follow.

Affinity Diagram

Before the team gets together to begin the process, write each consequence desired by consumers on a self-adhesive note sheet. Supply a large surface to which the note sheets adhere for use in sorting the consequences.

Next, assemble the team to conduct the process. The team consists of no more than six members from the larger service development team. Explain the affinity diagram process to them. Emphasize that they are to maintain silence throughout the sorting process to encourage creativity. Also, recommend that they move very quickly without thinking too long about any possible pairing or groupings. Like during a brainstorming process, speed prevents censoring ideas and aids creativity.

The team sorts the desired consequences into groupings. Each member looks for consequences that relate to the others in any way and places them near each other on the large surface. Use any pairing that comes to mind. If someone does not like where a consequence is, that person moves it. This process continues until the team has placed all consequences in groupings and team members have stopped moving the consequences around. Depending on the team and the consequences, this process can take considerable time!

Once they have completed the sorting, the team members select a consequence from each group to be the category title, placing it at the top of the group. This card best represents all cards in the group. Try to represent the essence of the category with the title card.

Customer Sort

We give each customer a deck of cards, each bearing one desired consequence. The customer sorts the cards into piles so that each pile represents similar consequences and differs from the other piles in some way. We ask the customer to choose a single consequence from each pile that best represents the desired consequences in the pile. This consequence, called the exemplar, becomes the category title. We keep it in the voice of the customer.

We record the consequences that the customer puts in each pile, along with the exemplar. Calculate the number of times you paired each consequence with every other consequence. You can analyze the data resulting from the customer sorts by hand or using computer software to do a cluster analysis. To do the analysis by hand, create a matrix with the consequences listed both across the columns and down the rows, in the same order. Draw a diagonal line through the cells where a consequence intersects with itself. Now use only the cells above and to the right of the line. Fill in each cell with the number of times the consequence for that row was placed together with the consequence for that column in a pile. The consequences that you paired together most often form the final groupings of consequences.

In general, those who have tried both approaches to grouping consequences say that the customer sort provides a clearer, more believable, easier-to-work-with representation of customer perceptions than the affinity diagram. However, the customer sort approach takes considerably more time to perform. The reason for this sort is to be able to prioritize the customer needs. We will eventually rank the customer needs in a 1 to 10 ranking with 10 being the most important to the customer. There is more to this process, and it is covered very well in the books in the References. From here we are ready to enter the quality house in the quality function deployment process.

ALTERNATIVE IMPORTANCE SCALES

Now let's go back to looking at how to measure the importance of a set of consequences desired by consumers. People commonly use four scales to measure relative importance: rank order, itemized rating, constant sum, and anchored.

The *rank order scale* lists consequences and asks the consumer to rate them in order of importance from one to the number of consequences listed, as shown in Figure 8.2. Consumers have little trouble understanding how to answer rank order questions unless the number of consequences gets large, especially larger than 10. On the other hand, they have no way of ranking two consequences the same if they feel they are equally important. A rank order scale provides an ordinal measurement. The proper measure of the average is the median. We should not use the results to multiply times brand ratings because of the nature of this measurement scale.

The *itemized rating scale* asks the consumers to rate each consequence on a specified scale of importance, as shown in Table 8.5. It is easy for the consumer to understand and answer. The consumer may give more than one consequence the same rating. However, the

---

Rank the following consequences of pizza delivery from one to seven according to how important they are to you. Give the most important consequence a seven. Then assign numbers to the others to indicate the order of their importance to you.

_____ The crust is good.

_____ My order is taken quickly.

_____ Delivery is quick.

_____ I can get my favorite toppings.

_____ The pizza is hot when I get it.

_____ I can order when I want.

_____ I save money.

Figure 8.2 Rank order scale.

Table 8.5   Itemized rating scale.

Rate each of the consequences given below, using the scale provided. Circle the number that best represents your feelings about the importance of that consequence.

Consequence	Not at all important	Slightly important	Important	Very important	Extremely important
The crust is good.	1	2	3	4	5
My order is taken quickly.	1	2	3	4	5
Delivery is quick.	1	2	3	4	5
I can get my favorite toppings.	1	2	3	4	5
The pizza is hot when I get it.	1	2	3	4	5
I can order when I want.	1	2	3	4	5
I save money.	1	2	3	4	5

choice of scale item names strongly influences the results. The discrete rating scale provides ordinal measurements. The proper measure of the average is the median. We should not use it in multiplication.

The *constant sum scale* gives the consumer a total number of points that is to be divided among the consequences to indicate their relative importance, as shown in Figure 8.3. Usually, we use 100 points or 100 dollars, making this scale realistic. An advantage over the rank order scale is that the consumer may assign the same number of points to more than one consequence and may assign zero points to one or more consequence. Unfortunately, this scale is more complicated for consumers to use, especially when the number of consequences does not divide evenly into 100. Often they rate each consequence on a scale of 100, making their questionnaire unusable. The constant sum scale provides ratio measurements. We may use the mean as the measure of average, and we may multiply the results times the brand ratings.

The anchored scale first asks the consumer to choose the most important consequence from a list and to assign ten points to that consequence, as shown in Figure 8.4. Then we ask the consumer to rate the importance of all the other consequences in relationship to the most important one on a scale of zero to 10. The consumer may rate more than one consequence

Divide 100 points among the following consequences of pizza delivery to show how important each is to you. You may assign a consequence from 0 to 100 points; just make sure that the total for all consequences equals 100.

_____ The crust is good.

_____ My order is taken quickly.

_____ Delivery is quick.

_____ I can get my favorite toppings.

_____ The pizza is hot when I get it.

_____ I can order when I want.

_____ I save money.

Figure 8.3   Constant sum scale.

Find the consequence in the list below that is most important to you. Assign it 10 points. Then assign from zero to 10 points to the other consequences to indicate how important they are to you in comparison to the one that is most important. You may assign the same number of points to more than one consequence.

_____ The crust is good.

_____ My order is taken quickly.

_____ Delivery is quick.

_____ I can get my favorite toppings.

_____ The pizza is hot when I get it.

_____ I can order when I want.

_____ I save money.

Figure 8.4   Anchored scale.

the same, allowing equality of importance. Instructions are very important for this type of scale so that every consumer assigns a 10 to at least one consequence—creating the importance anchor. A natural fear when using this scale is that the consumers rate all consequences as high in importance; in the author's experience, this rarely happens. The anchored scale provides a ratio measurement; we may use the mean as the measure of average, and we may multiply the results times the brand ratings.

Table 8.6 compares these four scales used for measuring importance. For our purposes, we want a scale that we may multiply times our brand ratings and that meets the criteria for metric statistics. Both the constant sum and the anchored scales meet these requirements. My coauthor of *Developing New Services* prefers the anchored scale because the consumer can apply it easily to long lists of consequences that often occur in service situations, and it is less confusing than the constant sum scale because it does not require the consumer to divide.

This provides a quick overview of the voice of the customer for you. The references will provide more detailed information on the process. The conclusions of this process will be used in the quality house of quality function deployment to provide the requirements for the key processes in the operation to ensure we will meet the customer's needs and then ensure customer satisfaction with the products or services.

Table 8.6   Comparison of scales.

Scale	Measurement type	Strength	Weakness	Average	Equality	Zero	Multiply
Rank order	Ordinal	Easy to understand	Short lists only	Median	No	No	No
Itemized rating	Ordinal	Easy to answer	Wording critical	Median	Yes	No	No
Constant sum	Ratio	Realistic	Confusing	Mean	Yes	Yes	Yes
Anchored	Ratio	Works with a long list	Anchor critical	Mean	Yes	Yes	Yes

---

CHAPTER QUESTIONS

1. What are the differences between attributes and consequences from the voice of the customer?

2. How is the affinity diagram used in developing the attributes from the customer?

3. What does the Kano model show us about customers' expectations?

4. Why do we need the customers to rank their needs and expectations?

5. How are consequences obtained from the customers?

6. What types of questions do we need to ask to learn about customer consequences?

7. Why do we need to use an anchored scale for the importance of consequences?

8. Why is it necessary to organize the voice of the customer's data?

9. What is the benefit of using focus groups?

10. What is the difference between the anchored scale and the rank order scale?

SUGGESTIONS FOR FURTHER READING

Allen, Derek R., and Tanniru Rao. *Analysis of Customer Satisfaction Data*. Milwaukee, WI: ASQ Quality Press 2000.

Bossert, James L. *Quality Function Deployment: A Practitioner's Approach*. Milwaukee, WI: ASQ Quality Press, 1991.

Day, Ronald G. *Quality Function Deployment: Linking a Company with its Customers*. Milwaukee, WI: ASQ Quality Press, 1993.

Fisher, Caroline, and James T. Schutta. *Developing New Services: Incorporating the Voice of the Customer into Strategic Service Development*. Milwaukee, WI: ASQ Quality Press, 2003.

Griffin, A., and J. R. Hauser. "The Voice of the Customer." Marketing Science Institute, Working Paper Report 92-106, 1992.

Naumann, Earl. *Creating Customer Value*. Cincinnati, OH: Thomson Executive Press, 1995.

Naumann, Earl, and Steve Hoisington. *Customer Centered Six Sigma*. Milwaukee, WI: ASQ Quality Press, 2001.

Woodruff, R. B., and S. F. Gardial. *Know Your Customer: New Approaches to Understanding Customer Value and Satisfaction*. Cambridge, MA: Blackwell Publishers, 1996.

9

Pillar Seven: Quality Function Deployment

The Twelve Pillars for Six Sigma Support and Implementation

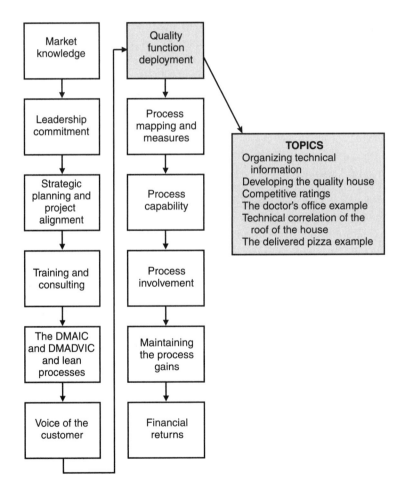

This chapter will cover the concepts of transforming the voice of the customer from the previous chapter into technical specifications or requirements for the operations side of the organization so processes and products may be designed to meet or exceed the customer's requirements. The tool used by Pillar Seven that will help us with this transformation is called quality function deployment (QFD) and is sometimes referred to as the house of quality. The founder of quality function deployment, Yoji Akao, described the QFD portion of the process as a method for developing a design quality aimed at satisfying the customer and then translating the customer demands into the design targets and major quality assurance points to be used throughout the service provision stage of the process.

Dr. Genichi Taguchi further developed the quality function deployment process in the 1970s. The process of filling out the matrix for this house and the establishment of the key processes or parameters for the process is relatively simple, but when one sees the completed matrixes it looks confusing unless you have been trained in the development of the matrixes and in seeing what the picture is telling you. We will briefly cover the establishment of this tool and how useful it is for the Black Belts. The references supplied at the end of this chapter can be used to obtain further knowledge of this powerful tool.

We will establish controls of each process to meet or exceed the process tolerances pointed out by the house of quality. The QFD process is most successful on new designs but can be used in reactive Six Sigma projects in order to define the critical processes and tolerances of parameters that must be held to ensure customer satisfaction. An example of the completed house is provided for your review. This example and other material in this chapter are taken from *Developing New Services.*[1]

Customer input is required for selecting the technical characteristics and for properly designing the service, process, or product. The left side of the quality house starts with the weighted or prioritized customer needs (the whats). These needs are the consequences derived from the interviews with the customers. The weighting of the customers' needs helps us with the selection of the critical issues for the technical requirements that we must meet in order to satisfy the customers' needs. These weightings, in turn, determine the weightings for the technical requirements. At this point, we have established the customer section of the house.

We set a goal of creating one to three technical requirements for each consequence (the hows). More gives us too many technical requirements to handle; less will not adequately provide for satisfying customers. Figure 9.1 shows the transfer of the hows from the whats.

Each technical requirement is a way that we can use (process or design) to meet the corresponding consequence desired by our customers. Each needs to be within our control and contain an attribute we can vary within our service or process. Each also needs to be measurable so we can set objectives and determine if we are meeting them.

ORGANIZING THE TECHNICAL INFORMATION

We use a creative process to organize the technical information that helps ensure that we properly develop and define the technical requirements. The tree diagram[2] is a good tool for developing the specific technical features that help meet the requirements of the customers. We cover the tree diagram process for generating the technical requirements next.

We use the tree diagram to create requirements in a way similar to the use of the cause-and-effect diagram to generate root causes. Figure 9.2 shows a template for a three-layer tree diagram. The tree diagram is useful for linking the want or consequence to the technical requirements while performing the analysis.

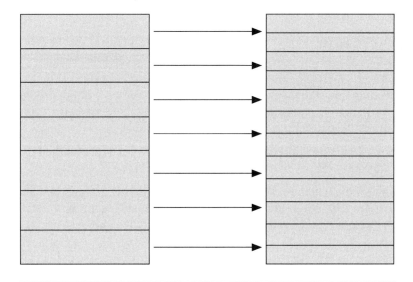

Figure 9.1 Provide one or more hows for each what.

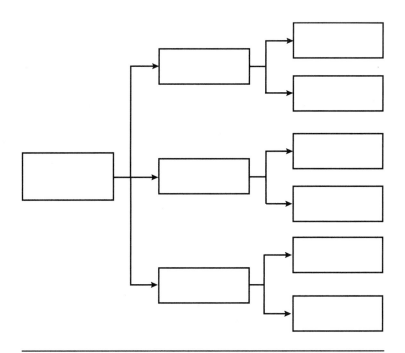

Figure 9.2 Three-layer tree diagram.

The rules for building a tree diagram are:

1. Choose one grouping from the completed affinity diagram of customer wants to expand into a tree diagram. (Each group can become the basis for a separate tree diagram.)

2. Agree upon one statement that clearly expresses the core issue, problem, or goal for the group selected. We can use the header card taken directly from the affinity diagram if it meets the team's approval.

3. Once we define this primary goal or issue card, we place it on the left side of a flipchart or table.

4. Identify all the elements or components related to this primary statement. Then brainstorm additional elements or components, using the existing card as a starting point. Record each new idea on an index card.

5. Identify the ideas most closely related to the central statement. Arrange them in a column to the right of the central statement, similar to a family tree or organization chart. These ideas represent the secondary level of detail on the diagram.

6. Add the elements related to this secondary level to create a tertiary level of detail. Continue until you have added all of the cards or recorded ideas to the diagram in a sequence that shows their relative level of detail. You may find a card does not belong on this tree diagram or that you need a new card to meet the specific goal or purpose.

7. Study the diagram for any holes in the sequence or the logic. You may review each branch by starting at the most detailed item on the far right and tracing the flow from more to less detail.

The process for developing customer requirements in the technical information matrix is to take the wants or consequences and align them with technical concepts.[2] We illustrate the results of this process for pizza delivery in Figure 9.3. Customers want hot, tasty pizza

Quick response	_____ Time to respond (cycle time)
	_____ Time to complete transaction
	_____ Time to deliver
Clean facility	_____ Cleanliness standards
Hot pizza	_____ Hot core bags
	_____ Speedy delivery
	_____ Cook at location
	_____ Cook on way
Fast delivery	_____ Air Express
	_____ Automatic sorting
	_____ Hand delivery

Figure 9.3 Pizza delivery service needs example.

delivered on time to their houses. The specific customer needs and expectations are:

- The pizza is cut all the way through the dough.
- The pizza is hot.
- The pizza tastes good.
- The pizza is done all the way through.
- Distinct sauce flavors and spices are used.
- The pizza is good every time.
- The pizza does not droop when picked up to be eaten.
- A variety of types is available.
- The sauce covers all of the dough.
- The pieces are cut uniformly.
- There are many choices for toppings.
- The sauce is not watery.
- The pizza is not stuck to the box bottom or the paper.
- The pizza is not doughy.
- The pizza is not greasy.
- Generous toppings are supplied.
- Generous cheese is provided.
- Fast delivery.
- Large topping pieces are provided.

The hot pizza delivery can be shown by using the tree diagram in Figure 9.4. In Figure 9.5, we look at another example of the tree diagram. For service processes, such as delivering a package, we need to offer alternatives that provide speedy and safe delivery based on a given price. The alternatives can be air, surface truck, small service car, bicycle, or a variety of hand deliveries. We must follow up on each of these ideas for feasibility before we consider them for inclusion in the technical requirements of the quality house.

THE DOCTOR'S OFFICE

The following example of the doctor's office looks at attributes and consequences in the reception area. From the consequences developed for a doctor's office reception and the importance ratings developed, the technical staff develops the requirements for meeting the needs of the patients. They and the doctors consider the processes that support the customer needs and develop the requirements for the process and the key measures for the process to be successful.

The list of needs obtained from the interview process is as follows:

- Length of time until appointment.
- Number of rings until the call is answered.

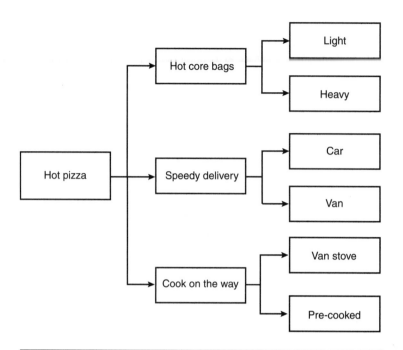

Figure 9.4 Tree diagram for developing technical ideas for a hot pizza.

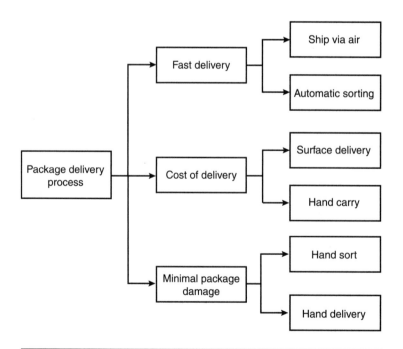

Figure 9.5 Example of a tree diagram for delivery of a package.

- Time on hold.
- I was passed from person to person.
- I was asked few needless questions.
- Use of automated phone system.
- Waiting time in office too long.
- Responsiveness of personnel too slow.
- Insurance coverage processing properly.
- Insurance company recognized by office.

From this list of attributes, the following consequences are developed:

- I got an appointment within a week of my call.
- I had my choice of days.
- I had my choice of times.
- I spent little time on the phone.
- I was asked if this was an emergency.
- I was not put on hold.
- I was in the doctor's office on schedule.
- My questions were answered accurately and timely.
- My insurance claim was processed properly.
- My insurance carrier provides coverage for the doctor.

Once you have developed the customer consequences from the voice of the customer and weighted them, you can fill in the left side of the house.

A receptionist handles the customer's need for an appointment with a doctor for a routine check-up or for a diagnosis of a health problem. Because the receptionist has a variety of options, she/he must determine which one or combination of doctors should be assigned to perform the routine exam or diagnosis. The development team must identify all the alternatives that exist for questioning the patient, and it must select the method that the receptionist will use to address the customer's needs. Team consensus helps in this process. For the appointment, they offer alternative dates and times. Figure 9.6 shows the quality house with the customer's desired consequences and the weightings the customers assigned to them.

DEVELOPING THE QUALITY HOUSE

Once we have completed the technical hows, we work on the relationships to the technical portion of the quality house. We can further understand the alternatives if we create a matrix of customer needs to possible technical requirements. This matrix process leads to alternatives that you can discuss with the design team before moving on with the selection of key design concepts that have the ability to meet the needs of the customer. The example in Figure 9.6 shows the matrix for the house of quality. Next, we develop the strengths

Technical Requirements / Customer Input	Weighting																	
Time to appointment	8																	
Number of rings	8																	
Choice of days	9																	
Choice of times	5																	
Short time to schedule	9																	
Criticalness of visit determined	10																	
Appointment made without interruption	5																	
Appointment time kept	8																	
All questions answered		9																
Insurance claims processed	8																	
Insurance coverage recognized	10																	

Figure 9.6 Quality house matrix with customer input and importance weightings.

of the relationships between the technical requirements and the customer consequences. The symbols used to indicate the strength of the relationship are:

None	=	No relationship	weight = 0
△	=	Small relationship	weight = 1
○	=	Medium relationship	weight = 3
◉	=	Strong relationship	weight = 9

We compare all relationships between the voices of the customer (needs) to the technical requirements (hows). Once we have completed this relationship matrix, we evaluate it for technical hows with no relationship to any of the wants (needs) of the customer. We need to question and eliminate these, if possible. This matrix will also point out whether we created too many requirements, or hows, during brainstorming. We should have filled in no more than 50 percent of the blocks and should have created a random pattern of filled-in blocks.[2] If this occurs, we will have to select the best choice of requirements to meet the customer needs.

The office personnel develop the processes to provide the consequences desired by the customer. First, they translate the customers' needs (consequences and attributes) into technical requirements using the brainstorming process. Figure 9.7 shows the results of their brainstorming process.

Their next step is to organize the technical requirements, using a tree diagram. Figure 9.8 shows part of the tree diagram they developed, and Figure 9.9 shows the design matrix log, which ties the voice of the customer to the technical how and how much, or measurement to be used, along with the value of the measurement (see page 110 for both figures). The tree

Time to appointment	Availability of doctor
	Type of care required
	Time required during visit
Number of rings	Responsiveness
	Phone locations
	Answering system
Choice of days	Doctors' flexibility
	Number of open slots
	Scheduler flexibility
Choice of times	Doctors' flexibility
	Number of open slots
	Scheduler flexibility
Short time to schedule	Scheduler availability
	Systems capability
Criticalness of visit	Asking the right question
	Determining the patient needs
No interruptions	Scheduler has the time
	System speed
	Scheduler capability
Appointment time kept	Doctors' availability
	Scheduler system capability
	Doctors' performance
Questions answered	Doctors' performance
	System scheduler capability
	Doctors' accuracy
Insurance claims processed	Systems scheduler capacity
	Scheduler capability
Insurance coverage	Scheduler capability

Figure 9.7 Results of brainstorming technical concepts.

diagram is also useful in describing which methods or techniques are required for satisfying the specific technical requirement chosen to fill the need.

Now the team must select the process that will meet the selected requirements and determine whether a measurement can be applied to each process. The methods used for this are to brainstorm the requirements of the process and choose the process that will meet the needs of the customer. The team then fills in the top of the house.

The cause-and-effect diagram shown in Figure 9.10 (see page 111) can also be used to evaluate potential hows for the top of the matrix within the house. This example shows the doctor's appointments issues.

The technically key characteristics or considerations are friendliness, time to obtain appointment, ability to help, knowledge about the problem, and courteousness. Using this material and information helps us build the quality house for the customer needs. Figure 9.11 on page 111 is an example of what the quality house looks like as they begin to build it.

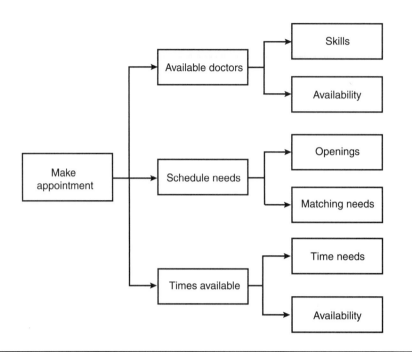

Figure 9.8 Tree diagram example for the doctor's office.

No.	Customers' Voice	Technical Requirements	Measuring Units	Value
1	No waiting in office	Scheduler	Time	Seconds
		Doctors' timing	Time	Minutes
		Process control	Checks per line item	Number
2	All questions answered	Operator training	Training time	Hours of training
		Training process effectiveness	Testing	Passing grade
		Insurance knowledge	Training time	Hours of training
3	Short time to schedule	Care available	Care types	Quantity of care types
		Doctor staff level	Number on staff	Quantity of doctors with skills
		Schedule flexibility	Scheduler and type of care	Ability to schedule type of care

Figure 9.9 Doctor's office customer design matrix log.

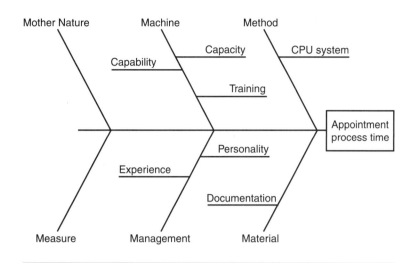

Figure 9.10 Cause-and-effect diagram for doctors' appointments.

	Material	Material	Methods	Methods	Machine
	System	Friendliness	Knowledge	Able to help	Time to appointment
Appointment					

Figure 9.11 Beginning of the quality house.

In order to verify that the appointment process performs well, they may have to run a study (experiment) that analyzes whether different experience levels, or knowledge levels and personalities, of receptionists greatly affect the time taken to make an appointment. The people who work as receptionists in the office should participate in the experiment.

The team establishes the methods and approach for the experimental design and the data to be collected. They select sample sizes, equipment, people to perform the experiment, and people to perform the test under controlled conditions. To evaluate the results, they need to obtain data from observers or blind callers.

They need to consider how to select the sample of callers in order to eliminate any bias and conduct a fair evaluation. They repeat this test and poll customers of a competitive doctor's office using the same customer input to obtain a competitive analysis.

Once they have completed the caller test, they run further tests to verify system capability and capacity of the process. They use this measure (capacity) for controlling appointment timing. Consider the following possible causal factors:

- Personality

- Healthcare experience

- Training

- Experience in the doctor's office

- Process knowledge

They study these variables to determine the optimum level for the receptionist. Through their experiments, they come up with the best selection for the five variables noted above. The design team creates the ultimate formula or recipe. Once it is in place, they control the recipe or the process. They eventually verify the sensitivity of the process to the five variables by conducting an experiment, if they have not completed one during the design process. They must consider the design of experiments throughout the construction of the quality house. Figures 9.12 and 9.13 show how the hows can be developed for the doctor's reception office.

To evaluate scheduler performance, they test the input checks performed, the database for procedure timing, and the ability to plan the output. They screen each doctor's abilities and match them to the patient's needs at the time of the call in order to understand the diagnostic requirements before scheduling the appointment. They also determine which process controls to put in place to ensure that they handle each patient properly and schedule appointments quickly and correctly.

COMPETITIVE RATINGS

The competitive analysis compares our delivery of desired consequences to that of our key competitors. Typically, we use a Likert-type scale of five points to measure customer beliefs for each organization. Likert scales are ordinal scales; the distances between the points on the scale may not be equal. The proper measure of the average is the median. The Likert scale is not metric, so we are breaking basic assumptions when we use metric statistics. Luckily, these statistics are not that sensitive to this type of failure. Researchers have found metric statistics used with Likert scales to be valid over many years of use.

			Doctors' training	**Process control**	**Process control**	**Process control**	**Process control**
	Schedule	**Schedule**					
	Training	Data accuracy	Diagnoses	CPU speed	Input accuracy	System capability	System training
No waiting time in office							

Figure 9.12 Doctor's office example of customer needs to technical hows.

Technical Requirements / Customer Consequences	Weighting	System available	Care available	Scheduler speed	Doctor training	Doctor staff size	Scheduler accuracy	Scheduler flexibility	Doctor flexibility	System capability	Operator training	System speed	System accuracy
Time to appointment	8												
Choice of days	9												
Choice of times	5												
Short time to schedule	9												
Criticalness of visit determined	10												
Appointment made without interruption	5												
Appointment time kept	8												
All questions answered	9												
Insurance claims processed	8												
Insurance coverage recognized	10												

Figure 9.13 Quality house with customer input and requirements on the doctor's office call.

The staff at the doctor's office developed a questionnaire to measure the importance of the consequences their patients wanted and to measure consumers' perceptions of how the office delivered these consequences. For comparison purposes, the questionnaire asked the patients to rate the office of another doctor or dentist on its delivery performance as well. Figure 9.14 shows their questionnaire.

They asked every patient who came into the office during the next week to complete the questionnaire while waiting to see the doctor. A staff member entered the data into Microsoft Excel and calculated weighted ratings and averages. Figure 9.15 shows the results. The average weighted ratings are virtually equal, not in agreement with the overall satisfaction ratings where the doctor's office scored higher than the competitors' offices. Two reasons for this disagreement are possible. First, some important consequence could be missing or some wording problem could exist. Perhaps someone reworded the consequences incorrectly. Second, the use of a variety of offices for the comparison measure could account for the disagreement. Using a variable comparison office would lead to greater variability in the data and could well account for the disagreement in this situation.

Using the requirements that were established for the doctor's office using the quality house, we can complete the measures for each feature or function and correlation matrix for the doctor's office processes to meet the customers needs. The technical team will evaluate the matrix for completion and note any deficiencies. The team then develops the measures at the floor of the house and the matrix correlation is filled in for the customer consequences to the technical requirements.

Find the consequence of making an appointment with a doctor in the list below that is most important to you. Assign it ten (10) points. Then assign from zero (0) to ten (10) points to the other consequences to indicate how important they are to you in comparison to the most important one. You may assign the same number of points to more than one consequence.

_____ I get an appointment within a week of my call.
_____ I am not put on hold.
_____ I am asked few needless questions.
_____ I have my choice of days and times.
_____ I spend little time on the phone.

Please rate how well we deliver each of these consequences when you call to set up an appointment. Circle the number below that best indicates how well you feel we satisfy each of the consequences. For comparison purposes, please rate another office on the same consequences; rate either another doctor's office or a dentist's office that you have visited in the past year. Use a scale of:

1 = Strongly Disagree
2 = Disagree
3 = Neutral
4 = Agree
5 = Strongly Agree

	Our Office					Another Office				
I get an appointment within a week of my call.	1	2	3	4	5	1	2	3	4	5
I am not put on hold.	1	2	3	4	5	1	2	3	4	5
I am asked few needless questions.	1	2	3	4	5	1	2	3	4	5
I have my choice of days and times.	1	2	3	4	5	1	2	3	4	5
I spend little time on the phone.	1	2	3	4	5	1	2	3	4	5
Overall I am satisfied with the appointment process.	1	2	3	4	5	1	2	3	4	5

Figure 9.14 Questionnaire for doctor's office.

The doctor's office example shows the entire process of taking the requirements from the initial planning matrix to the secondary parameters for the office to deliver to the requirements of the key processes and supply the customers' desired consequences. Figure 9.16 (on page 116) shows the original doctor's office example with a few additions.

From Figure 9.16, the staff took forward the highest priority technical requirements. Figure 9.17 (on page 117) illustrates some of the process parameters that the team developed. This part of the doctor's example also shows the relationship between the key technical requirements and the process parameters for those processes. The weight for the input row is determined by taking the final weight for the column from the planning matrix and dividing it by 10.

TECHNICAL CORRELATIONS FOR THE ROOF OF THE QUALITY HOUSE

We show the technical trade-offs at the roof of the house for the technical requirements chosen to meet the customer needs. Here we are looking for positive, negative, or no cor-

Technical requirements / Customer consequences	Weighting	System available	Care available	Scheduler speed	Doctor training	Doctor quantity	Scheduler accuracy	Scheduler flexibility	Doctor flexibility	System capability	Operator training	System speed	System accuracy
Time to appointment	8	△	○			◉	◉	○	◉	◉	◉		○
Choice of days	9		◉		◉	◉	◉	◉	◉				○
Choice of times	5		◉		◉	◉	◉	◉	◉				○
Short time to schedule	9			◉			◉			◉	○	◉	○
Criticalness of visit determined	10								○		◉		
Appointment made without interruption	5	○		◉			○	△		◉	◉	○	○
Appointment time kept	8					◉			○	△	○		
All questions answered	9				◉						◉		
Insurance claim processed	8	○								◉	◉		
Insurance coverage recognized	10		○		◉								
Value		↓	↑	↑	↑	↑	↓	10SEC.	↑	↑	↑	↓	↑
How much		System downtime in hours	Number of caregivers	1000 MHZ processor	Trained in necessary care	Number of doctors available	Software errors	Software capacity	Doctor care training	Number of software features	Training effectiveness	System response of 1 second	Software capability

Figure 9.15 The doctor's office call with the matrix completed with requirements, measures, and relationships.

relation between the technical requirements that we established to meet the customers' desired consequences as defined by the voice of the customer process. The roof is sometimes difficult to establish because we might not know the relationships or we might not be able to verify them. If this is the case, we will have to conduct further testing and correlation analysis for the variables (the technical requirements). The testing may be some form of comparison testing or designed experiments. The correlation analysis helps us establish good design parameters, which are required for meeting customer's needs and expectations. Since the process design specialists (engineers) provide the technical requirements to meet the customer consequences, they also determine the relationships or correlations that exist between each pair of requirements. This team leads the process for filling in the roof of the quality house.

Customer consequences	Weighting	System available	Care available	Scheduler speed	Doctor training	Doctor staff size	Scheduler accuracy	Scheduler flexibility	Doctor flexibility	System flexibility	Operator training	System speed	Training process	Screening process	Insurance knowledge
Time to appointment	8	●	●	●		●	●	●	●	●					
Choice of days	9	●	●		●	●	●	●	●	●					
Choice of times	5	●	●		●	●	●	●	●	●					
Short time to schedule	9	△	●		●	●	●	●	●	●		●			
Criticalness of visit determined	10										●		●	●	
Appointment made without interruption	5	●	●	○			●	●	●	●	●	●		●	
Appointment time kept	8	△			○	●	●	△	●	●	●			●	
All questions answered	9										●		●		△
Insurance claim processed	8	○									●		●		●
Insurance coverage recognized	10										△		●	●	●
Value		↑	↑	↑	↑	↑	↑	↑	↑	↑	↑	↑	○	○	↑
Final weight		268	324	86	215	351	396	332	396	396	370	126	333	297	171

Figure 9.16   Doctor's office technical requirements.

The development team should see how one requirement might affect another requirement as they determine the hows for the technical portion of the matrix. The direction and degree of the correlations between the technical requirements have serious impacts if one how affects another and can represent design difficulties. The hows that are related negatively with respect to others represent design bottlenecks that will call for special planning or design breakthroughs to solve the conflict.

In completing the technical correlation matrix, or roof, the team establishes tests using the requirements that affect the activity or function it is evaluating. The tests may require the development of an experiment to determine the interaction of the requirements on the output responses or dependent variables. Statistics and research design books develop the experiments we use.

The roof of the quality house (this may be why we call this matrix a house) quickly becomes the groups' design control method to ensure that we consider the interactions between the technical process parameters. These interactions will affect the customers' needs if we are not careful. The measures we established for these items are used now to our advantage to design the process so that the interactions have the least effect on the final process and, in turn, will provide the customers' desired consequences as well.

	Critical process specification	Weighting	System requirements	Scheduler requirements	Doctors' experience	Staffing system	Operator experience
System available		27	◉			○	◉
Care available		32		◉	◉	◉	
Scheduler speed		9	◉				△
Doctor training		22			◉		
Doctor staff size		35				◉	
Scheduler accuracy		40	△	◉			○
Scheduler flexibility		33	○	◉			
Doctor flexibility		40	○	○			△
System capability		40	◉				
Operator training		37					◉
System speed		13	◉	△			△
Training process		33		○			◉
Screening process		30		○			◉
Insurance knowledge		17		○			◉
Value			100 MHZ	10 sec	10 years	1 month	5 years
Direction			↑	↑	↑	○	↑
Weight			1020	1305	486	684	1416

Figure 9.17 Doctor's office process parameters.

Testing approaches to consider for determining the correlations between technical requirements are:

- Laboratory prototype evaluation
- Simulated operational performance
- Alpha test sites to evaluate performance
- Past experiences and test data

Now we take the pizza example and apply this approach to determine the correlation between the requirements we use to develop the pizza delivery process. Determining the relationships between the technical requirements is important when we develop the approaches used to create the consequences for our customers. The process team reviews all the possible correlations by checking each possible pair of requirements. The correlation symbols used for the roof are:

Correlation
High positive ✱
Low positive ×
Low negative ○
High negative ◉

Figure 9.18 shows a correlation matrix for the pizza example for your review and analysis.

We have filled in most of the roof correlations for the analysis of the pizza. Some other considerations may surface as we analyze the effects of the technical features associated with ordering, preparing, baking, and delivering the pizza. This correlation analysis is important to the design of the processes that will allow us to deliver high-quality pizza on time to meet various customers' needs. The trade-offs will be important to meeting customers' needs and the ability to deliver a service that will exceed what is available from the competition. The technical process owners and delivery personnel conduct this correlation analysis to be sure we have covered all necessary relationships between the technical requirements.

The staff of the doctor's office met as a team to consider the correlations between the technical requirements. They considered the relationship between each pair of requirements. Figure 9.19 (on page 120) shows the correlations they hypothesized. Even though they felt confident about the direction of the correlations, the team members recognized a need to study some of the relationships further.

THE FINAL QUALITY HOUSE FOR THE DELIVERED PIZZA

The quality house for the delivery of a tasty pizza is shown in Figure 9.20 (on page 121) as another reference illustrating the completed form. It may look very detailed and sometimes confusing if you are looking at the matrix without knowing how it was developed. Note the important points for the customer and the key processes that need to be maintained. The process parameters should be noted at the bottom of the matrix, along with the most important processes that will support the improvement of the delivered pizza.

The quality house has helped us deliver the key process parameters to operations or the design group of the organization. The development of the quality house and the use of quality function deployment will help the organization focus on the important factors of the processes. We should then be ready to determine where the existing process is for the important characteristics. This leads us to the next level in Six Sigma and future chapters.

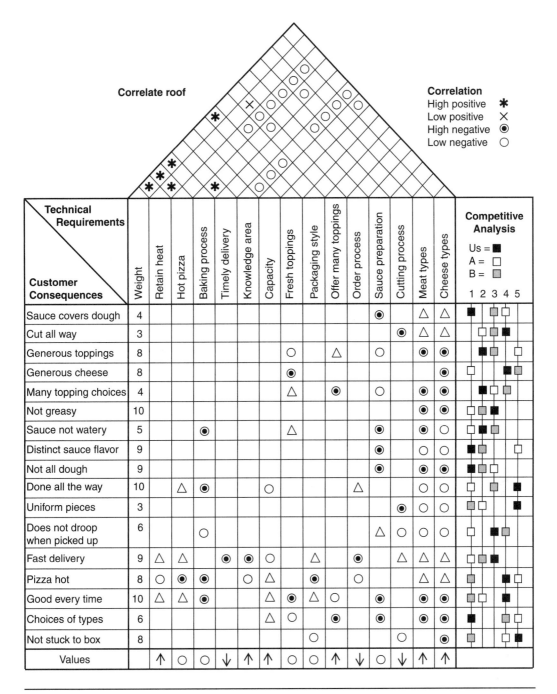

Figure 9.18 Portion of the finished pizza quality house.

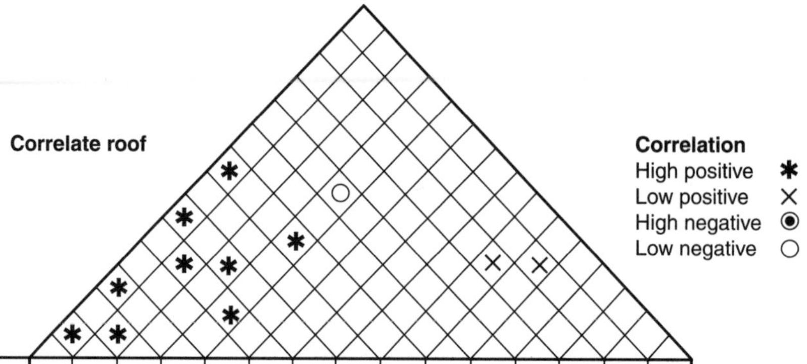

Figure 9.19 Portion of the finished doctor's office quality house.

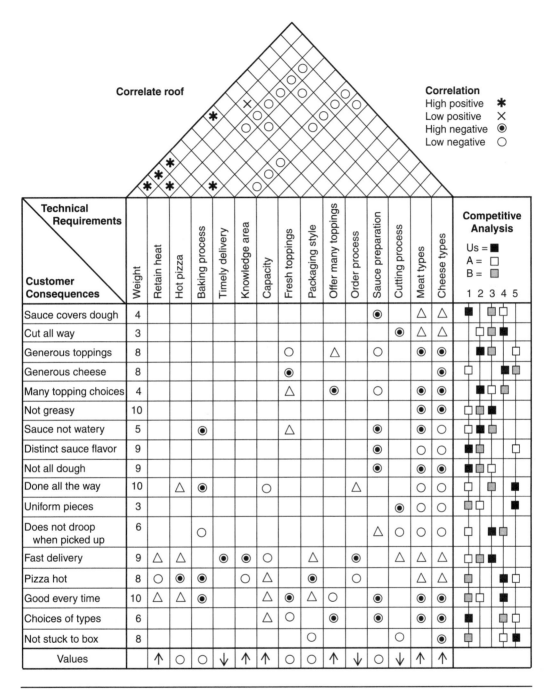

Figure 9.20 Portion of the finished quality house for a delivered pizza.

CHAPTER QUESTIONS

1. How are the "how" and "what" features developed to meet the customer's needs for the quality house?

2. What are some of the tests that are applied to determine if the how will be important in meeting the customer's needs?

3. What is determined from the roof of the quality house in quality function deployment?

4. What should the matrix of the customer's needs to the engineering hows tell us about the relationships and fulfillment of the customers' needs?

5. What is the importance of weighing the relationship between the customer's needs and the engineering hows of the process or features?

6. How does the measurement of the how help us in developing a good process?

7. When the matrix in the house is finished, how much of the need/how matrix should be filled in for the analysis?

8. What would happen if the customer's needs were not ranked by the customer for use in the quality house?

9. Do consequences or attributes work better as inputs into the quality house?

10. How is the cause-and-effect diagram used in the development of the quality house?

SUGGESTIONS FOR FURTHER READING

Akao, Yoji, Ed. *Quality Function Deployment: Integrating Customer Requirements into Product Design.* Cambridge, MA: Productivity Press, 1990.

Allen, Derek R., and Tanniru Rao. *Analysis of Customer Satisfaction Data.* Milwaukee, WI: ASQ Quality Press, 2000.

Bossert, James L. *Quality Function Deployment: A Practitioner's Approach.* Milwaukee, WI: ASQ Quality Press, 1991.

Day, Ronald G. *Quality Function Deployment: Linking a Company with its Customers.* Milwaukee, WI: ASQ Quality Press, 1993.

Fisher, Caroline, and James T. Schutta. *Developing New Services: Incorporating the Voice of the Customer into Strategic Service Development.* Milwaukee, WI: ASQ Quality Press, 2003.

Naumann, Earl. *Creating Customer Value.* Cincinnati, OH: Thomson Executive Press, 1995.

Woodruff, R. B., and S. F. Gardial. *Know Your Customer: New Approaches to Understanding Customer Value and Satisfaction.* Cambridge, MA: Blackwell Publishers, 1996.

10

Pillar Eight: Process Mapping and Customer and Process Measures

The Twelve Pillars for Six Sigma Support and Implementation

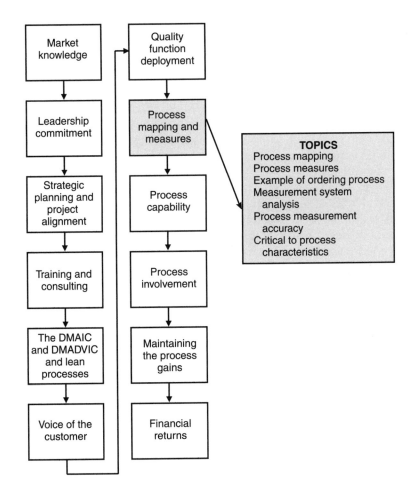

Now that the customer's needs and expectations are known and the key processes that will affect the customer have been identified through the QFD process, we need to ensure that we focus on the key measures within the process that will provide a consistent output to meet the requirements of the customer. This chapter will focus on the process mapping structure and the key measures for the customer and the key measures for the process that we must address to achieve customer satisfaction.

The subject of process mapping creation has been treated well in many other books. Only the use of the mapping process will be discussed here. The initial process map is usually called an as-is process map because it should outline the process that currently exists in the problem area that the Black Belt wants to address.

PROCESS MAPPING

The process mapping operation needs to assure the team that the as-is condition of the activities are documented and that each activity has the cycle time, cost information, and defect rates provided. The key parameters for each step, as well as the measured value used for performance analysis, should be identified. This chapter covers the identification of the measures for the process and the level at which it is operating when measured. The process map will identify the boundaries of the process we are evaluating and provide information about the input requirements to the process and the outputs provided by the process. To develop the process map, select the people within the process, the suppliers to the process, and the customers of the process for input. There are standard symbols to use for developing the map and the way the map is laid out. Most often we use activity maps, but we could use deployment maps and opportunity maps. These are discussed in more detail in the sources provided at the end of the chapter.

The high-level, or level 1 map, is usually called a SIPOC (supplier input process output customer) and looks at supplied input and other inputs such as trained labor to perform the operations within the process activity block. Figure 10.1 shows the major components of the high-level process or SIPOC. Figure 10.2 shows the example SIPOC for the activity map shown in Figure 10.3. Then we provide the activity to change the inputs and provide an output to the customer.

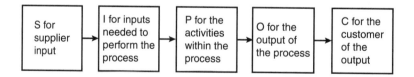

Figure 10.1 SIPOC flow of information or product for a process.

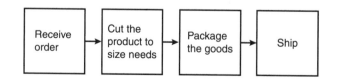

Figure 10.2 High-level SIPOC for the cut-to-size process.

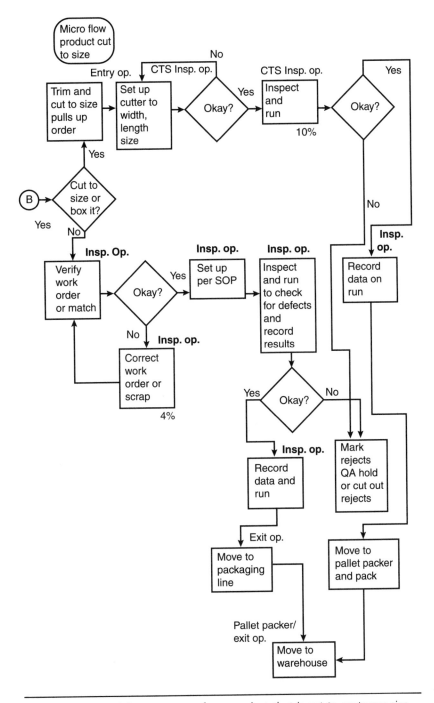

Figure 10.3 Level 3 process map for a product that is cut to customer size requirements.

The next flowchart that will be developed is the detailed process map with the level of detail required to determine the main checkpoints and activities to produce the output. Process mapping at this level, usually called level 3, will identify the events, inputs, and outputs of the previous steps required for providing the output to the process. This process map is usually detailed at the department level and is the how-to level for the activity. (The level 2 map usually deals with the between-department activities that occur during the sequential process from receipt of the raw materials to the shipment of the product.)

Level 3 maps identify all the steps in the process and display the complexity of the process. The key input variables, which may be controllable factors, noise factors, or standards for the requirements, will be identified. The steps used in the mapping process are to involve all the personnel who play a part in the process (the players). They will map the process, define the scope, document all the steps, list outputs, list inputs, and list the targets or operating specifications of the output of the process. A typical level 3 map is shown in Figure 10.3.

The process diagram will provide a lot of information about the process. Some example information follows:

- Minimum and maximum time of each step

- Minimum and maximum time of the entire process

- The areas that have issues to address that will decrease cycle time of the process

- The cost of each step

- Defect rate at points that are checked or tested in the process

- The total cost of the process

PROCESS MEASURES

The quality house in quality function deployment should lead us to the key processes and measures that are important to the process input or controls. Next we must ensure that all the measures that are important to the control of the output are considered and that they tie to the customer's key measures, taken from the voice of the customer(s), which analyze the customer input. The customer's key measures should be determined before this step. These measures are key to achieving customer satisfaction. The task at hand is to develop the customer's methods and measurement requirements that will be used to determine whether its needs and expectations are being meet. This can be as simple as copying the measures from the voice of the customer information or as complex as visiting the customer and detailing the ways in which the customer will verify the requirements have been met.

The voice of the customer, documented in Chapter 8, should lead us to the key CTQs for the customer base and market segments we decided to address. Each CTQ should have its own measure. We should have the parameter defined by the customer and determine how the customer will measure the CTQ. We must feel comfortable with the measurement process so that we can determine whether we can meet those needs. The more the customer uses attributes to measure the performance, the tougher the job we will have when determining or establishing measurement correlation. We will need to get as specific as we can on the customer measurement system. Let's look at some examples of CTQs and the measures assigned to them (Table 10.1).

Table 10.1 CTQs of the customer and related measures.

Characteristic	Measure
Weight of product	Plus/minus ounces of product
Speed of product	Plus/minus seconds
Percent defective	Defect rate
Color	Meets shade criteria
Shape (roundness)	Plus/minus millimeters
Flatness	Plus/minus microns
Made up room	Meets standard
Size dimensions	Minus zero plus 2 inches
Accuracy	Plus/minus 2 microns

The current measures of customer needs have to be addressed here so the organization can identify the true needs and the ways they will be measured.

We need to determine how we will verify that the end product or service will be checked or tested before we deliver the service or product to the customers. This should allow for the detailed investigation of the customer's measuring system and how we can duplicate or develop another testing or inspection method for output verification. A tree diagram could be used to develop the key characteristic and measures required for the customer to be satisfied. Consider the following critical to quality, delivery, and cost concepts throughout the cycle of the process to deliver a product to the customer.

EXAMPLE OF ORDERING A PRODUCT

When an item is ordered, product type, style, size, and color are specified through the order entry system. The scheduler will enter the order and schedule the product to be manufactured to the selected type, style, size, and color. Now the operation must ensure that the process controls will complete the part manufacturing process to the requirements specified. This is not always easy, because we need personnel who are familiar with the customer's needs, the process, and the input variables that will affect the output. The key is for the operation to relate to the customer order needs to the process capability to meet those needs. The voice of the customer must be established throughout the organization so that the personnel performing each function that affects the process in the delivery cycle will know how the process they are performing affects the parameters that lead to meeting the customer's needs. This is best accomplished by using the quality house built during the quality function deployment process. The need exists to identify process parameters that will affect the output of the process (which is required to meet the customer's needs). Then a capability study should be defined for these characteristics. The next task is to establish the key process characteristics that will affect the process in such a way that the output Y factor will be affected. This can be accomplished by using another QFD matrix in which we tie the CTQ to the critical to process (CTP) requirements. The next step is to determine the optimum level of the X factor in the process that will maintain the output consistency. Remember $Y = f(X_1 + X_2 + . . .)$.

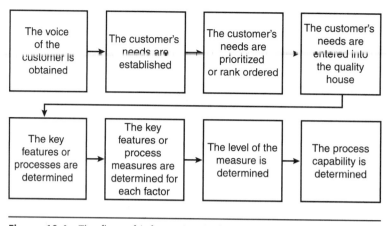

Figure 10.4   The flow of information in the customer and process measures development.

Figure 10.4 shows the flow of this information in the process. The information flow is usually controlled through the quality function deployment process.

If we use the QFD process for transferring the key customer needs to key processes and the process characteristics needs, the customer measures will be met. This leads to the key processes and their measures that need to be controlled in order to provide consistency in the process output. The key process measures must be discriminating enough to denote process variation.

MEASUREMENT SYSTEM ANALYSIS

It is good practice to perform a measurement systems analysis of the key process measures to verify capability of the measurement system. If the measurement system analysis shows that the measurement system is contributing more than 10 percent to the total variation of the process, the measurement system must be fixed. The capability of the measurement system ideally should be around 1 percent to 2 percent of the total variation. We will cover the measurement systems analysis using an example and MINITAB in Figure 10.5.

According to the study, the gage is acceptable with a measurement system variation of .16 percent and a study variation of 4 percent, which is the ratio of the measurement system standard deviation to the total observed standard deviation. This measurement is used to determine whether the organization can measure its process variation well enough to validate its process improvements. The only note here is that inspector one is reading one part differently from the other inspectors. We may need to follow up on the inspector issues.

Another example of a measurement systems analysis using MINITAB is for a destructive test of tensile strength (Figure 10.6). Because it is a destructive test, this example uses a nested test format in MINITAB.

This measurement system analysis is also acceptable with repeatability of 5.85 percent of the total variation of the parts being studied. The repeatability issue can be caused by the difference between inspector measurements, the instruments themselves, or both. It could also be caused by an interaction between the measurement instruments and the inspectors.

Gage R&R (ANOVA) for trial

Gage name:
Date of study:

Reported by:
Tolerance:
Misc:

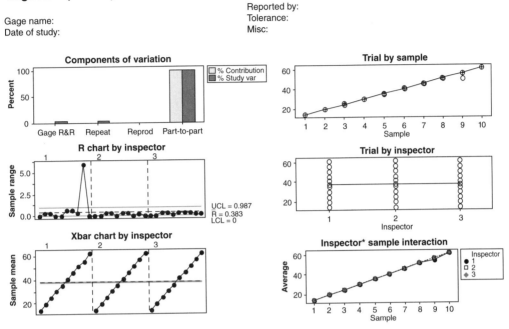

Figure 10.5   Measurement systems analysis for a typical torque gage.

Gage R&R (nested) for result

Gage name:
Date of study:

Reported by:
Tolerance:
Misc:

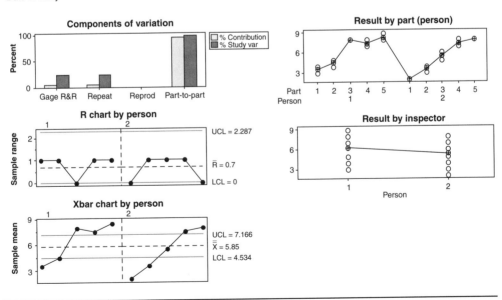

Figure 10.6   Measurement systems analysis for tensile test.

PROCESS MEASURES ACCURACY

If we follow the customer's measures, we can relate them to the key process measures required of our system. Let's compare some of the measures we introduced previously and how the process needs to be measured to achieve process control in Table 10.2.

Current process measures are developed to understand the present stage of development of the process and to look for actions required to improve the processes. Now we need to verify that we have all the measurements that are required to deliver the customer the product or service they expect.

The processes to be addressed for the development group are pointed out by the QFD matrix when the quality house shows a measurement that is not being captured from the process in the current situation. This becomes obvious when the measurement of the output that concerns the customer is not present or is not being recorded in the current process, but the quality house has defined it as a key process characteristic and a measurement has been defined. We then need to establish how the measurement will be made, by whom, and with what instrument. This will result in the measurement of the specific characteristic, using the proper instrument by people trained in its use.

Sometimes the opposite measurement situation occurs and we find that we are measuring and monitoring a parameter that will not affect the customer. The process parameter has no affect on the key customer needs but we are controlling it for some reason that is not definable. This measurement analysis continues for each step of the process flow. Now let's get back to the process map and the flow of the process.

CRITICAL TO PROCESS CHARACTERISTICS

The key measures of the process are the CTP characteristics that usually are derived from the quality house during the QFD process. These are the measures that need to be controlled in order to achieve the desired level of the process, which will attain customer satisfaction. These characteristic values are the measures that should be looked at for reduction in variation to provide consistent output to the customer.

Sometimes the key measures will be driven by other factors. Remember the function $Y = f(X_1 + X_2 \ldots)$ for the key variables that affect the output. We may need to experi-

Table 10.2 Measures and accuracies established for various customer needs.

Customer needs	In-process measures
Weight of product	Mixing to plus or minus .1 ounce
Speed of product	System clock rate plus or minus .1 second
Percent defective	Number of rejects per product
Color	Dye mixing rate RPM
Shape (roundness)	Cutting speed RPM
Flatness	Tool alignment parallelism
Made up room	Room cleanliness to standard
Size dimensions	Length in plus or minus 1/4 inch
Accuracy	Precision required

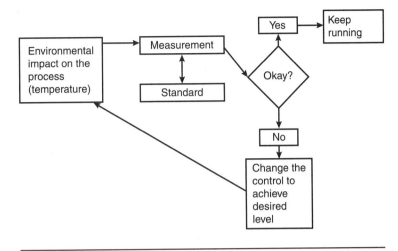

Figure 10.7 Measurement and feedback information for a closed loop control.

ment with the values of X to find the optimum level of X for Y output. In most cases we will find causation of the X values to Y output in the process. We need to maintain this key process parameter or parameters. We must maintain the key process parameters at the value or level needed to deliver the required output to the customer. Approximately 30 to 40 percent of the time we will need to establish test runs to verify the output parameter. The key measurers are controlled, as outlined in Figure 10.7, to provide the answers to process control.

The concept of determining the key control for the output is not new, but most organizations forget what to control or the level that is required. This is usually determined when the capability analysis is performed for the process output. The capability analysis process will be discussed in the next chapter. The important item to consider here is the type of data that can be obtained and whether it is continuous scale (variable) data or discrete (count) data that the process is working with during the data collection and analysis performance. The variable data will be easier to use for the analysis of the capability to deliver to the needs of the customers. The discrete data is useful and will allow the team to determine whether the proper data are available for the capability analysis. The difference in the count, ordinal, or nominal data we may be collecting is that they are less descriptive about the variation, causing the output to change or vary in results. Some examples of key characteristics to achieve a desired output are listed in Table 10.3.

With the key parameters chosen and the measures taken, we are ready to determine whether the process is stable and to find out the capability to deliver the output to the customer requirements. The stability of any process can be determined by using the pictures from histograms, frequency plots, and run chart or control charts that are capable of determining the current process characteristics that we are monitoring over time. We do not need to spend a lot of time on the tools for stability, but you need to know that 50 to 60 percent of the consulting work starts with unstable processes. Most processes are allowed to drift over time, and they are like the garden that has not been weeded. The weeds must be cleared before we start to grow vegetables. The processes that are not stable drifted to that condition because the special causes, and their root causes, were not found. We need

Table 10.3 Output measures for the customer and process inputs to the process.

Input	Output
Speed of machine	Tear force
Temperature of oven	Cure of material
Humidity	Moisture content of material
Pressure	Fill amount
Blend rate	Homogeneity of product
Flow rate	Material blend
Torque	Product fit

to put our troubleshooting hats on to solve for the special causes before we determine what sigma level we are operating at for the process. The stability of the process is important, and we usually use the charting techniques to find our answer.

The measure step of the Six Sigma process involves the collection of data, designing studies of data, and then summarizing and interpreting the data to support the decisions that need to be made about the process. We need to collect samples of product to measure on which to base decisions made about the process performance. The variable data will be continuous, having no boundaries between points and including most noncounting data intervals and ratios. The discrete, or attribute, data has clear boundaries and includes nominals, counts, and rank order data.

One of the key points of information to take away from this is the central tendency of the data, which is the mean or median data value. The process spread or variation of the process is also derived from the data set. For continuous data, we are interested in the standard deviation of the sample or population and the variances, which are determined from this standard deviation. We are usually concerned with the normality of the data and are trying to determine something about the population from a sample or perform comparisons of the sample to the population or other samples. The variance of the data is usually obtained during this data collection and analysis stage. We can then determine the probability that the value will be different from sample comparisons or from the sample population when comparing the sample to the population. The data are also analyzed over time in a run chart to determine whether process variation occurs over a set time frame. The measure of the sigma level for the process or performance at key steps in the process is appropriate at this time. We need to know at what sigma level the current process is operating so we may determine the gap that needs to be covered. The measured data needs to be in a form that can be stratified to perform analysis of the process performance and plotted to show a picture of the data. The data need to be turned into information that can be used by the project team. The best way to do this is to collect the characteristics data and collateral data about the process in a form that can be sorted and collated to show patterns for the analysis step of the process. The next chapter will cover this in more detail.

The measures of the process need to take into consideration factors that will affect the output of the process. These factors are derived from the key processes that have been determined during the quality function deployment process, which was discussed in previous chapters. We need to identify the key steps in the process mapping activity and where in the process the key parameters are being recorded and analyzed for capability. Let's look at a simple check-cashing process at your local bank in Figure 10.8. We can apply this use of the map to any process that has activities that add value to the output of the process. All work should be defined as a process so we can first understand the process, then determine the issues of the process, and, finally, verify cycle times and locate defects within the process.

The key checkpoints illustrated in Figure 10.8 are the length of the line when we enter the bank and decide to stay or leave and the presentation of account information, when the teller decides whether or not we can cash the check. This simple process shows the measures that must be in place for us to decide what action to take based on the data that it processed. The length of line will be evaluated in respect to the time it will take to cash the check. The measure of time will be determined by how long we can wait and how patient we are while waiting for the check to be cashed. Time is a subjective parameter that may change based on many input factors. The bank needs to obtain this information from the customer so it can measure the length of time a person may wait and take action before the limit is reached. Let's say that the maximum wait time should be three minutes before we reach the teller. The bank needs to measure this parameter and establish a head count limit for the tellers to ask for help with the lines. The next checkpoint in the process is when the teller verifies our account information and proceeds to cash our check. Now, the information within the account needs to be accurate and up to date. The accuracy of the system should be better than 0.1 percent and the account information needs to be current to the nearest minute. The bank's systems must be up to date with current data and must be available for the transactions 100 percent of the time. The account information needs to be updated and verified on a scheduled periodic basis. The key parameter of the system will be monitored and information provided concerning the reliability of the system and the accuracy of the data within the system. The critical features of the system or process must

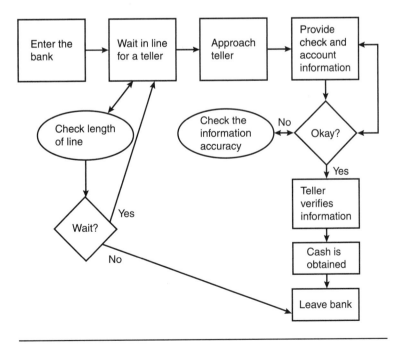

Figure 10.8 Flow of cashing a check at the bank with checkpoints.

be evaluated to meet the process needs. We need to count the mistakes of the process at each step within the process. Look at the check-cashing process in Figure 10.8 and determine the places were errors could occur and then determine the error rate at the time of developing the process map.

This example takes us through process mapping to measures of the process in the eyes of the customer and the personnel within the process. The critical stage in the mapping process is evaluating the present measurements that are in place and then determining whether they will meet the data needs to satisfy the customers. If there are gaps, we will need to close them before we proceed. This may require additional measures and measuring devices that will be put into the process steps. These critical measures will be derived from the define and measure phases and tied together for the analysis phase. The key items (CTQ and CTP measures) to consider in the measurement systems analysis for the process measures are:

- Accuracy and precision
- Instrumentation requirements
- Methods for taking the measurements
- Training for taking the measurements
- Sample selection and size
- Stability of the measurement system
- Linearity of the measurement system
- Repeatability of the measurement system
- Reproducibility of the measurement system

Measurement system analysis and data collection is probably the most important part of the define and measure phases of DMAIC.

In conclusion, we have covered the determination of the key process variables to be controlled from the quality house. With the parameters identified, we then need to measure the as-is condition of each measurement of each step in the process. Once the as-is conditions of the measures are known, we need to check for stability of the process parameter. Once process stability is known, we need to determine the capability of the process to deliver to the requirements of the customer or engineering specifications. This will be covered in the next chapter.

CHAPTER QUESTIONS

1. What is an as-is process map?

2. What is a CTQ?

3. How are CTQs transformed to CTPs?

4. What is the function of Y for the customer?

5. How are the process measures determined for the key processes?

6. What is important in the measurement system analysis?

7. How does the information flow from voice of the customer to the process capability study to verify we meet the customer requirements?

8. Why do we want to develop an as-is process map?

9. What is the difference between a SIPOC and an activity map?

10. What are some of the characteristics of the process that can be obtained from the process diagram or map?

SUGGESTIONS FOR FURTHER READING

Brassard, Michael. *The Memory Jogger Plus.* Methuen, MA: Goal QPC, 1989.

Breyfogle, Forest W., III. *Implementing Six Sigma,* 2nd ed. Hoboken, NJ: John Wiley & Sons, 2003.

George, Michael L. *Lean Six Sigma.* New York: McGraw-Hill, 2002.

Grant, Eugene L., and Richard S. Leavenworth. *Statistical Quality Control.* New York: McGraw-Hill, 1980.

Naumann, Earl, and Steve Hoisington. *Customer Centered Six Sigma.* Milwaukee, WI: ASQ Quality Press, 2001.

Wheeler, Donald J. *Understanding Variation.* Knoxville, TN: SPC Press, 1993.

11

Pillar Nine: Process Capability and Analysis

The Twelve Pillars for Six Sigma Support and Implementation

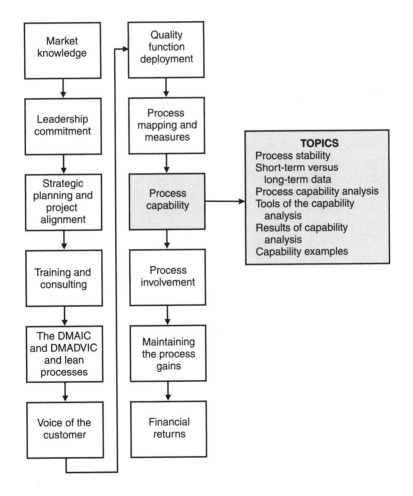

This chapter will highlight Pillar Nine, process capability and analysis of stability. The capability analysis of the process under study is very important if we are to understand the status of the existing process before we begin to improve it. The first step in this process activity is to verify process stability, as noted in the previous chapter. A simple Shewart chart analysis will allow for the analysis of the process stability. Process stability is verified by studying the short-term process behavior over the process output with short-term variability. We are evaluating the input variables that are key to the output performance response factor. Large swings in X inputs and individual X values beyond the control limits of the parameter under study indicate instability. The fundamental checks of Shewart chart rules tell you the story of process stability. Don't forget the run rules of process shifts, trends, too many or too few runs, and numbers of points one, two, or three standard deviations from the mean. These rules will help us understand whether some special causes are producing the instability of the process.

PROCESS STABILITY AND VARIATION

If the process is not stable, the task at hand is to reduce the variability or eliminate the causes of the variability based on the sporadic condition. This requires that we troubleshoot the process for causes of the sporadic conditions. We must eliminate the reasons for the causes of the sporadic conditions. We then will achieve stability of the process. I do not want to make this sound too simple, but it usually is easier to bring a process into stability than to improve the performance of a process that is stable.

Once process stability is achieved, we can begin to control the process through SPC or other controls and start the process of capability analysis. (Many books offer a thorough treatment of SPC.) If you need to know more about SPC charting of X-bar and range, X-bar and standard deviation, individuals and moving range, exponentially weighted moving average, C and U charts for defects, and P and NP charts for defectives, please read the sources provided at the end of this chapter. The attributes and variables charts, as they are called, allow for process stability analysis and process interpretation of performance and then control. Measures of mean and standard deviation are used in many of the calculations we are providing for the process. The initial job is for us is to understand the process. Then stability is analyzed using the rules of control charts to determine whether special cases are affecting the process.

Let's review some of the most used rules for charting. Any point outside the process limits is cause for concern about a special cause in the process. If a data trend of seven or more points occurs either up or down in a row, then something special is acting on the process. If eight or more points in a row are above or below the mean of the process, a special cause is shifting the process. We can evaluate the number of runs in a time-related chart for stability. The task at hand is to eliminate the reasons for the special causes in the process. This means that we must put on our troubleshooting hat to find the root cause for the special or unnatural variation in the process. If we had been weeding the garden during the year, the special causes would have been handled as they occurred and eliminated at the time of occurrence. If we are not weeding the garden, we wind up with a bunch of weeds and cannot distinguish between the good vegetables and the weeds. At the conclusion of the year we wind up with many causes of variance and lack control of the output.

Short-Term versus Long-Term Data

The next item to consider is how the short-term versus long-term data affects the process. This will be discussed later in this chapter, but for now we need to determine whether the data we are analyzing is collected from short-term process variation or long-term. To me, the definition of long-term data is data taken over the time frame of the process that will be able to tell me the effects on the processes of material variables, methods changes, measures changed, people differences, machine differences, or environmental changes. This means that natural variation of the process must be allowed to occur over a specific time frame while we measure the effects on the output. We then run a capability analysis on this long-term data.

PROCESS CAPABILITY ANALYSIS

Once we know that the process is stable, we are ready to perform the capability analysis of the process to deliver to the customer requirements. This means that we need to know the true customer needs as well as the specification of the characteristic and the true process mean and limits for the characteristic under study. We then compare the voice of the process against the voice of the customer to determine the capability of the process. All that is happening here is the comparison of the limits of the process to the limits of the specification. It is important that the limits of the process be created from the natural variation of the process. The ratio that is created forms a comparison that is easy to calculate and relate to the customer's needs. The real problem in this analysis is the ability to come up with accurate and reliable data for the process. It is crucial that relevant process variables are identified for measurement and that the measurements taken are precise enough to ensure that the data obtained produces an accurate calculation of the standard deviation. This standard deviation will be used to calculate the comparison of the process spread to the specification for the analysis of the process capability. The sample selection process for the data collection also needs to be verified.

The capability of the process will be analyzed with regard to these simple comparisons:

Design capability:

C_p = Upper spec. limit − lower spec. limit ÷ 6 × standard deviation of the process

Process capability:

C_{pk} = Upper spec. limit − mean of the sample ÷ 3 × standard deviation

This C_{pk} value is determined for the lower specification, too, as noted below. The lowest number for C_{pk} value is used for the process capability analysis.

C_{pk} = Mean of the sample − lower spec. limit ÷ 3 × the standard deviation

The higher the number in the capability analysis, the better our ability to meet the customer's needs, assuming we have the proper specifications from the customer or engineering and an accurate process standard deviation. Note: The lower C_{pk} value is taken as the process capability when taking the process centering into consideration. When considering capability analysis, we need to always improve upon results of less than 1.33, with results below 1.00 being serious and requiring that action be taken on the process variation or centering of the process. A value of 2.00 or higher gets us to the Six Sigma levels for the process. With the process capability completed, we are ready to analyze the process for improvements to output consistency.

Many of the processes that are evaluated for capabilities are not stable and, when stabilized, are found to be controlled too poorly to provide good capability. It has been my experience that about 40 percent of processes evaluated are unstable. The weeds have grown and we need to weed out the process to obtain stability, finding the special causes of variation and eventually getting the process to stabilize. The capability improvements come from reduction of the variation during the process of the key variables that affect the output and the centering of the mean of the process to the target. Sometimes the analysis will not lead us to the key factor or factors that affect the process output. In these cases the design of experimentation will be required to determine the factor or factors that affect the output. The process of designing and analyzing a number of factors can become complex. The complexity of the process will affect the type of experimentation that will be required to determine the variables that need to be controlled. We may also use multiple regression analysis to determine the important X factor(s).

Short-term capability studies are measures using the short-term process standard deviation. These values are usually free of the subgroup-to-subgroup change in data and look only within group data variation. The long-term capability study uses the long-term standard deviation data. This analysis takes into consideration the data between and within subgroups. The ratios of customer- or engineer-specified tolerances to six standard deviations of the process are used for the capability study.

Capability Analysis Examples

Let's look at some examples of actual data analysis for this capability study, using a software tool, MINITAB.

The process example in Figure 11.1 was run using MINITAB software and demonstrates the process with a poor capability. The spread of the process exceeds the specification, and we have a high failure rate below and above the limits, as defined by the customer or engineering. We need to reduce the variation of the process to bring it within the limits or change the limits if they are not meaningful to the customer.

We must investigate how the specifications were obtained and sometimes spend time with the customer to observe the use of the product, feature, or service. Once we know that the specification is good, we identify which variables within the process affect the output the most and we develop ways to eliminate or reduce the variation.

The next capability analysis, shown in Figure 11.2, displays the output of MINITAB for a process that is not centered and would be improved if we could just center the voice of the process closer to the target of the customer or the nominal of the specification. This distribution is not perfectly normal but will probably fill out with more samples. The overall capability takes into consideration the spread of the process over time or how the standard deviation will change over time as we assume a normal curve for the output data.

The next example, shown in Figure 11.3 (on page 142), displays a process well within specification and with a variability that is tightly held about the mean of the process and somewhat centered to the specification.

These tools of charting the process and looking for special causes and causes of variation are very important in ensuring a stable process. The capability study compares the stable process voice to the voice of the customer through the specification. This is the first major hurdle in the Six Sigma improvement process. If the capability analysis shows a need

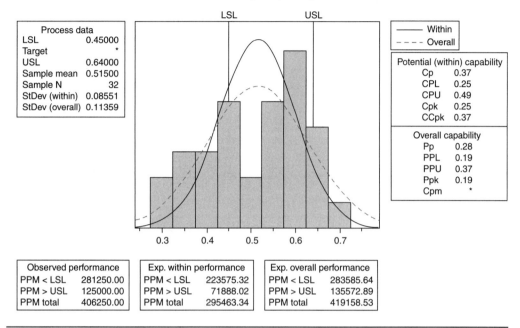

Figure 11.1 Capability analysis of response data from a bonding process with bond strength in Newtons.

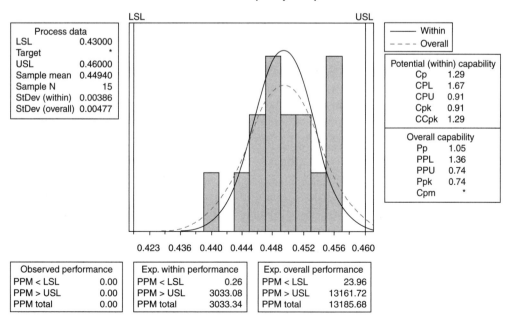

Figure 11.2 Bond strength capability analysis of another material using a different process.

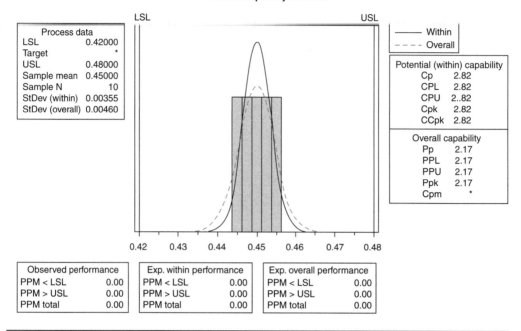

Figure 11.3 Capability study of the bond process, which was adjusted for improved performance. Note the very tight distribution without any tails to the data.

for improvement toward the Six Sigma level (not all processes need to achieve the Six Sigma level), we are working with common cause variation within the process. Sometimes this is more difficult to do because the inherent natural variation of the process requires designed experimentation to determine the source of the variation and the level at which the factors must be in order to achieve reduced output variation. The task for the Black Belts is to reduce the causes of variation in the inputs to the process, the key factors within the process, or the extraneous factors that affect the process output. It has been my experience that most of the variation can be reduced by implementing changes to the input materials and the methods used within the process. These include the training of the operators of the process, maintenance of the equipment, and the measurements of the process. Only about 25 percent of the time will we need to invest in different equipment or facilities.

Tools of the Capability Analysis

The basic tools used to improve the capability of the process are the run charts, control charts, cause-and-effect diagrams, the five whys, the tree diagram, and the frequency or histogram charts.

This chapter may seem simple when reviewing the ratio of the specification to the process variation, and the page content may not seem to do it justice, but it is the most important phase of the DMAIC process. If we have processes that are not in control or are not stable, we have to address the sporadic causes of the variation affecting the process. In other words, we need to hire someone to weed the garden before we plant something new. This analogy should indicate that we need to put the process under statistical control before we begin to estimate the sigma level of performance and attempt to improve it.

The capability analysis that does not meet our expectations of 3, 4, 5, or 6 sigma must be improved during the analyze phase of DMAIC. Our job is to find the causes of variation that are affecting the capability—the previously discussed sporadic or common causes.

Understanding the Results of Capability Analysis

Planners using processes that are not stable will have causes that affect performance of the output, and customers will see inconsistent quality and will eventually leave in favor of the competition. How would you feel if you bought a product or experienced a service that was at 1 or 2 sigma level of performance? Your dissatisfaction would leave you wondering whether you need to buy this product or service again. This variation in the experience of the product performance or service performance causes the customer to leave for other alternatives. The customers will not return unless they experience worse service or performance at the competition. It's your job to ensure the consistency in the performance so the customers will not even consider leaving you for a product or service of the competition. The most important part of this Six Sigma process is to reduce the variation of the process inputs and parameters.

The capability analysis of the process leads to the sigma level of the process. Some common levels of performance that industry could have over the years are listed in Table 11.1.

Most customers were satisfied with 3 and 4 sigma levels of performance until they either saw a need for or experienced performance in the 5 and 6 sigma levels of performance. Customers today are raising the bar on performance expectations. Organizations that produce products or offer services to future customers must assure themselves that they understand the customer's changing needs in this area.

The capability analysis study must be performed on all the key parameters of the process under investigation. These key parameters are usually pointed out to the organization from the quality function deployment tool we talked about in Chapter 9. All the parameters need to be evaluated to ensure customer satisfaction. Another item to consider is the measurement system analysis (MSA) of the current measurement system used to obtain the data for the capability analysis. We need to be assured that we are obtaining accurate and precise data. We need to obtain an MSA result of 1 to 2 percent of the total variation based on the precision and accuracy of the data.

Another Capability Analysis Example

Let's look at a simple explanation of the capability analysis study, using a check-cashing process (Figure 11.4).

We need to identify the key steps in the process, such as the wait in line and the account information. These steps will need to be evaluated to ensure that the process will provide the service the customer is looking for. The wait in line could be measured by time

Table 11.1   Common sigma levels with capability ratios.

Capability ratio	Sigma level
1.00	3 sigma
1.33	4 sigma
1.67	5 sigma
2.00	6 sigma

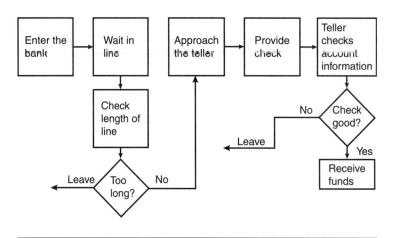

Figure 11.4   Flow of the check-cashing process in a bank.

in minutes and the patience of the customer. The account information will be measured by the balance in the account and the amount of cash the customer is trying to obtain. These critical features of the process must be evaluated to ensure that the process can meet the customer's needs. A measurement systems analysis must be performed before we conduct the capability analysis for the process under study. We are interested in wait time and account accuracy.

The first step is to consider the length of time spent waiting in line. A study produced by the organization determined that most people would be willing to wait at least four minutes. This time would vary depending on the patience of the customer, usually determined by the customer's need to proceed through the line quickly because of other commitments. This is a subjective patience factor. With this figured into the picture, the wait time is generally two minutes. The teller needs to ensure that the wait time does not exceed two minutes. If we get close to this time level, the teller needs to call for another teller to handle the overload. Now we are ready to check the process with a stopwatch at different times of the day to evaluate the performance and calculate the capability to meet the two-minute need. We will now look at a capability study performed on the time in line in Figure 11.5.

The capability study performed on the length of time in line for the teller at the bank has shown that we are at .85, which is less than a 3 sigma level of performance. We can see that the X-bar and R chart shows a data point outside the limits, and therefore the process needs to be reviewed for improvement. When we find the problem in the line time, we can proceed to recheck the capability.

Let's look at an example of measurement system analysis that should be performed before we perform the capability study on a torque gage, using MINITAB, in Figure 11.6 (on page 146).

As explained in the previous chapter, this information will tell us how much variation is introduced into the measured data by the measurement system. As we start to contribute more than 10 percent of the final data variation by the measurement system, we may not be reading the true measurement values for the process. (This all depends on our needs.)

According to the study in Figure 11.6, the gage is acceptable with a measurement system variation of .16 percent and a study variation of 4 percent, which is the ratio of the measurement system standard deviation to the total observed standard deviation. This measurement is used to determine whether the organization can measure its process variation well enough to validate its process improvements.

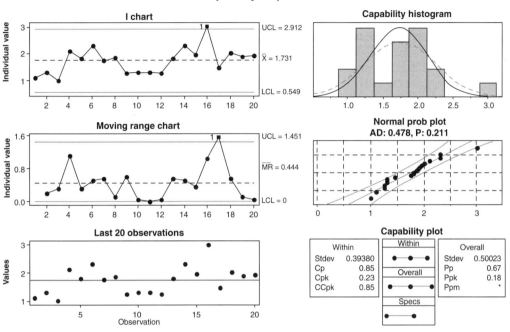

Figure 11.5 Capability study performed on the length of time in the bank line.

Another example of measurement systems analysis using a destructive tensile testing result is shown in Figure 11.7 (on page 147), as we discussed in the previous chapter.

Now let's return to the check-cashing scenario and consider the evaluation of the account information and the ability to cash the check. We are looking at the check validation process. The check may not be cashed if errors exist in this process. Some of the errors to consider are:

- Not enough funds in the account.

- Wrong account number is keyed into the system.

- Customer provides wrong account number.

- Account balance is not updated.

In any of these outcomes, the customer will not receive the cash until the problem is rectified. The first problem is in the customer's hands. The customer must decide to ask for less cash if the funds are not present in the account or move on. The next two problems should be cleared up quickly by a change in the account number. The last problem needs to be resolved by the bank's systems update. The speed at which the system is updated now and in the future will help satisfy all parties in the check-cashing process.

These simple examples show the approach we must take to close the gap between the needs of the customer and the performance of the process. The major intent of this chapter is to point out the need for the project team to understand the capability of the process to meet the needs of the internal and external customers and how the measurement systems analysis will validate the measurement system. Then, if the gap is too wide, with a performance at 3 or 4 sigma level, we need to improve it. The first step is to have stability.

Gage R&R (nested) for result

Gage name:
Date of study:

Reported by:
Tolerance:
Misc:

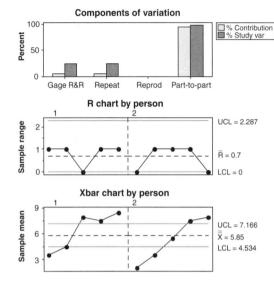
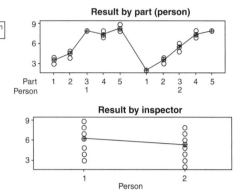

Gage R&R

Source	VarComp	%Contribution (of VarComp)
Total Gage R&R	0.432	0.16
Repeatability	0.432	0.16
Reproducibility	0.000	0.00
Inspector	0.000	0.00
Part-To-Part	268.073	99.84
Total Variation	268.505	100.00

Source	StdDev (SD)	Study Var (6 * SD)	%Study Var (%SV)
Total Gage R&R	0.6576	3.9454	4.01
Repeatability	0.6576	3.9454	4.01
Reproducibility	0.0000	0.0000	0.00
Inspector	0.0000	0.0000	0.00
Part-To-Part	16.3729	98.2376	99.92
Total Variation	16.3861	98.3168	100.00

Number of Distinct Categories = 35

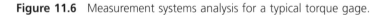

Figure 11.6 Measurement systems analysis for a typical torque gage.

Gage R&R (nested) for result

Gage name:
Date of study:

Reported by:
Tolerance:
Misc:

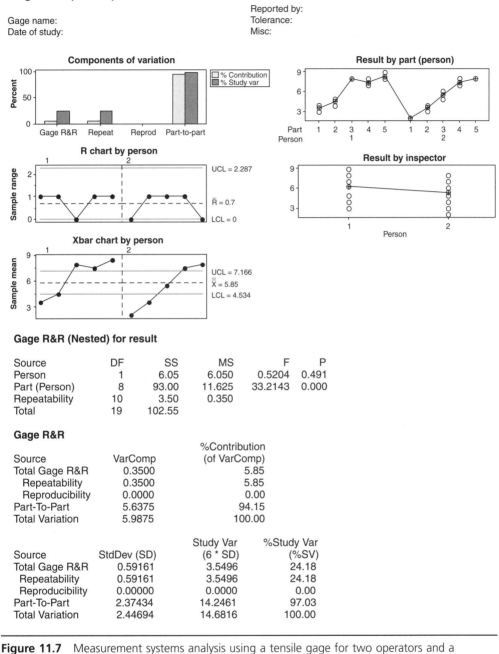

Gage R&R (Nested) for result

Source	DF	SS	MS	F	P
Person	1	6.05	6.050	0.5204	0.491
Part (Person)	8	93.00	11.625	33.2143	0.000
Repeatability	10	3.50	0.350		
Total	19	102.55			

Gage R&R

Source	VarComp	%Contribution (of VarComp)
Total Gage R&R	0.3500	5.85
Repeatability	0.3500	5.85
Reproducibility	0.0000	0.00
Part-To-Part	5.6375	94.15
Total Variation	5.9875	100.00

Source	StdDev (SD)	Study Var (6 * SD)	%Study Var (%SV)
Total Gage R&R	0.59161	3.5496	24.18
Repeatability	0.59161	3.5496	24.18
Reproducibility	0.00000	0.0000	0.00
Part-To-Part	2.37434	14.2461	97.03
Total Variation	2.44694	14.6816	100.00

Figure 11.7   Measurement systems analysis using a tensile gage for two operators and a destructive test.

CHAPTER QUESTIONS

1. What is the significance of performing a capability analysis using the C_{PK} versus the C_P study?

2. How do you determine which capability you need to achieve as you continually improve toward the Six Sigma level of performance?

3. Is Six Sigma capability equal to a C_{PK} of 2.0 or better?

4. What are the potential causes of poor process capability numbers?

5. In Figure 11.1, what needs to be addressed to achieve a process capability of 1.33?

6. What is being compared in the capability study?

7. What does a capability of .67 mean to you?

8. Why should planners be concerned about a processes capability?

9. What should a Black Belt do to improve capability of a process?

10. How is short-term capability different from long-term capability?

SUGGESTIONS FOR FURTHER READING

AT&T Technologies. *Statistical Quality Control Handbook.* Indianapolis: Western Electric Company, 1956.

Besterfield, Dale H. *Quality Control.* Englewood Cliffs, NJ: Prentice-Hall, 1986.

Bossidy, Larry, and Ram Charan. *Execution.* New York: Crown Publishing, 2002.

Brue, Greg. *Design for Six Sigma.* New York: McGraw-Hill, 2003.

Eckes, George. *Making Six Sigma Last.* New York: John Wiley & Sons, 2001.

———. *The Six Sigma Revolution.* New York: John Wiley & Sons, 2001.

George, Michael L. *Lean Six Sigma.* New York: McGraw-Hill, 2002.

Grant, Eugene L., and Richard S. Leavenworth. *Statistical Quality Control.* New York: McGraw-Hill, 1980.

Harry, Mikel, and Richard Schroeder. *Six Sigma.* New York: Doubleday, 2000.

Naumann, Earl, and Steve Hoisington. *Customer Centered Six Sigma.* Milwaukee, WI: ASQ Quality Press, 2001.

Spande, Peter S. *The Six Sigma Way.* New York: McGraw-Hill, 2000.

Wheeler, Donald J. *Understanding Variation.* Knoxville , TN: SPC Press, 1993.

12

Pillar Ten: Process Solutions and Improvements

The Twelve Pillars for Six Sigma Support and Implementation

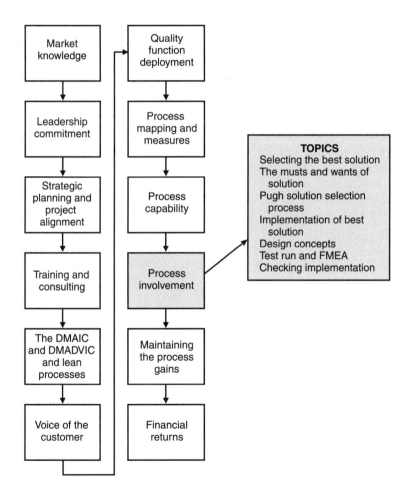

This chapter covers Pillar Ten and the improvement efforts that need to be put into place to solve the problem that was selected and defined when the team charter was developed. The problem identification process leads to a project charter that the team should be able to achieve. When we have reached this stage of the Six Sigma process, the sporadic and common causes are identified and we try to determine the best solution to eliminate the sporadic or common cause, or at least to identify its origin in the process. The tools listed in Appendix B are used to find the root causes of sporadic and common cause variation. The next step to improvement is to identify the best solution to sporadic and common cause variation. This will require some of the tools discussed in previous chapters. The use of control charts, histograms, and frequency plots will help us identify the common variation within the process. The use of cause-and-effect diagrams, tree diagrams, and the five whys will enable the team to identify the areas to address for causes and improvement or where more data is required. The determination of the cause of variation is more difficult, and we usually need more data. This additional data should lead us to determine which factor affects the output variation the most. Then we can determine at what level to maintain the factor to achieve improved performance. Improved performance can be achieved only if we have established the key parameters to maintain the output.

SELECTING THE BEST SOLUTION

To obtain the best solution for a specific problem, we should use the tools of brainstorming ideas, idea box generation, brain writing, Pugh analysis, analogies, or other creativity techniques. We will not take the time to discuss these in detail here because the methods of idea generation differ in many ways and are discussed in detail in the sources provided at the end of the chapter.

During the improvement process, we will select the best solution for eliminating the root cause of the problem. To ensure that we have picked the proper solution, we need to make sure that we include all the proper stakeholders in the development of the solutions and in the selection of the best solution. One way of doing this is to develop a stakeholder or person requirements matrix. Let's look at a typical matrix in Figure 12.1. This matrix allows the team to indicate which stakeholders need to be involved in the improvement phase and which ones might have a need to know but little involvement.

The improvement process requires us to identify the numerous X factors to control for consistency of output. The factors chosen to be controlled will have to be verified by a sample run with the changes in place. We may use multiple regression or designed experiments to note the X factors that contribute to the output. Often we need to run some experiments to achieve the desired improvement the team needs to show for the project. The implementation step also requires that we determine which solution is

Involvement ⇒	High need	Medium need	Low need
Stakeholder ⇓			
Purchasing	XXX		
Plant		XXX	
Engineering			XXX

Figure 12.1   Person requirements matrixes that will help the team include the right people in the improvement efforts.

applicable to the problem we are trying to solve. Now that we have come this far, we will need to use tools that will allow for the selection of the best solution based on some selected criteria for the decision. The criteria are usually in the form of "musts" and "wants" that are weighted for purposes of the selection process. The weighting will be allocated based on the want level as developed by the process owner and the customers. Let's look at an example of a weighted matrix.

The generic matrix in Figure 12.2 helps the team define the best approach to take and identify the people who need to be involved in the selection of the best alternative solution. The criteria weightings are determined by the team, and each team member can select

Criteria ⇒	A = 1	B = 3	C = 2
Solutions ⇓			
New equipment	1	0	1
Modified equipment	1	1	0
New method	1	0	0
Total	3	3	2

Figure 12.2 Solution selection matrix for improvement of the process.

the solutions that best meet the criteria. The matrix is then used for the total analysis as voted on by the team.

The Musts and Wants of the Solution

At this point the team should list the musts, which the alternatives must meet in order to be included in the implementation, and consider the wants for the process or project. The wants can be prioritized on a numerical scale of 1 to 10, with 10 being the highest weight for the feature or function of the alternative. The musts and wants should be measurable and verifiable. The team can establish a matrix to evaluate the musts and wants against the alternative solutions. The team should eliminate all the alternative options that fail the musts and that score low on the wants list. The remaining options will have data collected about the

Computer brand	HP	Dell	IBM	Local
Must cost less than $2000	$1895	$1595	$2000	$1780
Must weigh less than 4 lbs.	3.5	3.1	3.9	4.0
Must be 2.2GHZ	1.9	2.3	2.1	2.5
Must have modem	Yes	Yes	Yes	No
Must have CD writer	Yes	Yes	Yes	Yes
Highest RAM Score 10	532 Score = 10	532 Score = 10	256 Score = 5	256 Score = 5
UBS port Score 8	Yes Score = 8	Yes Score = 10	Yes Score = 10	Yes Score = 10
Fast modem Score 5	56K Score = 5	56K Score = 5	56K Score = 5	56K Score = 5
Maximize HD Score 10	10G Score = 5	30G Score = 10	6G Score = 4	10G Score = 5
Totals	28	35 Winner	24	0

Figure 12.3 Selection process for an office computer.

financial results, technical facts, and the capability to perform to the requirements. Kepner and Tregoe used these methods in their problem-solving process. Let's look at an example of this approach for the purchase of a portable computer for my office in Figure 12.3.

After the final solution is selected, the team assesses the possible outcomes of the solution. These outcomes are the risks or faults that may exist when the changes are implemented. A list of possible threats should be developed, and a determination of how potential risks or threats will be overcome should be made. The next task for the team is to perform a failure mode and effects analysis (FMEA) on the new process or product changes to ensure that new problems are not introduced by the changes made from the selected solution. I have personally experienced a solution that caused more of a problem to the customer's needs than the original problem that was to be solved.

Pugh Analysis Solution Selection Process

The Pugh analysis, developed by Stuart Pugh, is a tool that will help with the design or redesign process. It helps us select the critical items for the design. The steps for this analysis are:

1. Obtain the design criteria from the customer wants, needs, consequences, and expectations.

2. Include functions, or features, that will enhance the customer criteria.

3. Develop a group of design concepts that will satisfy the customer criteria.

4. Use a matrix to list the criteria and concepts for correlation.

5. Select one of the concepts as a datum against which to compare all other concepts.

6. Evaluate each concept against the datum as better (+) or worse (−).

7. Record the team's decisions.

8. For each column, determine the total number of pluses, minuses, and equals.

9. Improve the concepts that are the best.

10. Continue the process of synthesizing the concepts until the best one surfaces.

Figure 12.4 shows an example of the Pugh analysis concept. The pluses and minuses in the matrix refer to the standard oven used to cook the pizza that presently satisfies the customers. The new processes add to or subtract from the standard. An S indicates that the process will not add or subtract from the standard because the customer is already satisfied or the item is the same as the standard chosen.

The winning solution is the new oven design to meet the needs of the pizza shop owner.

The Implementation of the Best Solution

The improvement process will review for alternative solutions before we select the improvements to be made to the process under study. The solutions can be obtained by using the matrix of musts and wants or by a formal Pugh analysis. The best solution is then piloted to determine whether it resolves the original problem. Once the process improvement is noted, we are ready to consider the full implementation of the solution selected. The process will be validated for the improvement, and then controls will be put in place to maintain the improvements. The implementation plan will be put together once we have tested the best

Concepts	New oven design for the baking process	Existing oven	Purchased oven
Requirements			
Musts:			
1. Temperature of pizza	+	S	−
2. Tastes good	+	S	+
3. Sauce not watery	+	S	+
4. Generous toppings	S	S	S
5. Done all the way	+	S	−
Wants:			
1. Distinct sauce flavor 9	S	S	−
2. Good every time 10	+	S	+
3. Not greasy 10	+	S	+
4. Fast delivery 9	−	S	−
Wants totals:	11		2

Figure 12.4   Pugh analysis concept example.

solution for the problem. The plan for implementation must have enough detail to achieve the outcome expected from the changes to the process or product. The implementation plan should contain the resources, funding, and changes to be made to ensure proper implementation. The items to consider for implementation are:

- Procedural changes
- People issues
- Equipment resources
- Training requirements
- Policy changes
- Procedural changes
- Capital funding
- Production requirements based on commitments
- Equipment changes
- Measurement changes
- Environmental changes

Some of the items to consider in the selection process for the best solution are the clarification of objectives of the project and then prioritization of the key objectives for the customer and the project. Sometimes the objectives can conflict and must be sorted out for the specific project. We need to search for alternatives that will solve the issues or causes that were developed for the project.

We must gather all the facts about the alternatives that exist to solve the problem and, if needed, use some of the creativity tools we mentioned earlier to determine other alternatives to the solutions. It will benefit the team to determine the consequences for implementing the alternatives and test the general purpose of the project to determine whether divergent issues exist and to ensure that the line item objectives for the project can be met by the alternatives. If the team needs more objectives than those stated by the project charter, they could select the personnel with the appropriate knowledge and use brainstorming to obtain a list of other objectives.

Now that the implementation process contains the acceptable solution and the plan to ensure that it will go in place with minimal effort, it is ready for review. The process should be reviewed for potential errors, using the FMEA tools and the pilot run techniques.

DESIGN CONCEPTS

We will use the critical criteria from this process to develop the design concept proposal in block form for all the functions, or features, that must be developed or improved. A block diagram of the design concepts will show how the design fits together. This diagram can be used both to develop the design and to analyze it.

The block diagram helps develop a common understanding at a high level of how the process is currently operating, or is required to operate, and how major work groups within the process interact or interface with outside organizations. The diagram traces the paths that materials and information will flow between suppliers' inputs and the final outputs. The diagram includes the blocks of activities required. The following is a step-by-step process for the development of the block diagram:

1. Define the purpose and boundaries of the process.
2. Draw a box containing columns for each major work group within the process and list the customers and suppliers external to the process.
3. For each input to the process, identify the supplier.
4. For each activity defined, determine the output it produces, the activity or customer who receives the output, and the individual or group that performs the activity.
5. Label each new activity box and continue generating information or workflows until all processes are connected together.
6. Verify that the members of each work group are reflected by the block.

Figure 12.5 shows a block diagram for a service of producing a document for a customer.

For the technical developments, we consider balancing the requirements to the established targets. This could lead to further testing or trial runs of the process. We must develop checks and balances of the performance against the targets we established during the matrix development.

TEST RUN AND FMEA

Before we implement any solution, we need to test the solution to verify that the problem will be resolved and evaluate the new process for any new failure types. Two analysis tools

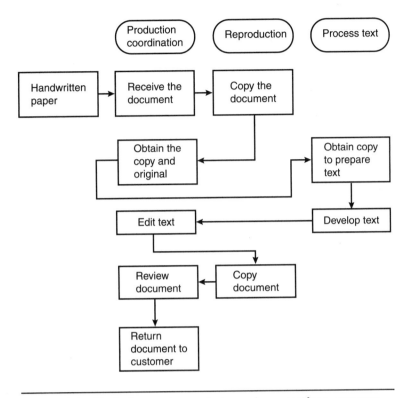

Figure 12.5 Block diagram for producing a document for a customer.

can determine whether the new process will perform better than the old: pilot lots, or test runs, and an FMEA for the new design and/or process. We need to review the test run results and FMEA results to ensure that the changes will resolve the problem and not cause other problems. If the problem was defined properly and the cause of the problem found, the implementation process of the selected solution requires support of the necessary resources to find the best solution and implement it successfully.

The implementation phase requires that we consider a planning methodology to ensure that the changes are put in place and that improvements in the output are noted. Some items to consider here are the use of Pert charts or Gantt charts for planning purposes. Microsoft Project also works well. The planning process should alert us to the needs or resources required. Even if the planning process is informal, it will alert you to the tasks that have to be completed, the people who are required, and the capital investment that may be required. The process of planning probably provides the most benefit because it allows the project team to consider the alternatives as well as the steps required for completing the project. The timely availability of the right resources will allow the team to meet the implementation plan.

The process improvement phase of DMAIC can involve correcting sporadic causes in an unstable process or reducing variation in a stable process from common causes, or both. Usually the sporadic causes are easier to solve and sometimes less costly to improve and implement than common causes. This does not mean that sporadic causes of variation in a process do not require a Black Belt to solve the problem because it should be easier to solve. Unstable processes are usually at that level because the process was left to wander without controls or necessary attention. This occurs when we become lax about supplied goods requirements or find a better price at a new supplier or the supplier lost control of the process and we are not paying attention. The organization may not be paying attention to maintenance requirements or new employees are not receiving the proper training to run the process. Sometimes the cause is the measurement equipment that may be out of calibration or that has drifted over time. The improvement phase will then require changes in supplied goods, process equipment, measuring equipment, training, or methods of running the process.

The common cause variation of the process will be improved when the natural process variation is understood and then reduced. It usually takes more time to learn which factors within the process and which input factors to the process (X factors) affect the output Y factor and how much variation will be allowed in order to achieve a consistent process output. The improvement phase will reduce the variation of the dominating X factor, therefore reducing the Y factor variation. Some important items to consider in the implementation phase are:

- Use creative methods to develop alternative solutions to solve the problem.

- Use a formal selection process to find the best solution.

- Plan for the implementation of the solution.

- Provide all necessary training and documentation for implementation.

- Test run the solution selected to determine the results and verify implementation.

- Implement changes in the standardized forms.

- Implement standards.

The improvement phase must come up with the best solution to resolve the stated problem. After the implementation of the solution, we must be able to show that the factor measured has improved. The improvement seen in the measured factor should be 10 times that of the initial measures of the projects that the Black Belts are trying to resolve. Some examples to consider for improvement project results are:

- Reduced cycle time to produce the product or provide the service

- Increased capacity to produce or deliver the service

- Reduced waste in the process

- Reduced variation in key X factors

- More consistency in output to the target requirements

- Increased profitability

The improvement phase also allows us to test the need for change and the amount of change required for achieving the intended results over the long haul. The main points that support this phase are the good planning, leadership, negotiation, and management skills of the Black Belt. Most projects fail in the analysis and the improvement phases because we do not have the proper skills and data to pinpoint the root cause of the problem. Sometimes the best solution is not selected for the original problem as defined by the team in the charter. We need to concentrate on the improvement phase, using creativity to find potential solutions. We must determine some criteria, determined by the team and management for the organization's selection of the best solution. This involves selecting the proper stakeholders of the process. Most teams are not patient enough to cover the creativity process, and the solution to the original problem may be selected by emotions, or feelings. The reason for this is that the team has not worked with the creativity tools. The team usually has an idea of the best solution for the causes identified in the analysis process. Another reason is the need to act quickly to remove the causes and implement changes.

Some organizations jump from the define and measure phase to the implementation phase, assuming they know the solution to the problems that have been picked by the management staff. The way to ensure that we do not jump to solutions too fast is to identify the critical X factors that affect the output characteristics we want to control for the customer. Some processes may have 10 to 20 variables that can affect the output and require complex analysis techniques. We need to determine the key X factors that affect the Y factors output, using the function of X equal to the Y output, $f(X) = Y$. The tools that allow us to obtain the answer to this function are the designed experimentation process, regression analysis, and the ANOVA process. Sometimes we can develop test runs or simulation techniques to test the answers to the X factors.

The outcome of the improvement phase should also help us determine the operating tolerances for the X factors that should be in place in order to realize optimum levels for the Y output. The X factors are determined to provide the best consistency to the process outputs. The other part of this process is to confirm the results that should be obtained when the solutions are selected and are implemented permanently into the process. After the implementation, new process maps are created. Control charts and process capability will be revisited to ensure the changed process will meet the needs. Sometimes confirmation experiments or test runs are performed. This phase may require validation of the measurement systems analysis for the key measures, that the results show that process capability has increased, and that the current data are collected properly to support the improvement.

The optimum robust settings for the process are needed in the improvement phase in the key areas that were addressed in the define phase using the VOC process. Remember that we cannot lose sight of the customer's needs in the improvement process and that we must center the process voice to the customer's voice.

Another insight that comes from the improvement phase is that we may use the concepts in other development areas for new products or processes. We must look at products being developed for new markets or customer bases that the organization will be selling to soon. The organization needs to look at the design process to ensure that the new products and processes will achieve a higher sigma level of performance than the previous projects and designs. (Refer to the DFSS process, described in Chapters 6 and 20, for new designs.)

The process improvements must compare to results of some of the initial tools used in the measure phase. These may include run charts, Pareto charts, control charts, frequency graphs, histograms, and capability analysis. The improvement needs to be verified, and the savings obtained will be recorded by finance. This will ensure that we realize the desired financial returns along with the process variation reduction for the key characteristics of the process.

The implementation phase must contend with possible resistance to change in the process or product. The resistance to change or change management must be covered in the Black Belt training. The cultural issues of the organization need to be considered when we are implementing Six Sigma and when the changes for the project are implemented. We need to convince the people involved to implement the remedy to the problem. The practical issues that affect implementation will need to be considered. How can the changes be implemented efficiently and effectively? Some of the items in the following list should be considered when determining reasons for resistance to change within the organization:[1]

- The current beliefs of the organization and employees.
- The current habits of the employees.
- The current practices of the organization and the employees.
- Traditions of the organization shared by the group and taught to new members.
- Experiences of the employees.
- Defense of vested rights in the organization.
- Intrusion by outsiders is felt by the organization as a negative.
- Resentment of exclusion from the planning or implementation.
- Embarrassment at the magnitude of change not seen before.
- Past failures with similar initiatives.
- Uncertainty of the change taking place.
- Comfort with status quo and habits of the past.
- Conflicting messages from management on change.
- Not being part of the process change.

CHECKING THE IMPLEMENTATION

The measure of our success will be based on the ease of implementation of changes, the improvements made to the process, and changes to the bottom-line profitability. Each project must help satisfy the customers, improve a key process that affects the customers and costs, be measurable, and provide more profits to the organization or savings to the customers.

The improved process output should be monitored for a good period based on the time it takes for the process to produce a complete cycle. This could be hours, days, or months. We should also sample enough of the process and its output characteristics to ensure with 90 percent to 95 percent confidence that we have changed the output.

CHAPTER QUESTIONS

1. What would happen if your project team did not apply the implementation phase successfully?

2. What is the benefit of a Pugh analysis?

3. Who should be involved with the implementation phase of DMAIC?

4. How do you verify that the implementation phase was successful?

5. What must the team do if the implementation phase is not successful?

6. What does a design block diagram do for the DMAIC process?

7. What indicators should be used to display the improvement results?

8. What tools should be used for planning the implementation?

9. How do we overcome resistance to change?

10. What types of resistance will we see during the implementation of the changes to a process?

SUGGESTIONS FOR FURTHER READING

Besterfield, Dale H. *Quality Control.* Englewood Cliffs, NJ: Prentice-Hall, 1986.

Bossidy, Larry, and Ram Charan. *Execution.* New York: Crown Publishing, 2002.

Brue, Greg. *Design for Six Sigma.* New York: McGraw-Hill, 2003.

Eckes, George. *Making Six Sigma Last.* New York: John Wiley & Sons, 2001.

————. *The Six Sigma Revolution.* New York: John Wiley & Sons, 2001.

George, Michael L. *Lean Six Sigma.* New York: McGraw-Hill, 2002.

Grant, Eugene L., and Richard S. Leavenworth. *Statistical Quality Control,* New York: McGraw-Hill, 1980.

Naumann, Earl, and Steve Hoisington. *Customer Centered Six Sigma.* Milwaukee, WI: ASQ Quality Press, 2001.

Spande, Peter S. *The Six Sigma Way.* New York: McGraw-Hill, 2000.

Thomas, D. W. AT&T Technologies. *Statistical Quality Control Handbook.* Indianapolis: Western Electric Company, 1956.

13

Pillar Eleven: Maintaining the Improvement

The Twelve Pillars for Six Sigma Support and Implementation

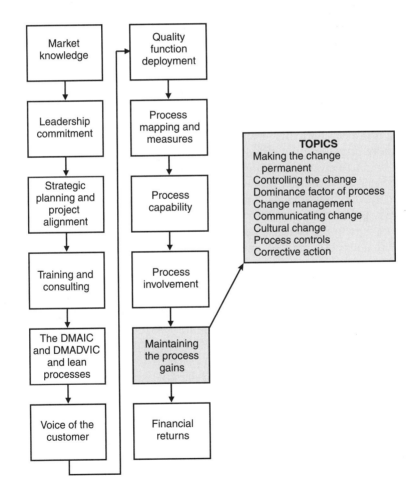

This chapter highlights Pillar Eleven and the ways we can permanently maintain the improvements to the process output achieved during the improvement phase. To protect the gains in process improvement, we must consider the type of change being made and determine how we will avoid backsliding to the original problem level of the process performance. Many improvements fail over the long run because we did not take the time to ensure that the change would be maintained. The maintenance of the gains can be as simple as using a new method or machine, or as complex as mistake-proofing the process.

MAKING THE CHANGE PERMANENT

If the change is part of a machine or equipment modification, usually training is all that is needed to make the change permanent. When the change is in methods or the way we perform a task using the existing equipment, training alone may not hold the change in place. It would be too easy to go back to the original level. The way to make the change stay in place is to change the measures that are being taken and monitor the measurements or performance by using the new measurement system. Another way is to not allow the error to occur in the first place. To do this we need to mistake-proof the process error. Dr. Shingo discusses this very well in his book and provides some of the methods of providing mistake-proof concepts.[1] The results that we are looking for in the process performance or the output of the process should require a change to the performance measures.

If we change the methods permanently, the operators cannot return to the original way of running the process. Old habits are hard to change unless the new method will benefit the operator more than the old method or unless the operator was the one suggesting the change. Some ways to eliminate old habits in a process include changing the methods of operation, the tools used, and the procedures used. Therefore we need to audit the process changes or change the measures used to determine performance status. We can then evaluate the process performance against the new measures. Let's consider the methods of measurement change in the following example:

In setting up a process, the line speed could be set up wrong and cause rejected product output. We could measure the line speed and compare it to the high- and low-limit specification. If the speed is not within the limits, the process would not be allowed to start. We could also leave this check in place while the process is running; when it passes either of the limits, the process is automatically stopped until the operator brings it back into control. This can be used along with the process control documentation.

To recap, the changes made to the process with automatic means will stay in place, and changes that are soft in nature will not stay in place. If we can go back to our old habits easily, we will not change the way we perform the operation.

CONTROLLING THE CHANGE

To maintain the improvements made by the DMAIC process, we need to consider the type of controls that will be installed and the measures used. We can also configure the new step or use different methods in the process. The use of control charts and control plans can ensure that we monitor the new process. If changes occur, we will have a reaction plan for maintaining the gains made by the initial changes. Sometimes the team will need new training, instructions, and methods to ensure that the new process will be implemented and maintained properly. Another approach is to establish new measures that will indicate whether a cause enters the process. The best implementation action is to change the equipment so that the operation will be maintained permanently. A proper solution and control method will ensure that the new process will maintain its improvements.

The outcome of the control phase is the establishment of methods that will ensure that the new process will continue to supply the product or service to the customer's requirements. The capability of the new process should be evaluated, and the measurements should prove out improvements to the indicators selected. The control of the changes should have a corrective action plan for when the indicators note a change in the output parameters. One of the team's tasks is to consider what aspects of the improvements are reversible when the operators are not familiar with the need for the changes and the benefits of the changes. Sometimes the people are comfortable with the old way of doing things because of habits formed by the operators. Resistance to change is caused by some of these issues and the fact that people fear how the unknown change will affect them. It is the team's responsibility to include the proper personnel in the solution selection and implementation process to reduce resistance to the change. There are indications that personnel are sometimes angered that they did not recognize the need for the improvements, and this causes resistance to the new process. To help with the implementation and to hold the gains in the process improvements, we need to line up all the technology changes and have a plan for training and installation. We need to make the changes a turnkey implementation and foolproof the new process so errors will not occur. All the procedures and instructions should be completed and implemented. Training should be provided on the new process. We need to be present for the installation and observe the implementation. The team needs to audit the outcome of the changes and implementation. We need to explain the reasons for the changes to the people who will help in the implementation and control of the new process. The team must insist that the new process be followed and change the indicators or measures to ensure that the change is monitored.

DOMINANCE FACTOR OF THE PROCESS

The control of implemented changes will require us to understand the process dominance factor if the changes are to be felt by the output. The dominance factor is what affects the process output most. This dominance factor will be derived from the material used, the set-up of the process or the equipment, and the tooling within the equipment. Sometimes the operation will be dominated by the operator and his or her skill in performing the tasks of the process. A good example would be a welding process. Welding requires a skilled person who can operate the welding machine. The machine set-up, type of rod used, the part(s) set-up, and the operator skill must be present. The operator would need to understand the reasons for the types of changes being implemented and agree with them.

The one item we tend to forget in the improvement phase is the need to fail-safe the process against errors or mistakes. This means that we must consider the redesign of processes and product to eliminate errors, signal the process operator when an error occurs, and provide the configuration control. We need to consider automating the process in order to control the characteristics of the process automatically. The process should contain as much automation as possible, with state-of-the-art equipment to standardize the repetitive process activities and to ensure that we will obtain the changes required for the output to be more consistent to meeting the customer's needs.

CHANGE MANAGEMENT

The change management process must be considered and support provided for the change to hold the gains from the implementation. To change the organization, we must consider organizational values and beliefs and what changes will be required to these values, as well as changes that will be required of management at the process level. The management team needs to consider providing awareness training to ensure all employees understand what the organization is doing with the Six Sigma process. The executive team also needs to understand the process and be able to support it as we implement the changes. The executive team needs to be committed to the Six Sigma process and have the patience to allow the teams of Black Belts and Green Belts to perform the steps or phases in the DMAIC process.

The executive team needs to be open to the change required to become customer and process focused. They also need to establish measures and expectations of the new process performance required for improvement. The executive team will need to follow up on the status of projects and the implementation of the changes within the organization as well as process improvements. For process changes we need to consider what training, procedures, measures, and resources are needed to support the team.

The Black Belt, as the change manager, needs to understand the project focus on teams and team skills. The Black Belt also will need to know how to handle conflicts and resolve outstanding issues with the team. The art of negotiation and team facilitation will be required in the changing environment. We will not cover these in detail here, but the sources in the references will allow the reader to obtain the best practices on these subjects. For now, let's cover an overview of the change management process.

The resistance to change will affect the implementation process and must be overcome by the Black Belt and the team. One way to accomplish this is to involve those who will implement the change in the solution selection and the planning for implementation. The people affected need to feel secure about the changes; if they have a hand in the decisions about the change, there is a better chance that it will be supported. The use of force field analysis might help the team or Black Belt understand the resistance that has to be overcome.

COMMUNICATING CHANGE

Effective communication with management, employees, and team members will help the Black Belts implement the change. One key point here is to back up any change with data and information that show the benefits of the change. This will help everyone understand the expected outcome after the changes are made and reduce fear of the change. Critical to the communication process is the need for the Black Belts to learn to become good listeners so that they hear the facts from the resistors and the people who will help in the change process. This allows the Black Belts time to address the concerns and to counter resistance with facts and information that will overcome the reasons for the resistance. The Black Belts need to figure out what needs to be controlled or countered to stop or overcome this resistance. The following are potential reasons for resistance:

- Beliefs of the employees and the organization

- Habits of the employees

- Values of the organization and the employees

- Practices of the organization
- Traditions of the organization and the employees
- Values shared by the group
- Values and beliefs taught to new members
- Experiences of the employees

THE ORGANIZATIONAL CULTURAL CHANGE

The change management process needs to consider the cultural change that may be required at the organization level to be able to support the Black Belts and their projects. To perform the higher level of management change, we need to acknowledge the beliefs and values of the organization that are obtained through strategic planning. Once we have completed the strategic plan, we can use the outputs from the process to evaluate where the organization presently stands. We can then develop a force field analysis that may need to be implemented to overcome the present values and beliefs. This part of the process is critical to sustaining the continuous improvement efforts for the Six Sigma process. If we do not cover the strategic issues format in this process, we may not establish the lists of values, beliefs, and sometimes artifacts that are of the old culture. If we want to make the best of the implementation process for Six Sigma, we need to assure ourselves that the new values and beliefs can be put into place.

For the organization to overcome some of its reasons for resistance, the management team will need to draw on its knowledge of the Six Sigma process concerning the customer, the process focus, and the strategic planning process. This means that the executive team will need to ensure that the strategic planning process considers how the new agenda will be set in place if we need to overcome resistance to a change. This is the higher-level management change process. The change management process will require the support of the executive team. The use of force field analysis will help the Black Belts and the teams learn more about the forces that support the change and the forces that resist it. This tool is effective in identifying the areas that need to be addressed. The sources at the end of this chapter should help with further study on the change management process.

It helps achieve proper change implementation when the Black Belts have good management, leadership, and negotiation skills to overcome conflicts. Black Belt training should teach these skills or at least discuss the concepts. In some organizations, more training will have to be provided if the Black Belts are to be effective at change and change management. The change management expert I always looked too is Rosabeth Moss Kanter.[2] Especially in her book on confidence, she covers the change management concept very well.

TYPES OF PROCESS CONTROLS

To maintain the goals, we can provide control with feedback from the output of the process, which is compared to a standard; action is taken based on the results of the comparisons. An example of this process is displayed in Figure 13.1.

In Figure 13.1, the effect of the process is measured with specific sensors that record the performance of the output. This output is compared with the expected standard. If the measured output differs from the expected standard, we need to have a control plan that

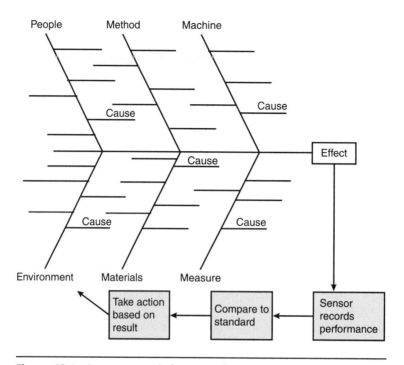

Figure 13.1 Process controls for a specific process.

indicates what should be done when out-of-control conditions occur. If we can provide automatic feedback to the process, it can self-adjust to control the process. The importance of automatic control cannot be overlooked, because it will produce the best benefit in controlling the process.

The control plan helps manufacturing hold the gains and consistency of the process output to the requirements. There are many ways to provide a control plan. These include making the plan part of the standard operating procedures, providing a measurement control plan for product dimensions, and standard process control plans for the process at the various steps in the process. We usually see these plans being attached to the process flowcharts and indicating in which areas process checks are to be made, how frequently to make those checks, and what instruments to use for the checks. Along with the areas to measure, there usually is a reaction plan detailing what to do if the parameter being measured does go out of control. An example of the layout is provided in Figure 13.2, showing how the control plan and its reaction plan may look in application.

The control plan must outline the steps to take to perform the measurement, how to take the measurement, and what should be controlled to maintain the process output to the requirements. The documentation of the control plan must be simple so that the operator can easily understand how to use the control.

During the controls phase we can use the list of actions that are identified in Figure 13.3 that facilitate implementation of process control.

Figure 13.3 shows the best approaches for keeping the process gains. The first item requires the team to put an action in place that will eliminate, or mistake-proof (Poka-Yoke), the process so the error will not occur in the first place. This level of action allows for a change that will eliminate the errors or the reason for the process variation. If we cannot eliminate the step in the process or redesign the product to eliminate the material or compo-

Process/Part Number	Process Name	Operation	Originator
Characteristics:	Process Step	Measurement	Instrument
Diameter	Twenty-one	Shaft Diameter	Micrometer
Sample Size	Five Consecutive		
Control Method	Process Speed		
Reaction Plan	Change process		

Figure 13.2 Typical items in a control plan.

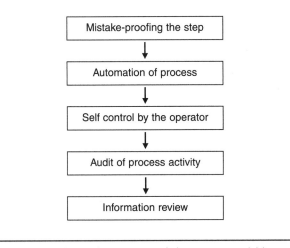

Figure 13.3 Actions taken to control the process activities go from bottom to top.

nent variance effects, the next approach is for the team to focus on automating the process. If the technology or costs prohibit the automation of the process with automatic feedback, then we must at least notify the operator of the machine that the error has occurred and we will not process any more goods or services until it is corrected. The variance must be rectified within the process or the product before the operator restarts the machine cycle.

Part of the Poka-Yoke process is the use of statistical process controls, alarms, stops, and machine controls to allow us to note the change and to stop the process so corrective action can be taken. The methods of doing this are the error-proofing, or Poka-Yoke, approaches. When error-proofing the process, redesign the process to eliminate the error if possible with the current technology. Another approach is to find the error when it occurs and then configure a control mechanization and design new equipment as necessary to eliminate the error. A third approach is to use the next steps of process automation, self-control, or auditing practices to control the process and the product performance.

CORRECTIVE ACTION PLAN

For controls to be effective, we need a corrective action plan for when a process shift is detected. A control plan should be developed for each process activity that can be verified before, during, or after the activity of the process takes place. A control plan should be in place for all of the process activities or steps. In fact, every key process should have a control plan attached to the process flowchart. The control plan should be looking at the dominance factor for the process to be controlled. This process dominance can come from one of the following areas and is where the controls need to be applied:

- Material dominance
- Tooling dominance
- Set-up dominance
- Equipment dominance
- Operator dominance
- Measurement dominance

The control portion of the DMAIC process must find the best approach that will allow the gains in process improvement to be maintained. The steps or stages of control need to be evaluated based on the technology available, cost to control, and ability of the operators to perform the controls necessary for the output to become successful. Let's consider different types of controls that could be used for this phase. The automation of a process will usually solve much of the variability of the process if the automation equipment can maintain stability over the environmental and operating ranges seen by the equipment. An example of the automation process is the automobile braking system, which most of us can relate to. If we need to stop our automobile, we must rely on our reflexes, the brake system reaction time, and performance of the system to stop the automobile. We could automate the braking system to perform a gradual stop once we trigger it. We could even automate the entire system by providing sensors that would monitor the automobile's performance, the conditions of the environment, and the operator's performance within the system. The system would then take over, just as an airplane's autopilot will fly a plane. This means that the braking system could be totally automated and eliminate human decisions if sensors could be supplied to control the automobile.

At this point in the DMAIC process we should be reaping the benefits of the reduced variation within the process. The control phase is the final phase of our process. Now we are ready to consider more improvements in the same process or selecting another key process problem to consider.

CHAPTER QUESTIONS

1. When should process controls be put into place?

2. When should SPC not be used as a control approach?

3. What might happen if you miss the control phase of the DMAIC process?

4. What does the step function of control offer us in this phase?

5. What are some of the skills that the Back Belt needs to understand to help in the implementation and control phases?

6. What is the process dominance factor about in DMAIC?

7. What kind of change management skills will Black Belts require?

8. What is meant by self control?

9. Why do Black Belts require good listening skills?

10. What is Poka-Yoke?

SUGGESTIONS FOR FURTHER READING

Besterfield, Dale H. *Quality Control.* Englewood Cliffs, NJ: Prentice-Hall, 1986.

Bossidy, Larry, and Ram Charan. *Execution.* New York: Crown Publishing, 2002.

Brue, Greg. *Design for Six Sigma.* New York: McGraw-Hill, 2003.

Eckes, George. *Making Six Sigma Last.* New York: John Wiley & Sons, 2001.

———. *The Six Sigma Revolution.* New York: John Wiley & Sons, 2001.

George, Michael L. *Lean Six Sigma.* New York: McGraw-Hill, 2002.

Grant, Eugene L., and Richard S. Leavenworth. *Statistical Quality Control,* New York: McGraw-Hill, 1980.

Naumann, Earl, and Steve Hoisington. *Customer Centered Six Sigma.* Milwaukee, WI: ASQ Quality Press, 2001.

Spande, Peter S. *The Six Sigma Way.* New York: McGraw-Hill, 2000.

Thomas, D. W., AT&T Technologies. *Statistical Quality Control Handbook.* Indianapolis: 1956.

14

Pillar Twelve: Planning for Financial Returns, Recognition, and Rewards

The Twelve Pillars for Six Sigma Support and Implementation

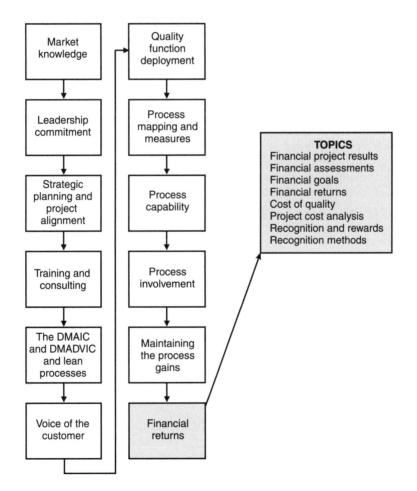

We will now cover Pillar Twelve, which focuses on the financial results to be obtained from the Lean Six Sigma process implementation. In order for the Six Sigma DMAIC process to be successful, we have to provide a return on the investment made in training, problem solving, and changes that are implemented to the processes. The best way to show this result is through the return on investment analysis. This analysis is best performed with the help of the professional financial personnel within the organization. The Black Belts should take counsel with the controller of the plant, or division, to arrive at the methods and the target numbers that will prove out the gains of the project. The gains of most projects consist of reduced rejects, increased throughput, increased capacity, and, sometimes, increased market share. These successes must be discussed but, let's face it, the project must save the organization money. I have heard of Six Sigma companies saying that they might have gone out of business if they had not followed this improvement process. This is a testimonial for the Lean Six Sigma approaches.

FINANCIAL PROJECT RESULTS

Successful Black Belt projects can usually be accomplished by producing several of the following attributes of success by the end of the project:

- Simpler and easier process steps
- Reduced process down time
- Reduced rework and scrap
- Higher efficiency
- Reduced cycle time for the process activities
- Process capability to deliver what the customer wants and needs
- More knowledgeable workers of the process and customer needs
- Development of the knowledge worker skills
- More consistent practices
- Increased profits
- Happier workforce
- Increased capacity
- Reduced operating costs

Let's get back to the financials issue. There are many claims of the savings provided by the Black Belt and Green Belt projects. When first starting out, it should not be a problem for your Black Belts to provide a savings of $100,000 to $250,000 on the average project. So, with 10 Black Belts, the total savings to the bottom line can be anywhere from $1 million to $2.5 million annually. If Black Belts can complete two to three projects per year, they can return millions of dollars to that bottom line. An organization can probably continue this type of savings per project for the first three to five years, depending on process complexity and size of the company. If DFSS using the DMADVIC process is applied by the organization, the future retroactive project savings may be reduced in favor of proactive design projects. Realize that we live in a continuously improving society, which changes its mind on wants and needs. This means that there will always be projects to improve a characteristic or the need for a new characteristic that is important to a customer. This raising of the bar for key characteristics will occur for all businesses. The organization will need to keep focused on the customers' needs to ensure that every change is noticed. Sometimes the organization itself causes the bar to be raised by the improvements it has made. Realize that this is a never-ending change. The organization's listening posts need to pass the news along as soon as a new technology is available for meeting the customer's needs in a better or cheaper way. It is your job to stay ahead of the raising needs or change those needs to new levels for your customers.

FINANCIAL ASSESSMENTS

The financial assessment of the organization should include all expenses incurred for the training, time spent on the project, consulting costs, and capital expenses. The savings will be taken from some of the areas in the following list. The organization must establish the methods for evaluating the financial success of the Six Sigma projects. Some points to consider are:

- Inventory carrying costs
- Overhead burden rate savings
- Capacity improvements from increased throughput
- Reduced scrap costs
- Reduced rework costs
- New product introduction cost reduction
- Reduced component costs
- Market share increases
- Profit increases
- Less expenses to customer good will
- Lower service costs
- Reduced warranty costs
- Reduced headcount
- Capability improvements

FINANCIAL GOALS

This item must be considered in this financial Pillar Twelve to determine what the goal should be for the return on investment for the Six Sigma program and, in turn, for the Black Belt and Green Belt projects. In my experience, organizations have wanted at least a 15 percent return and, in some cases, a 20 percent return on their investments. I have always tried to stretch out the 20 percent return on investment (ROI) and can assure you that this is achievable with the MBNQA Criteria, when tied to a good quality system and the tactical tools of Six Sigma and lean concepts. I have not seen too much attention given to these ROI values lately, but if your company is given a 5 percent return on an annual basis today, I am sure the company will take it. This is why I have a hard time when the executive staff has not provided the resources for full-time Black Belts to take on the improvement efforts and the engineering staff looking at DFSS as an asset to the design process. Each Black Belt project should bring in $100,000 savings after expenses. Green Belt projects can bring in $10,000 to $50,000. I cannot predict whether these types of savings will continue after the program has been in place for five to ten years because the organization's culture should have changed to focus on the customer requirements, the key processes, and the metrics to the point where we are preventing problems and thus the reactive way of operation will not exist to the extent it exists in the beginning.

FINANCIAL RETURNS ANALYSIS

The financial returns must be greater than the time spent on the project, resources used, and capital investment put into the project. The Black Belts must become familiar with the questions to ask when researching the sources of savings for the cost analysis. The accounting department will usually help in the cost analysis process. The management staff needs to know the financial as well as the process improvements that are being made during the project implementation.

The financial savings potential should be established during the development of the project charter and verified during the implementation phase. The Black Belt must take the lead in the project definition to provide the savings projection. The importance of the results must be stressed with the team. All projects must reduce variation in the process, which will produce a financial return to the organization in one of the categories we covered earlier in this chapter. One way to ensure that the financial return will happen is to provide a project selection process that aligns the project with the strategic issues important to the business. An example of the kind of data to collect is provided in Figure 14.1.

Most financial departments should be satisfied with an ROI analysis based on incurred costs versus the annual savings realized from the project. Returns of 20 to 30 percent are not unheard of and they can be greater once the Black Belts are running more projects. The ROI can be based on the length of time of the project, the achievement of the objectives, the best solution selection process, the cash flow from the selected alternative, comparisons of the solutions, and the best selection approach. Therefore, phase 4, the improvement phase, should be followed closely to achieve the desired ROI of the organization. As mentioned earlier in this book, full-time Black Belts working on key processes will show faster results. Most organizations have a hard time with the full-time Black Belt position, so part-time positions will have to suffice at the start. All that happens is that the financial returns and cultural change to a problem-solving process takes longer to set in place within the organization. I don't think the full-time Black Belt position will be hard to justify once it is recognized that each full-time Black Belt will save at least $1 million dollars a year for the organization. This is hard to turn away from once the process is shown to work. So probably we need to consider the opportunity based on the strategic plan and reassess the use of some of the Black Belts on a full-time basis to solve most strategic project issues.

Project Title:	Project Scope:
Project Leader:	Project Team Members:

Finished goods costs
Work in process costs
Supplier costs
Direct Labor:
   Headcount reduction
   Cycle time savings
   Overtime
 	
Current: _____
 	
Proposed: _____
	In-process material costs
	Maintenance costs
	Inspection costs
	Overhead:
	   Purchased services
	   Supplies
	   Building facility costs
	   Travel costs
	   Overtime
	
	Current: _____
	
	Proposed: _____

Standard Material Savings: Purchase price: _____ Scrap: _____ In-process scrap costs In-process rework costs	Logistics: Freight costs: _____ Inventory costs: _____
Project expenses: Training costs Consulting costs Capital costs	Project resource costs: Team project time costs Project production costs New process implementation costs

Figure 14.1   Typical Black Belt project form for financials.

THE COST OF QUALITY

The use of the cost of quality reporting will usually show organizations the tip of the iceberg in quality costs, of which the failure and appraisal costs could be saved. These costs can improve the bottom line and are usually better at providing results on the earnings than on increased sales. In my experience, the typical $1 billion gross sales organization will have a savings potential of $20 million to $100 million. To verify this opportunity, we need to have a rough idea of what the present cost of quality is in failures internally and externally and the appraisal costs. I am not suggesting that a full-blown cost of quality program be established, but that the cost accounting department sort the existing costs into categories that will allow the Black Belts to sort out this cost information. We need to look at the budget process for the costs incurred by process complexity, rework, scrap, and product returns or recalls. Some of the sources at the end of the book and this chapter will go into more detail on the categories of costs. My experiences, when working with Phil Crosby Associates, were that the opportunity is in the area of 10 percent to 20 percent of gross sales. This savings is from the support processes as well as the manufacturing operation. An example of the areas to search for opportunity costs is provided in Figure 14.2.

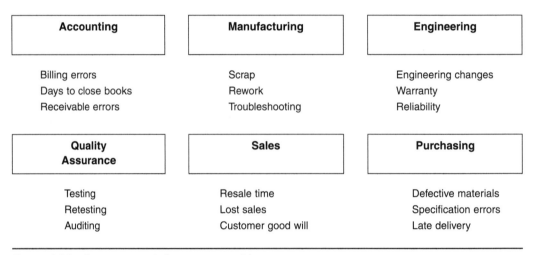

Accounting	**Manufacturing**	**Engineering**
Billing errors	Scrap	Engineering changes
Days to close books	Rework	Warranty
Receivable errors	Troubleshooting	Reliability

Quality Assurance	**Sales**	**Purchasing**
Testing	Resale time	Defective materials
Retesting	Lost sales	Specification errors
Auditing	Customer good will	Late delivery

Figure 14.2 Areas to search for costs caused by errors.

Do not let the Black Belts or Green Belts go forward on projects without seeing a potential savings for the effort. If you fail to address this area in the beginning of the project, the program will start to fail. For the organization to become more profitable, the executive team must insist on a reduction in variation of the key characteristics and reduced costs in operations. The cost of quality is one area to investigate for these savings. The cost of quality consists of the following:

1. Cost to maintain customer needs

    • Conformance

      —Appraisal/audit

      —Prevention

    • Nonconformance

      —Redoing

      —Failure

2. Total costs of quality:

    • Price of nonconformance

    • Price of conformance

3. Prevention costs:

- Things we do to prevent problems from occurring
- Cost to get things done right (usually 1 percent to 3 percent of sales for world-class companies)

4. Waste costs:

- The things we do over because they were not performed right the first time
- Cost to do things wrong (ideally 0 percent but usually you attain .25% of sales level for world-class companies)

Some points to consider for the cost of quality are:

- Differences to consider for the costs of quality:

  —Large manufacturing (500+ employees): 10 to 20 percent of sales

  —Small manufacturing (less than 500 employees): 5 to 15 percent of sales

  —Service (all types): 10 to 40 percent of sales

- Reduction in the cost of quality to bring the savings to the bottom line:

  —A dollar saved is equal to a dollar earned

  —Usually it takes $10 to $100 in sales to return the same amount to the bottom line

Cost of quality is not an absolute performance measurement. It is an indication of where corrective action should be taken and is usually controlled by the controller. One way to look at the costs of quality is depicted in Figure 14.3.

PROJECT COST ANALYSIS

The typical cost analysis approach considers the total investment in the project and savings from the project. The savings must be verified by reducing the cost of producing the product, by increasing capacity to produce more products, or by reducing overhead costs. All the savings must show up on the bottom line. Some costs to consider in the analysis of the project are: Black Belt, Green Belt, champion, and executive training costs; project time for the team; capital equipment needs; process change costs; project expenses; and the personnel costs for the project. Some areas to consider for the cost of quality are: what the conformance costs will be, audits, quality education, prevention methods, tests, verification, reviews, checking, and inspection. The nonconformance cost areas will be: rework, reprocessing, retesting, retyping,

Figure 14.3 The flow of the quality measures to the cost of quality to the bottom-line results.

expediting, inventory, down time, and warranty costs. There are other areas to capture costs related to the project, and they are:

- The number of engineering change orders
- Claims processing costs
- Laboratory testing
- Specification changes
- Lost time
- Supplier costs to do business
- Design reviews
- Cost in closing the books
- Missed schedules
- Sorting
- Customer cost of ownership
- Audits
- Legal cycle time for patients

RECOGNITION AND REWARDS

The organization must not forget to address the recognition of and rewards for the projects completed by the Black Belts and Green Belts. This is required as part of the financial analysis pillar. The organization now has the tough job of recognizing the successful efforts of the Black Belts and Green Belts. Most recognition can be as simple as a dinner party with presentations from the Black Belts or as complex as providing a percentage of the project savings to the team. The recognition part of Pillar Twelve is very important to sustain the Six Sigma process. We briefly covered some of the recognition methods in Chapter 2. Let's take a moment to cover the extremes of the range for recognition and their benefits and pitfalls. At one end of the spectrum is the payment of a percentage of the savings for each successful project, in the range of 5 percent to 10 percent. At the other end of the spectrum is the chance to keep your job if you are successful.

The provision of a percentage of the savings of the bottom-line results has been tried in many suggestion programs. It works, but must have a set of rules and an administrator to implement it in larger organizations. Although this is probably a preferred method, it can create extra overhead and sometimes morale problems. The next best approach might be to provide a set bonus for successful projects at the end of the fiscal year.

The do-nothing approach for the Black Belts and their teams could become another morale problem unless we develop a Black Belt classification and job work instruction that is rated by personnel in an effective salary range. I guess this is better then doing nothing for the Black Belts.

In the recognition process, we need to focus on teamwork success as well as the project success. The return on investment for the organization as a whole must be in the range of 15 percent to 25 percent or we are not using the skill level of the Black Belts and Green Belts properly. I would review the selection processes for the projects, Black Belts and the Green Belts first to see whether these processes are failing to deliver the proper projects and the proper use of skills. The other area to investigate is the linkage of the project selection process to the strategic plan.

The Black Belt projects should provide a savings of $100,000, or at least $50,000, per project. If you have not achieved this kind of return, the project selection process or Black Belt skills are not being used properly. Green Belt projects on specific department issues may not contribute as much of a savings as some of the Black Belt projects. This is because these projects reduce or control issues within the department. These projects will reduce variation, but the savings may be smaller and the focus is on the specific department issues. Most Green Belts should be working with Black Belts on the Black Belt projects to help achieve a quicker return of the selected projects that are aligned with the strategic plan and the goals and objectives of the organization. The Black Belt projects will be completed in a more timely fashion and bring the $100,000 projects to successful completion at a faster pace.

For any process or program, there should be recognition when we are performing well. This must be considered if the Black Belt projects are providing bottom-line results in the range of $50,000 to $250,000. If we don't recognize the Black Belts, they will have plenty of opportunities to leave and join other organizations. This part of the Six Sigma process (recognition) is sometimes forgotten. This will be discussed in more detail in Chapter 18, which is on the pitfalls of Six Sigma. Celebration is needed if we are to remain on the continuous improvement path. Consider some of the following methods for celebration and rewards when successful projects are completed in a timely fashion:

- Classification as a Black Belt with commensurate salary change
- Acknowledgement from the CEO and president
- Family and officers dinner celebration
- Sabbatical or vacation trips
- Bonus program
- Promotion program
- Return of percentage of savings
- Gift certificates
- Future promotions within the organization
- New job classification

The key to the celebration process is to take time out to acknowledge success and recognize the efforts that have provided positive results to the organization.

RECOGNITION METHODS

We need to ensure that the management team, sponsors of the project, and champions keep up with the project status and provide the proper compliments at the proper time during the project. Some methods of reviewing the projects and providing recognition are the following:

- Storyboarding the projects in a war room
- Project presentation and recognition to the management staff
- Formal presentations and dinner celebration
- Plant presentations and party
- Interface with the management team
- Percentage of the project savings as reward
- Special organization privileges

We need to consider another problem with recognition, which will affect the team spirit of the organization. Most projects will require help from Green Belts and other personnel within the organization. Usually a team is required for the Black Belt project. This means that when we consider the results of the project and the possible recognition that the entire team must be considered in the recognition process. This is one area where I have seen some deficiencies in the recognition process. The team may not be considered when the Black Belt is presenting the results of the successful project. The many team members should be included in the recognition and in any ceremonies that are provided for the results. The Black Belt needs to be recognized for the leadership role he or she has played in the team process, but the team members need to be recognized for their contribution to the results. These project teams are usually cross-functional people from different parts of the organization who are brought together to work on a common problem. This team is usually under the direction of the Black Belt. This is another reason why the Black Belt selection process must be performed with care.

We have to consider that a team is neither a committee nor a group that meets for the need of the group. They usually meet to accept the common goal of resolving a specific problem within the organization. Well-formed teams are a performing group who work together, using their diverse skills to address issues during the process of improving a situation or solving a problem.

CHAPTER QUESTIONS

1. Why do we want to perform an ROI on the Black Belt and Green Belt projects?

2. Who should be involved with the financial analysis for each project?

3. Who should report on the financial status of the projects?

4. What are the key components of the cost of quality?

5. Why do we need to reward success?

6. What factors need to be considered for the financial evaluation of the project?

7. What are the typical savings per year per Black Belt?

8. What project costs and organizational savings should we capture?

9. What cost centers should we be concerned with in the financial analysis?

10. What other benefits beside financial returns does Six Sigma bring to the organization?

SUGGESTIONS FOR FURTHER READING

Brue, Greg. *Design for Six Sigma.* New York: McGraw-Hill, 2003.

Eckes, George. *Making Six Sigma Last.* New York: John Wiley & Sons, 2001.

———. *The Six Sigma Revolution.* New York: John Wiley & Sons, 2001.

George, Michael L. *Lean Six Sigma.* New York: McGraw-Hill, 2002.

Grant, Eugene L., and Richard S. Leavenworth. *Statistical Quality Control,* New York: McGraw-Hill, 1980.

Naumann, Earl, and Steve Hoisington. *Customer Centered Six Sigma.* Milwaukee, WI: ASQ Quality Press, 2001.

Ross, Phillip J. *Taguchi Techniques for Quality Engineering.* New York: McGraw-Hill, 1998.

Spande, Peter S. *The Six Sigma Way.* New York: McGraw-Hill, 2000.

Welch, Jack. *Jack: Straight from the Gut.* New York: Warner Business Books, 2001.

15

The New Paradigm of Six Sigma

PROCESS FOCUS

The new paradigm for the Six Sigma program is to focus on the process rather than the functions within the organization. This is a difficult change for some organizations. Two reasons for this difficulty are that the various departments are developed in a silo fashion and that we tend to focus on the discipline of the function such as materials, quality, and engineering rather than on the process that needs to be accomplished. The discipline of the function gets lost in the process and is hard to maintain. My experience with this functional-to-process shift has been that the organization becomes more efficient and customer focused but the needs of the discipline are lost. The way we overcame the discipline loss was to create task groups that shared the movements and ideas of the discipline in a committee or association format. They met monthly or quarterly to keep abreast of the field. We do not need to create committees for all the functions, but a corporate-level quality or materials function group might keep up with the discipline and involve all of the other process personnel to keep them in tune with changes in the functional disciplines.

STRATEGIC PLANNING

The organization must perform some form of strategic planning process for the proper alignment of project selection and resources to important drivers of the operations performance. In most organizations the company is trying to perform retrospective Six Sigma, which means it is trying to fix existing problems based on a crisis that exists. The reason the crisis exists is that the organization did not meet performance requirements. If the requirements and the process controls had been understood, the causes would not have occurred or would have been resolved as they occurred. The organization needs to focus on the key processes that will deliver the performance requirements and to ensure that controls are put in place to exceed the requirements. The only way I know of obtaining this direction is by going through a planning process that identifies what is critical to the success of the organization and making sure that we concentrate on these areas for the improvements. It is astonishing to talk to personnel who do not realize the direction the organization is taking and how it will need to proceed for growth. The Black Belt projects should support the goals of the organization and provide a savings and improvement in the key processes.

CUSTOMER FOCUS

The next task for the organization is to attend to customer satisfaction and focus on the customer's needs and expectations. Because this is time consuming and sometimes difficult, an organization often does not take the time to understand and focus on the customer's needs. The sales- and engineering-driven companies sometimes feel that they know the customer base well enough to describe their needs and expectations. This may not always be true. I have seen failure to identify the customer expectations occur in many cases because organizations were not attentive to the customer. Needs are usually easy to define and obtain, but obtaining expectations takes a good question list and interview process. The methods of obtaining the voice of the customer were covered in detail in Chapter 8. If we do not perform this step on new products or review them on existing products, we will miss the mark.

DATA AND INFORMATION FOCUS

The next major change for the Black Belt team and management team is the use of data to determine present and future conditions of the process rather than ideas or hunches. The people in a Six Sigma organization become more critical of the use of data to make decisions. The establishment of measures for the organization's dashboard and the key processes is critical to the success of the Six Sigma improvement process. Most organizations have measures, but we must make sure that they are the right measures for achieving the organization's strategic goals and the goals of the Black Belt projects. Some organizations find that tracking these measures is a new paradigm. Measuring key indicators for success means that the dashboards must align with the goals of the organization. The key process indicators align with the dashboard. The Black Belt project results must help the indicators of the dashboard and key processes move in the right direction for improvement. The dashboard and key process principles were covered in Chapters 3 and 4.

The measures discussed above must be derived from the strategic planning process. Strategic planning must be considered important by the executive management team and sometimes is another paradigm that needs to be overcome. The strategic plan is important in setting the direction for the organization. The planning depth will depend on the type of business and the size of the organization. Chapters 3 and 4 covered this subject in enough detail, but most organizations do not take the time to plan; even if organizations do plan, listening posts are not in place to provide the information for the development of a good plan. Planning and measurement development takes time that most staff members do not seem to have.

IMPROVEMENT FOCUS

The next shift in thought (paradigm) is to establish goals for the Six Sigma process that will offer 10 times the improvement. Think about it! If I am at 3 sigma and I can improve to 4 sigma, the improvement will be more than 10 times the current process performance level for defect rate or process cycle time. Setting strategic goals seems tough, but with the proper attitude it can be achieved. This is what Bob Galvin saw in the Six Sigma approach at Motorola in the early 1980s. Ten times improvement can be achieved with the tools available for problem solving and continuous improvement. Part of the paradigm shift is the thought that improving from the 4 sigma to 5 sigma level of performance is better than a process that is at 5 sigma and is not improving. The customer will notice the improvement. The goal should be to achieve the Six Sigma level of performance for all key processes.

PROBLEM-SOLVING PROCESS

Probably the most difficult change for some individuals is the shifting to a problem-solving DMAIC process to evaluate a problem, find its root cause, and select the best solution for eliminating or controlling the cause. The DMAIC principles and process must be followed for the improvement to take place. This requires a disciplined approach and the attitude that the change can be achieved. For new designs, the DFSS concepts using the DMADVIC process should be followed to prevent the installation of new processes that will probably add to process variation. These processes are defined in detail in Pillar Five (Chapter 7). The change that must take place is the patience to get to the root cause and the ability to understand how to analyze the process to achieve the answer about variation. The use of statistical thinking, process variation, and statistical tools must find the data leading to the real causes. This requires an ability to search for multiple reasons for the problem and select the one or two reasons that cause the problem to exist. Many times individuals will skip the steps of the process, which leads to the wrong cause and therefore the wrong solution.

Most personnel within the organization feel that they understand the processes well and they can move from problem definition to solution selection and improvement without a disciplined approach. Even the organizations that have a disciplined problem-solving process, such as the automotive seven D and eight D processes, feel this is effective. Even with these processes, many of the problems are not resolved because the team or individual assigned to the problem does not determine the root cause of the problem. In some cases the best solution is not determined, because we are under pressure and time constraints to resolve the issues that present manufacturability issues. The problems that are identified are sometimes described as symptoms and thus are not properly identified, thwarting the effort to collect the proper data for analysis of the problem. The time constraints to perform the proper analysis lead to poor decisions. We always seem to have the time to perform the analysis over again but do not have the time to perform the right analysis and do it right the first time. If we could just obtain a more disciplined approach to the problem-solving process, we would be eliminating the errors, or at least identifying them as they occur and resolving them faster. The other problem in the typical problem-solving process is the lack of corrective action to solve the problem. This also would be solved by a disciplined approach such as the Six Sigma process improvement approach.

CULTURAL CHANGE

The organization must consider its present culture and the culture required to implement and support the continuous improvement Six Sigma process. This means that the present culture must be recognized and the new culture required to support the process be understood. This usually can be accomplished during the champion training process. I would suggest that in the champion training, the organization should review the current strategic plan and update it if necessary during or after the training. If a strategic plan does not already exist, a separate two- to three-day planning session must be established. Highlights of the process are covered in Chapter 4. This plan will allow the executive team to focus on the metrics of the dashboard during the champion training and help with the alignment of the first Black Belt projects to the strategies.

PROJECT SELECTION PROCESS

Many organizations need to rethink the projects selection process and ensure that they pick projects that will support the vision and mission. If this process is not followed, the Six Sigma process will start to fail in two to three years. The projects selected may not need the skill levels of the Black Belt, and therefore projects will be completed without the returns expected. This is why I feel that Drucker's knowledge worker idea will surface as we follow the Six Sigma process. The Black Belts will use their knowledge to ensure that the project selection process is focused and the projects selected will bring in the results projected. If we develop the right projects around the planning process, the improvements will become a success and drive the organization in the right direction.

If we do not select the right projects, we will improve the wrong processes, and the bottom-line results or ROI we expected will not be obtained. These ROI issues were discussed in more detail in Chapter 14.

DATA ANALYSIS

Another factor to consider is the need to have people who have the skills to identify opportunities, analyze the data and develop information about the processes under study. The knowledge worker will become the logical and analytical thinker who will help improve operations and customer satisfaction. We must be patient enough to allow this person to grow and learn the proper tool set and the right characteristics to control the key processes and business drivers.

Executive management who are leading an organization using the MBNQA Criteria and the Lean Six Sigma process will be more dynamic, and they will find the process to be satisfying to the entire executive team. This executive team will need to understand the MBNQA Criteria and the Lean Six Sigma process, support it, and provide the resources to sustain the process. It is exciting to see the solving of problems that organizations have lived with for 10 to 15 years. The true causes are now being resolved. The typical office day will become more enjoyable, and things finally will be completed right the first time.

KNOWLEDGE WORKER

The next area of change is the knowledge worker concept that I see developing from the Black Belts. The people being trained within the organization become more familiar with the organization's processes and key business drivers, and thus more valuable to the organization and knowledgeable about the organization. The Black Belts also become experts in problem-solving methods and understand the use of statistics in data analysis, which is required to determine the direction to take to improve the process. This knowledge worker will help the organization improve the key processes, which will link to the key process measures and the operations dashboard metrics. When this occurs, the industry, customer, and company knowledge will be used to meet or exceed customer expectations.

TEAMWORK ENVIRONMENT

Although most organizations will not need to call teamwork a paradigm shift, many organizations really do not have teams. What they have are groups of people meeting to discuss issues and sometimes perform some activities to improve the processes. I am not being negative toward teams, but the definition of a team is usually two or more people getting together to work toward a common, accepted goal. Most teams are created without good charters and direction to resolve a specific problem or create a new product or process. Sometimes poor team performance is caused by the lack of a good facilitator and/or leader to direct and support the team process. Teams require a reason to bond together to work in a common direction or toward an agreed-upon cause. A good facilitator will present rules to govern meetings and communications, to make decisions, and to go about solving problems. The team needs to be able to work together and keep the project on track. The Black Belt needs to be able to handle and resolve conflict. The styles of collaborating, compromising, competing, accommodating, and avoiding conflict will help in handling teams and team meetings. We should also consider conflict intervention methods, ranging from doing nothing to using direct methods to halt or control conflict.

The Black Belt needs to be able to handle self-directed teams, which are put together to manage the work direction of the process that is being reviewed and controlled. The lean program relies on this self-directed team to improve processes by eliminating complexity, reducing waste, and decreasing cycle time. Good meetings with these teams will have ground rules, agendas, and the following roles assigned before the meeting: leader, facilitator, timekeeper, scribe, and minute taker. Many times I see teams meeting as a group but not functioning as a cohesive team working toward a common goal. The team leader and facilitator (one person may fill both roles) must work together to produce efficient meetings and keep the team focused to bring in timely results.

We must be sure that the Black Belts and sometimes the Green Belts know about teamwork and well-functioning teams. We may need to add the training for teamwork and facilitator roles to the Black Belt training agenda if the organization has not invested in this training before. Most Black Belt training provides an overview of good teamwork and how to handle teams and meetings in general. Most organizations provide team training for employees, but they forget the need for excellent team facilitators to lead the teams. Teams become groups of individuals meeting to discuss issues without direction. They need to be directed and challenged to follow a disciplined approach toward a common goal. The team training provided for the Black Belts should focus on the ground rules of teams, the conflicts that may occur, and how to facilitate the team process.

PREVENTION-BASED THEORY

The last paradigm shift to consider is for the organization to establish a prevention- or knowledge-based prospective improvement system to ensure that new products or processes will be released at the Six Sigma level. All new development projects will use the concepts of concurrent engineering and the DFSS (DMADVIC) process. This paradigm shift must be taken seriously or we will continue on the retrospective Six Sigma approach forever.

If you follow the paradigm shift of the subjects discussed in this chapter within your organization, the key processes and business indicators will improve and we will control the key business drivers.

These paradigm shifts must be considered before or as you are implementing the Six Sigma continuous improvement process. If you do not change from functional to process thinking, or focus on the customer, or use data for decision making, or use a good planning process, you may be left behind. Don't forget the criteria to run your total business as presented in the MBNQA. Organizations' customers are constantly looking for value and consistency of output, which will be achieved by using the Twelve Pillars of Six Sigma.

CHAPTER QUESTIONS

1. What are the paradigms that must be overcome for the proper implementation of the Six Sigma process?

2. How does the knowledge worker concept from Dr. Drucker fit into the Six Sigma process?

3. What are the key items to consider in moving to a process-focused organization?

4. What are the dashboard measures that the organization should consider?

5. How can the organization become more process focused?

6. Why do we need data to make decisions in the Six Sigma process?

7. How does sharing the strategic plan help with the Black Belt project selection process?

8. Does the organization need to move from a functional structure to a process or focused factory structure to implement Six Sigma?

9. Why is measurement of the processes and the business so important to the success of Six Sigma?

10. What other paradigm shifts might come out of the Six Sigma process?

11. What are the cultural issues most organizations will have in implementing Six Sigma?

12. Who needs to take the lead in handling the paradigm shift?

13. How does the organization determine the key business drivers and key processes to focus on for improvement?

14. How can the organization overcome the present paradigms?

15. Why is there a need to develop good teamwork facilitation skills?

SUGGESTIONS FOR FURTHER READING

Bossidy, Larry, and Ram Charan. *Execution.* New York: Crown Publishing, 2002.

Breyfogle, Forest W., III. *Implementing Six Sigma,* 2nd ed. Hoboken, NJ: John Wiley & Sons, 2003.

Drucker, Peter F. *Management Challenges for the 21st Century.* New York: HarperCollins, 1999.

George, Michael L. *Lean Six Sigma.* New York: McGraw-Hill, 2002.

Imai, Masaaki. *Gemba Kaizen.* New York, McGraw-Hill, 1997.

Naumann, Earl, and Steve Hoisington. *Customer Centered Six Sigma.* Milwaukee, WI: ASQ Quality Press, 2001.

16

The Knowledge Worker and Six Sigma

The knowledge worker concept is based on the knowledge that a Black Belt picks up as he or she works on projects that address customer needs, process capability, and key measures of the process and the organization. The Black Belt soon learns what is an improvement characteristic to the customer and what must be controlled within the process to meet or exceed those characteristics. The Black Belt becomes the subject matter expert on the process, its measures, and how they relate to the customer's needs. With this knowledge base, the Black Belt will be able to relate the customer CTQs with the CTPs of the process. This correlation is sometimes missed by many organizations. The Black Belt needs to understand the methods and machine variations that relate to the key process parameters. The environmental and material issues also need to be tied to the output variation of the process. These connections, which must be developed, require knowledge about material and chemical characteristics, input changes to the equipment, and changes in methods that will directly affect characteristics of the product output. The Black Belt will need to understand how variations in all areas of the process will affect the output of that process. In essence, the knowledge worker is created in this process of continuous improvement.

BLACK BELT CREDENTIALS

It can be seen that the Black Belt becomes very knowledgeable about the key processes of the organization. They learn how the processes are measured and how the inputs to the process must be controlled. Having the problem-solving skills, the knowledge of statistics, the data requirements to gain information, and the key measures, the Black Belt will become the new knowledge worker for that particular process, product, or service. This is an important asset to the organization. The communication process of the Black Belt becomes critical for the success of the projects. So, the criteria for Black Belt selection should ensure that the individual selected would be a good communicator. The effective communication of projects can be learned as the Black Belt progresses through training and project work. This person continues to become more valuable to the organization.

The Black Belt soon becomes the expert on the process used for specific products or services. Using the Black Belt training, the Black Belt can now improve the process and put the proper controls in place to maintain a consistent output. There may be a problem, however, if the Black Belt does not have the ability to use the tools or the comprehension to learn the process technology. This is why the Black Belt selection process is so important. The Six Sigma organization must establish a set of criteria that will be used to select candidates for the Black Belt training and continuous improvement efforts. Some items to consider are:

- Logical thinker
- Computer literate
- Good statistical thinker and analyzer
- Desire to improve the status quo
- Leadership skills
- Stay-with-it attitude
- Lots of energy
- Open-minded individual
- Good communicator
- Good listener
- Team player
- Respected by peers
- Company loyalty
- Desire to learn
- Good engineering fundamentals
- Good negotiator
- Knowledge about the business

The organizations that are implementing Six Sigma approaches must be sure that the Black Belt selection process will support the knowledge worker concept. In other words, the selection process must filter out the candidates who do not have the skills, desire, or capability to become an excellent Black Belt. Black Belts must also be able to make decisions based on knowledge gained from the customers, process technology, materials, and product characteristics. If the organization keeps improving processes by using Black Belt projects, they will become the process experts for all processes across the organization. They will become the organization's future knowledge workers. These subject matter experts still require the help of team members with specific expertise, but the Black Belt keeps gaining knowledge about the customers, processes, operations, and engineering.

KNOWLEDGE WORKER REQUIREMENTS

The knowledge worker will be required to maintain the key processes for the organization and ensure that process stability can be held or controlled. Knowledge workers will need to provide a control plan for the processes and show the linkage of the process output to the organization's business drivers. The Black Belt and Master Black Belt will have the best chance of filling the knowledge worker position for the organization. The more process, business, and market information that the Black Belt gains, the more dependent the organization will become on them to use the information to improve operations and customer satisfaction. The best data I can provide on this subject is the fact that most Black Belts are in demand by service and manufacturing industries to support their operations. The best approach for an organization is to grow its own knowledge worker in the industry and market that it participates in. The need for knowledge workers is even broadening into the healthcare and education fields. This problem-solving knowledge worker will become an asset to these organizations. So now is the time for you to learn and understand the Twelve Pillars of Six Sigma and develop your own approach to improving the processes that are key to your business.

The career path for this knowledge worker may be through the engineering ranks in design, development, process engineering, manufacturing engineering, process development, or quality engineering. The other path could be operations management, planning, materials management, quality assurance, or process support. The organization must consider the separate paths for the growth of the Black Belts as they grow into the knowledge worker position.

THE BLACK BELT AS THE KNOWLEDGE WORKER

The knowledge worker ties to categories 5 and 6 of the MBNQA process and applies the skills of the Back Belt to the tactical side of the improvement process. These combinations help the organization improve its operation.

The knowledge worker is a natural tie to the Six Sigma Black Belt concepts. The Black Belt who works full-time as the problem locator, problem solver, and change agent will be an asset to the organization and himself or herself. If the Black Belt has the proper attitude and aptitude, the projects taken on will be a success, the Black Belt will learn, and soon the individual will become the subject matter expert to the organization. The challenge to the organization is how to keep this person happy and challenged. This may be a good time to review Chapter 14 on financial gains and recognition.

The organization has to consider how it will reward the knowledge worker/Black Belt. The first step is to establish criteria for awarding the Black Belt certificate. The criteria might be the number of successful projects with a passing grade on the Black Belt training examination. The Black Belt who becomes the knowledge worker will need certain skills, abilities, and the drive to succeed. This person will have to want to learn and apply different skills required of the key processes of the business. The desire to learn, improve the operations, and serve the customer will help make the person successful in Six Sigma and at the organization. There may be many avenues to success within the organization, and the Black Belt will know how to succeed in any of them. Choosing the Black Belt becomes a challenge for the organization. The rest of the recognition process available is covered in Chapter 15.

FACTS ABOUT THE KNOWLEDGE WORKER

Knowledge workers should be able to fit into any part of the organization as long they have the background and the desire to succeed on the path they have chosen. The size and complexity of the organization will affect a knowledge worker's ability to succeed. The more complexity, the more skills or aspects of the business will be required of the Black Belts.

The size of the organization will mean that it will be harder to learn all the aspects of the organization. The organization must decide how to select, train, and support this process. It is suggested that the executive team establish the selection criteria based on the business factors and organization needs. The 11 items we need to know about the knowledge worker, as proposed by Peter Drucker,[1] are as follows:

1. In the knowledge worker position, we need to know what the task is before we can consider the results or productivity issue of the process.

2. The productivity improvement is now passed on to the individual knowledge worker.

3. The knowledge worker will manage himself or herself.

4. Continuing innovation has to be part of the work, the task, and the responsibility of the knowledge worker.

5. Knowledge worker productivity requires that the knowledge worker is both seen and treated as an asset rather than a cost. It requires that knowledge workers want to work for the organization in preference to all other opportunities.

6. Productivity of the knowledge worker has to aim first at quality, not minimum quality, but optimum or maximum quality. Only then can we ask what is the volume of the output.

7. Knowledge workers are responsible for their own contributions, and knowledge worker decisions are made on what to be held accountable for in terms of quality and quantity in respect to time and to cost.

8. Knowledge workers have to have autonomy, and that entails responsibility.

9. Continuous innovation has to be built into the job.

10. Continuous learning and teaching have to be built into the job.

11. The disagreements on quality must be resolved. The difficulty is not measuring it. The task definition will help in defining quality.

The knowledge workers will have to manage themselves and will face new demands, which are:

- What are my strengths and how do I need to perform work in this position?
- Where do I belong within the organization?
- What is my contribution to the organization?
- They will take relationship responsibility for processes.
- They must plan for the second half of their lives because they will not be with the organization that long.
- They need to ask, "How do I learn?"
- They must analyze their values in relation to the organization's values.
- They must develop relationship responsibility.

The technologists that we know today as the process engineer, the quality professional, and the manufacturing engineer are knowledge workers. They think about both knowledge needs and manual work. They are the biggest group of knowledge workers. As Drucker pointed out, knowledge work is a system.[1]

> The work itself must be structured and part of a system. Making the knowledge worker productive requires changes in attitude by the knowledge worker and the organization. Knowledge worker productivity will be the 21st century's biggest problem.

If the organization depends on state-of-the-art technology, the number of Black Belts and the skills required of the Black Belts will need to be narrowed to the key technologies used by the organization. This means that the Black Belt will be specialized. Then the knowledge worker will become more specialized in a specific field. Now is the time to consider the approach that you will take as you embark on the Six Sigma process. I believe that the Black Belts are headed toward this knowledge worker concept.

THE KNOWLEDGE WORKER AS THE CHANGE AGENT

Drucker states, "We cannot manage change" but "we can be ahead of it." It is popular today to lead change and not be worried about resistance to change. Drucker is indicating that we must be ahead of the industry or market and be able to anticipate change. Once we understand the needs of the market and the customer, we can prepare the organization for this change. This will require the organizations to have policies to handle the future requirements and systematic ways to anticipate change along with the methods to introduce the change into the organization. Then the organization needs to balance the change with some continuity within the organization to provide the change without losing the positives that are working. The organization needs to understand what old habits or methods or products they need to abandon in favor of improved methods or products. The key is to know what success requires and make sure that change addresses the future needs of the market and customers. This idea parallels what we are trying to accomplish with the Twelve Pillars of Six Sigma and lean. We can exploit the market and customer analysis of the Six Sigma process to develop the true needs of the market and customers and then be ready for the needs of the market ahead of the competition.

The strategic planning portion of the Third Pillar will provide the vehicle to stave off the old problems and then feed the new opportunities for the organization. This all ties together to allow the organization to keep ahead of the changing needs of the market and the customers. Then the proper products or services will be provided as the need is established. With the first six pillars in place, the organization can be prepared for future needs with changes to existing products or processes and the development of new products or services. The organization will succeed in being the change leader and can staff itself accordingly for the opportunities of the future. This is why so many organizations that rise too fast lose market share in the future. Forgetting that the marketplace changes, they ignore the customers and market until change has arrived and they are playing catch-up to the competition. We must build upon the present success rather than become complacent.

Sometimes the organization must create change with innovation to meet the new needs of the marketplace. This means that the new design process must be in place as we provide new products with DFSS and DMADVIC. The organization will have to create windows of opportunities, using the information from the listening posts in the market and customer areas. This again comes from the first three pillars of Six Sigma. Let's look at these concepts of opportunities from Drucker's[1] viewpoint. Windows of opportunities that exist for the organization include:

- Use the organization's own unexpected successes and unexpected failures to grow from, but also use the unexpected successes and failures of the competitors.

- Incongruities, especially in the process, whether of production, distribution, or customer behavior.

- Process needs now and in the future.

- Changes in the industry and market structures.

- New knowledge.

The change leader, who will be the Black Belt if developed properly, will be looking at two budgets. They are the budget to operate the business normally and the budget to determine the future needs of the market and customers as values and technology advance in society. The challenge for the leadership will be to handle the Black Belts and the business properly so change can be designed into the business and processes but still maintain the continuity inside and outside the organization. Drucker puts it this way: Change leaders must design for change and require continuity. Change and continuity are poles rather than opposites. This must be balanced. One way is to make partnership in change the basis of continuity relationships. The reason I tied the Black Belt position to the knowledge worker is that it fits Drucker's idea for the future. The organization will depend on the knowledge worker to sustain its future and its operations. These knowledge workers may become internal or external consultants to the organization. The skills developed will be a necessity for the organization of the future. The process must be effective and controlled to meet or exceed the requirements and provide an output of consistency in product. The knowledge worker will help provide this efficiency and effectiveness.

CHAPTER QUESTIONS

1. How does the Black Belt become the knowledge worker of the future?

2. Why is the Black Belt considered to be the knowledge worker that Dr. Drucker is talking about for the next century?

3. Why must the Black Belt become the knowledgeable person about the customers, processes, and technology?

4. Why is the Black Belt selection process critical to Six Sigma success?

5. Why do we need to consider a carrier path for the Black Belts?

6. What skills are needed to become a Black Belt?

7. What subjects must the Black Belt master to become the knowledge worker of the future?

8. When should an organization consider adopting the knowledge worker concepts?

9. What kind of knowledge requirement will this knowledge worker position need?

10. How would we determine if a person could fit the knowledge worker position?

SUGGESTIONS FOR FURTHER READING

Drucker, Peter F. *Management Challenges for the 21st Century.* New York: HarperCollins, 1999.
Eckes, George. *Making Six Sigma Last.* New York: John Wiley & Sons, 2001.
Spande, Peter S. *The Six Sigma Way.* New York: McGraw-Hill, 2000.

17

The Tool Sets Used for Diverse Industries

Tools alignment by industry can be a tricky subject because many of the tools can be used by all industries and service, government, and not-for-profit organizations. We will look at some of the differences in types of organizations, but we need to consider the fact that every organization could benefit from the use of all the tool sets discussed in this book. Let's first look at the difference between service organizations and manufacturing organizations. We should realize that many manufacturing organizations also provide a service to customers along with products.

MANUFACTURING ORGANIZATIONS

Manufacturing organizations spend most of their time looking at internal process variation by using statistical tools to find, understand, and control variation. Most of the areas that we focus on for complex processes are listed in Table 17.1.

The areas usually missed in the manufacturing sector are the use of project charters to determine the problem, voice of the customer to verify the needs and expectations, quality function deployment matrix to create the CTP criteria, cost of quality at the front end for opportunity costs, solution matrix for the selection of the best solution, should-be or could-be maps, and comparison testing at the back end. The should-be map is how the process activities should be in place for best performance. This is discussed in more detail in Chapters 10 and 21. Simple manufacturing processes usually do not use advanced tools such as the t-test, designed experiments, and regression analysis. The support services to the manufacturing sector are usually forgotten in the Six Sigma improvement efforts. Support services such as information systems, human resources, accounting, maintenance, and building services contain more waste and errors than in the manufacturing sector. I would like to suggest that the Black Belt project selection process include key processes within the organization's support departments. These areas sometimes have a cost of quality, failure rate, and acceptance cost in the range of 30 percent to 40 percent of the department's budget.

SERVICE ORGANIZATIONS

The service industry can usually improve processes by using measurement systems analysis, run charts, frequency plots, Pareto analysis, as-is and should-be mapping, capability analysis, and solutions matrixes.

Table 17.1 Areas of focus for the phases of DMAIC in manufacturing.

Define phase	Measure phase	Analysis phase	Improve phase	Control phase
• Project charters and problem definition • Voice of the customers • Cost of quality • Quality function deployment • Affinity diagrams • Process as-is map • Documentation review	• Run charts or time charts of data over time • Histograms or frequency charts for the picture of variation for continuous data • Measurement systems analysis • Control charts for discrete and continuous data • Lean waste concepts • Tree diagram • Sampling plans • Pareto charts	• Cause-and-effect analysis • FMEA • Scatter plots to develop correlation • Capability analysis • Comparison testing • ANOVA • Design of experiments • Chi-square tests • T-tests • Regression analysis • Lean demand flow concepts	• Idea generation process • Solution selection matrix • Measuring results • Pugh analysis • The should-be process map • Lean 5S process and SMED concepts	• Control charts • Documentation and change process • Training • New methods to the process

The selection of tools differs to fit the complexity of the industry. If you review the list of subjects in Chapter 7, you will note that many of the tools are used in a sequential problem-solving process. Therefore, more tools will be used as the processes become more complex. The transactional situations for most services will use less of the tool set than complex manufacturing, development, and testing processes.

The service industry usually works with the discrete data of several transactions. The tools will move toward the discrete side, such as P and C charts for defectives and defects. The measurement systems analysis will require us to use the Kappa or attribute method of analysis.

This is the perfect time to ask for training and the training material that will support your process needs. The training provider should be flexible enough to provide examples of all applications of the tool set for your industry. The DMAIC and the DMADVIC processes require tools that support the define phase such as voice of the customer interviews and affinity diagrams. In the measure phase they require Shewart charts, run charts, frequency plots, dot and box plots, and histograms. When we get to the analyze phase, the tools can become more sophisticated and statistical, such as regression analysis and ANOVA techniques. In this phase we really need to take advantage of the options to get to the root cause. Some of the options are: cause-and-effect diagrams, five whys, tree diagrams, frequency plots, stratification of the data, Shewart charts, run charts, t-tests, and capability analysis. The implementation or improvement phase uses tools that enable the team to pick the best solution to the root cause of the problem. In this phase we use decision matrixes, idea generation tools, process should-be maps, and measurements to ensure that the changes meet the needs of the process. The control phase uses the proper tools to maintain the process improvements: proper documentation and a change control system, as well as training processes on methods and the steps to verify that the controls are maintained throughout the process. Some of the tools that can differ in use based on need are listed in Chapter 2 and classified by DMAIC phase use.

The tools used by industry will be affected by the user's knowledge of the Six Sigma tool set, the process, and the customer's needs. If we are looking at a problem concerning cleanliness of rooms in a large hotel, we would start with the process flowchart, voice of the customer CTQs, and the process CTPs. Then we would evaluate the methods for checking cleanliness. We would then use an attribute chart to identify the current measurement for made-up rooms. As we start to analyze the data, we might use the Pareto principle to determine what causes unmade rooms and then work to reduce the variation in the process. For this type of problem we may not need to use the advanced statistical tools. The flowchart, Pareto chart, cause-and-effect analysis, or tree diagram will get us to the root cause of the problem. If we find that an equipment problem or materials problem is causing the variation, we may need to dig deeper into the causes. Possibly a designed experiment will be required.

As another example, let's look at the problem of too many knitting machine stops in a textile mill. The same up-front tools as listed above will provide the information about the customer's requirements on good doffed fabric with stops causing streaks in the final roll. The Pareto chart will help us find the reasons for stops. We would then use a cause-and-effect analysis to develop potential causes for the major reasons for stops. The cause-and-effect diagram will lead us to the areas to collect more data on the reasons. We may use the t-test or ANOVA to try to locate the differences in knitting machines, yarn, or set-up of the machines. These differences will lead us to the most likely cause of the variation that results in stops. We may need to run a designed experiment to verify the cause and establish the optimum level for key process parameters. In this case we may need to use more of the advanced statistical tools that will help find the causes of the problem and verify them to the team. These tools might be: regression analysis, designed experimentation, comparison t-tests, and ANOVA. The rest of the tools in the improve phase will be similar to the ones used in the hotel room example, but there may be differences in the methods in the control phase. The control phase may use different approaches to error-proof a process or use control charts to control the process. In the knitting machine example, we may use a control chart for control or change the machine setting, or operation, to eliminate some variation during the improvement phase. If so, we do not need to control a feature. In the case of hotel rooms, one control could be verification of the training for the housekeeper. We are looking for ways to standardize the room make-up for made-up rooms.

The major differences in tools for different organizations are caused by complexity of the processes and the technology in use within the process.

SERVICE AND NOT-FOR-PROFIT ORGANIZATIONS

Most service and not-for-profit organizations can succeed with lean process tools first, and then follow up with Six Sigma tools to reduce process variation in the key process steps. All these processes will be supported by the MBNQA Criteria for running the business. The lean tools are process value stream mapping, the five S's of the workplace, possibly kanban, kaizen blitzes, flow processes, and takt time calculations. The goal is to reduce waste and non-value-added steps in all processes being studied. Muda (waste) can be observed at the process level and reviewing activities, within the process. Waste is covered in more detail in Chapter 21.

Once lean has been applied or implemented in conjunction with, or after, the lean approach, we must start the Six Sigma problem-solving process. We will then reduce the variation of the process and the total lead time of the process.

CHAPTER QUESTIONS

1. What is the major difference between the service industry and manufacturing industries tool sets?

2. How does the cost of quality fit into the tool set for the Six Sigma process in all industries?

3. How does process complexity play a part in the tool set required by the Six Sigma process?

4. Which of the tools listed in this chapter might be used by not-for-profit organizations?

5. Would the government be able to use these tool sets for improving processes?

6. Why would most of the tools fit any type of industry?

7. Why does the service industry tend to use discrete data?

8. Why has a tool set been established for the Six Sigma process?

9. What is the lean tool set?

10. How does the Black Belt know which tool to use?

SUGGESTIONS FOR FURTHER READING

Brue, Greg. *Design for Six Sigma.* New York: McGraw-Hill, 2003.

Brossidy, Larry, and Ram Charan. *Execution.* New York: Crown, 2002.

Eckes, George. *Making Six Sigma Last.* New York: John Wiley & Sons, 2001.

————. *The Six Sigma Revolution.* New York: John Wiley & Sons, 2001.

George, Michael L. *Lean Six Sigma.* New York: McGraw-Hill, 2002.

Grant, Eugene L., and Richard S. Leavenworth. *Statistical Quality Control,* New York: McGraw-Hill, 1980.

Imai, Masaaki. *Gemba Kaisen.* New York: McGraw-Hill, 1997.

Naumann, Earl, and Steve Hoisington. *Customer Centered Six Sigma.* Milwaukee, WI: ASQ Quality Press, 2001.

Spande, Peter S. *The Six Sigma Way.* New York: McGraw-Hill, 2000.

18

The Pitfalls of Implementation

This chapter describes some of the problems you may have with the Twelve Pillars of Six Sigma, which can cause failure in the implementation process. This might be thought of as the dangers of not meeting the Six Sigma needs. The first obvious potential failure is lack of the executive management team's support and understanding of the Six Sigma process and concepts for improvement. The executive team must be fluent in the Six Sigma process and its technical tools to be able to support the tasks in the process. Knowledge of the Six Sigma process and its implementation requirements will help produce successful teams and projects. The executive team must support this process to succeed in the improvement of key processes. The following are some areas to address in the management support area:

- Resources to work on the project
- Capital when required for the project
- Accounting resources for financial analysis
- Six Sigma awareness training for the facility
- Six Sigma champion training
- Black Belt consulting time
- Black Belt selection process
- Black Belt training
- Master Black Belt training
- Green Belt training
- Green Belt selection process
- Project selection process
- Recognition

EXECUTIVE COMMITMENT

All executives should participate in at least a one-day overview training session and should strongly consider the three- to four-day champion training. Another area for potential failure is the definition of the problem based on the project selection during the define stage. The Black Belt needs to articulate the project scope and problem definition to be able to set the direction for the data collection phase of the project. Sometimes this articulation is not completed well and we need to redefine the project later as we collect more data. This is not detrimental to the project, but it does lead to delays in project progression. The project charter should contain a one-sentence problem definition; the goals and objectives that will be achieved, the measures required, and the resources needed; and an outline of the plan. The SIPOC should be developed and become part of the charter. The executive team should be selecting projects that will support the mission, goals, and objectives of the organization. They should be reviewing the project selection process and the project progression.

When the executive team changes for any reason, the Six Sigma commitment should be revisited to check for any lack of support. The biggest challenge is to obtain the executive team involvement with the planning, selection processes of projects and Black Belts, and the training required for them. The philosophy of Six Sigma must be ingrained within the organization by the management team. It sounds like some organizations seem to be doing the training but the executive team is not making the expenditures necessary for more training, consulting, and resources to set the improvements in place because of a lack of follow-up and support for the process. Sometimes the biggest obstacle to the improvement process is the executive staff's lack of understanding of Six Sigma's process requirements for improvements to take hold. Most executive teams have a set agenda, and without a broader knowledge of the Six Sigma process and the support for the Twelve Pillars, the improvements will be short lived. The process will die within three to four years. Some executives may be using the process of Six Sigma as another tool to reduce headcount, and sometimes this is what happens, but it creates a morale problem. The continuous improvement and problem-solving process must be integrated into the organization, and this can be accomplished only by executive involvement and commitment. Some organizations are starting to see some dropoff of the support because of a lack of patience and understanding of the improvement process. One way to determine the level of management commitment is to have an outside consultant audit and analyze the present business and quality systems.

PROVIDING THE DATA AND INFORMATION

Another area of concern is the availability of the data to address the problem. Sometimes the Black Belt is not able to readily obtain the data for the project. The data are not available or are difficult for the Black Belt to retrieve. This does not happen too often, but some projects drag on because of the lack of accurate and reliable data. Most information systems and metrology personnel can help. The data collection processes become important in the define, measure, and analyze phases of the DMAIC process. If the team has difficulty defining or obtaining the true process measures, it may be difficult to pinpoint the problem areas and causes in the analyze phase. The lack of data can be detrimental to the team. The team should understand what data are required and what information is needed before they start to collect it. The data collection process must be able to provide the information that leads the team in the right direction in its search for causes of the problem and improvements required to resolve them. They must be able to check the process for stability and its capability to meet the needs of the customer.

CULTURAL CHANGE

The Six Sigma process requires changes to customer focus, process focus, and metrics focus and a problem-solving discipline. This is why some organizations' executive teams will not change. It takes time for the organization to listen to the customers, understand them, and set a strategy to meet their needs. These are the reasons why some Six Sigma programs change slowly. The silos of functions within the organization have a hard time adjusting to the process focus and becoming process owners.

PROJECT SELECTION PROCESS

The executive team, along with the champion and sponsor of specific problem areas, selects the projects in most organizations. Without alignment of the objectives and goals of the organization to the strategic plan, these projects are given low priority by middle managers who want to see improvement in their specific area. This sometimes leads to projects being selected in order to please an individual or satisfy a department's need. This can lead to poor alignment of projects and low return on investments. The executive team must be involved with the decision process for the Six Sigma process improvements to occur. Each project must be selected against a set of criteria provided by the executive team. If the selection process is not in place, the organization will look as if it is using the Six Sigma process to reduce headcount, overload an already loaded staff, and control pet projects. This can be detrimental to Six Sigma improvements. The risk during the project selection process is that the wrong projects will be selected. Projects that are not aligned properly with the organization's needs, even if successful, will not improve the dashboard indicators that are important to the organization. If the selection is properly completed during the strategic planning process, the dashboard indicators must improve for the organization to be successful.

PROJECT REVIEW

The next area that can cause failure is the lack of project review activities and updates by the executive team. Projects can drift or require added support or resources to see them through to completion. Sometimes a Black Belt project will take on a life of its own, and if we do not follow the progress of the project, we may be feeding the prolonged life of the divergent activities. Project reviews help the team display the current progress, the difficulties encountered in any stage of the improvement process, or the success that has been realized. Management can help with the progress and resolve specific issues that the team may be facing. If the executive team does not review the projects, the team may stray from the goals and may not receive the support needed to resolve the problem.

The key point to review concerning the project is the progress made during each phase of DMAIC and DMADVIC processes. The alignment of the projects to the strategic plan and the operation's needs will help support the eventual success of the project's outcome.

BLACK BELT SELECTION PROCESS

If the organization does not select the knowledge workers of tomorrow as Black Belts, it will be looking at potential failures in the Lean Six Sigma implementation. A set of criteria discussed in Chapters 5 and 6 must be provided and the candidates interviewed by the Six Sigma coordinator and some members of the executive council. If we fail to select the right Black Belt candidates for the training and process improvement efforts, we will jeopardize the strategic plan and the success of the program.

CONSULTANT SELECTION PROCESS

Selecting the right consultant for your business must be part of the executive council review. One item to consider is a consultant's knowledge about the business and the key processes of the organization. Another factor is the individual's credentials as a Master Black Belt and the ability to train the employees you select to become the knowledge workers of the next century. The organization's success depends on this selection process.

APPLYING THE TOOLS

The Black Belt can also fail to apply the proper tools when required in any phase, but especially in the analysis phase. This means that the causes of the problem are not really resolved. This is especially true if special causes are present for the process under study by the team. The application of the Black Belt tools must be reviewed and required on specific projects to ensure that Six Sigma tools are used and that they are properly applied. The data may be improperly displayed, failing to show patterns that will lead to potential causes. This may require using several tools until we can learn something from the data. After two or three projects for each Black Belt, they should understand the principles and should have had a chance to apply most of the tools. They also should have a better understanding about process variation and the tools that will help them determine whether the variation exists and how to find the specific X factors that are causing the variation of the process output.

PROJECT TIME

The next type of problem that may be experienced is the amount of time that the Black Belt needs to uncover the potential problems to provide for a successful project completion. If the resources and time are not made available to the Black Belt team, the project will take longer than anticipated and the return on investment anticipated will be lower. This can cause some project teams to lose enthusiasm for the improvements, and the Six Sigma effort can ebb. To achieve success, we need to spend enough time on the problem analysis to quickly identify areas of opportunity, find the root causes, and select the best solutions to resolve the issues in the problem statement. There will probably always be controversy on the issue of using full-time versus part-time Black Belts on projects. It is my feeling that bigger and faster returns are found when using full-time Black Belts. The organization should plan on at least 1 percent of the personnel being trained as Black Belts and having at least two full-time Black Belts at each location. In larger plants the number of full-time Black Belts can be increased based on complexity of the processes and the number of processes.

RECOGNITION

The last item we will consider is recognition, which is not always provided to successful Black Belt projects. All successful project completions should be provided with a celebration of some kind. Without some form of recognition, we will have morale problems within the organization. We need to provide the recognition discussed in detail in Chapters 4 and 5. Recognition is important to the success of any effort, and especially the Six Sigma efforts because of the financial visibility brought into the picture during and at the end of the project. Without rewards, the effort might lose its effectiveness. Recognition does not have to be all financial, although money is nice. We can provide storyboards of projects in an open area for all the employees to observe. We can create an internal network or website to keep track of all the projects. The future projects may depend on the knowledge gained by the personnel within the organization.

As a conclusion to this short chapter, let's cover some of the areas where teams will have problems in the implementation of the Six Sigma pillars concepts or any other continuous improvement process. The following are some of the issues associated with the implementation of Six Sigma:

- Loss of self-esteem among the team members.
- No significant changes to the process are implemented.
- No negotiation on the projects during implementation.
- No emphasis on human resource skills.
- Lack of management skills.
- Leadership involvement and support are missing.
- Lack of teamwork within the executive team and/or the Black Belt teams.
- Poor selection of Black Belts.
- Project selection process failures.
- Lack of bottom line results because of support issues.
- Poor communications within the organization and the Black Belt team.
- Lack of recognition for the team.
- Lack of middle management support for the projects and the Black Belts.
- Teamwork and leadership is missing in all levels of the organization.

CHAPTER QUESTIONS

1. Why will the Six Sigma process fail if the executive management team is not committed to the process? What does commitment mean here?

2. What is the benefit of knowing the Six Sigma process and being able to support it?

3. What is the problem with the lack of data for a Black Belt project?

4. What is the potential affect of the lack of project alignment with the strategic plan?

5. Why do most projects have a difficult time in the define and analysis phases of the Six Sigma process?

6. When must the executive team be involved with the Six Sigma process?

7. Why must the Black Belt be able to apply the tools of Six Sigma to the process?

8. Why does the Black Belt need time to evaluate and improve the processes?

9. Why is recognition even a concern for the Six Sigma process?

10. What can happen if the Six Sigma Black Belt selection process fails?

SUGGESTIONS FOR FURTHER READING

Bossidy, Larry, and Ram Charan. *Execution.* New York: Crown Publishing, 2002.

Brue, Greg. *Design for Six Sigma.* New York: McGraw-Hill, 2003.

Eckes, George. *Making Six Sigma Last.* New York: John Wiley & Sons, 2001.

———. *The Six Sigma Revolution.* New York: John Wiley & Sons, 2001.

Imai, Masaaki. *Gemba Kaizen.* New York: McGraw-Hill, 1997.

Marash, Stanley A. *Fusion Management.* Fairfax , VA: QSU Publishing, 2003.

Naumann, Earl, and Steve Hoisington. *Customer Centered Six Sigma.* Milwaukee, WI: ASQ Quality Press, 2001.

Spande, Peter S. *The Six Sigma Way.* New York: McGraw-Hill, 2000.

19

The Successes That Can Be Achieved with Lean Six Sigma and the Knowledge Worker

The successful Lean Six Sigma or continuous improvement process will reduce variation in your process steps. This reduced variation will provide process output consistency, increased capacity, reduced operating costs, reduced material costs, and sometimes increased throughput in the process. The most important part of this process improvement program is the hassle-free operation that will surface because the reasons for variation have been eliminated, or at least reduced to the point that the output is consistent. The planners of the process output will be able to predict the output better, with more consistency for product shipments.

THE KNOWLEDGE WORKER

The other aspect of success realized from this improvement process is the development of the knowledge worker for the organization. The knowledge worker position will become critical to manufacturing and service industries that depend on process performance to meet the customer's needs. This person becomes knowledgeable about the organization's key processes, key customers, and key drivers. Knowledge of the key business and process drivers will help the organization control the process variation. The knowledge worker will have focused on the process parameters that will affect the process and any external noise factors that will also affect the output. The operations people should be able to plan better, sales should be able to sell to the requirements, and management can coach and lead the operations to success. The knowledge worker will help lead product or process performance to deliver to the customer's requirements.

REDUCED COSTS

The other success for the organization will be reduced operating costs, which can be transferred to higher margins for operations or a reduced price for the customers. This is what most people within the organization are looking for from the Twelve Pillars of Six Sigma. This will occur only if we select the proper projects, choose the right Black Belts, and align the selected projects with the goals and objectives of the organization. If you use the Twelve Pillars concepts presented in this book, the results will be realized within nine to twelve months. The returns can be slower or faster based on the amount of time given to the project and the resources needed for the project team. The executive team can decide at what pace they wish to proceed and the amount of savings they desire. The executive team will be able to focus on this pace based on the processes that need to be improved and the level of the dashboard indicators that must be achieved. Remember, the opportunity for most organizations is 10 percent to 20 percent savings from gross sales. This savings will come from manufacturing, support processes, and eventually from suppliers. The dashboard indicators will also improve based on the project selection process.

PROCESS CHANGES TO IMPROVE

Through experimentation, the effects will be realized for the key processes and the level of the process factors determined to obtain the best response. Another benefit will be the understanding of how the process factors can change as customers' needs change. This will allow the organization to determine how the process can be adjusted for the varying needs of the customers. This adjustable and agile process is necessary if a company is to be competitive. This can be very profitable for the organization. The agile and cost-effective organization will be able to lead the way in its marketplace. The organization can be a low-cost, high-quality producer. If you can maintain this new level of performance, you will have the edge to fend off competition and prevent it from eroding your market share.

PROFITABILITY

If the alignment of the projects to the objectives and goals is achieved, the reduction in waste, increased capacity, and improved planning will lead to a more profitable bottom line. Every dollar saved will hit the profit side of the balance sheet. Usually it takes $10 of sales increase to show the same $1 bottom-line profit that can be obtained by the improvement projects.

Some secondary rewards are derived from the Twelve Pillars of Six Sigma. The Black Belts and the project team become more knowledgeable about the market, the process, the suppliers, and the end customers. The teams become integrated into the organization and process. This all helps your organization become more focused on the key processes and the key customers. This can be very profitable for the organization. The new improvements in the process help with process efficiencies too.

The best improvement is when full-time Black Belts have taken projects that provide savings of $100,000 to $250,000 for medium to large organizations with somewhat complex processes. My definition of medium to large is more than 500 employees. This savings is balanced against the costs of the project. I have personally seen projects realize savings in the $2.5 million to $5 million range, but these occur only once a year at the start of the program or from potential new markets obtained through the DFSS process. In smaller organizations, the savings will vary from $20,000 to $50,000, depending again on complexity of processes and the opportunities for improvements. Sometimes the smaller organizations will have the benefit of seeing the savings hit the bottom line sooner and can easily justify two or three full-time Black Belts from the start of the implementation process. The major difficulty for smaller organizations is the implementation of the MBNQA Criteria to run the business.

If the initial projects are not saving $100,000 to $250,000, the process is not working and someone must check the process. I would suggest that a Six Sigma coordinator be appointed to put the measures in place for the Twelve Pillars of Six Sigma. With a measure in place for each pillar, the depth of Six Sigma knowledge within the organization, and the number of Black Belts and Green Belts with projects to meet the goals, the process is ready for constant evaluation. A senior staff member who will be at the Master Black Belt level of training and know about the processes of the organization should staff this coordinator position. We have to be careful that the position does not create a bureaucratic function and create excess overhead for the organization.

THE TWELVE PILLARS OF SIX SIGMA

The integration of the Twelve Pillars into the organization will provide for the foundation and processes to continually improve and maintain them for the long haul. If your organization realizes a billion dollars in gross sales, you have the potential to save $100 million to $200 million with the Twelve Pillars to support the Six Sigma philosophy. The executive team needs to work with the Six Sigma coordinator to ensure that the project selections will allow these savings to occur.

Now let's look at how a small company and a large company would typically approach the savings and process variation reduction. A small, $2 million to $10 million company would have savings opportunities of $100,000 to $1 million if two or more Black Belts work on several projects during the start-up years. What this means is that two or three Black Belts working with five to ten Green Belts will allow the team to capture $100,000 to $1 million the first year and subsequent three years. The problem for the small company is to support the use of full-time or part-time Black Belts devoted to the improvement of the process when they are needed to keep the present processes flowing. The part-time Black Belt position should work for your small companies. It is usually seen that the use of full-time Black Belts will return five to ten times their salary in a year. This may be hard to support at first for the small organization. The key is to obtain the Black Belt training at a public course or to find the training at one of your key suppliers. The customer or supplier may charge for the course or at least ask that the first projects will affect their operation and provide savings to them. Either way you approach the training, you are on your way to the Twelve Pillars of Six Sigma.

The final results of your Six Sigma projects at large companies will depend on the use of full-time Black Belts or part-time Black Belts within the plants and operations. The part-time process will provide slower results from the process improvements made. As we discussed before, we can save millions of dollars for an organization that has a billion dollars in gross sales. General Electric started to save up to $1 billion after operating in the Six Sigma mode for five to seven years. Many large companies such as ABB, Allied Signal, Honeywell, American Express, and Bank of America are saving millions because of the improvements made within their organizations. The process works for small and large companies, and the savings are proportional to the size and complexity of the processes. The results may be based on the projects selection process as well as the Black Belt chosen to run the projects.

IMPLEMENTATION APPROACH

Consider one more approach to the implementation of the Twelve Pillars of Six Sigma. One implementation plan that works is to implement the Baldrige Criteria followed by a good quality system, and then the people who manage, support, and run the process are trained to be Black Belts and continue in the same positions but use the tools of the Six Sigma process to improve the performance of processes. Before starting any implementation process, we may need to perform a gap analysis of the present systems in place against the Baldrige Criteria, the quality system against the ISO elements, and the business system's performance. An outside consultant familiar with the Baldrige Criteria, the ISO standards, and the business factors that will affect the future best accomplishes this gap analysis.

The successful projects will use the proper tools to locate the customer needs, translate the voice of the customer to the process key measures, and focus on those measures for the project. The most critical item is the analysis phase to determine the root cause of the problem selected. It does not become apparent that the tools were used wrong or the proper tool was not used until you get to the implementation phase and verify the results. Selecting good Master Black Belts helps in the detection of potential problems in the methods or tools being applied to the projects. If the projects are successful and the results are as expected, the Six Sigma process is on track.

The evaluation process we discuss in Chapter 20 should show how the organization performs in respect to achieving the 1 percent Black Belt level of participation as a ratio of the number of total employees. Our walk-around should show the spread of knowledge regarding process variation, sigma level of performance, and understanding defects as they relate to the customer. Project results should be positive and Green Belts should be supporting Black Belt projects and even taking on some of their own projects in their specific process areas. The executive team should observe that key indicators of the dashboard are continuously improving. The employees should see fewer process hassles and more process consistency.

People should start asking to learn more about the Six Sigma way and show signs of concern for the processes and meeting customer's needs. The operations personnel should recognize how the process measures affect customer needs and, in turn, customer satisfaction. We should be pleased with the business results and the change in the business drivers. The personnel will become aware of future needs and learn how to control the process inputs and process variables to become consistent with output performance. This means that operations can control their destiny.

To succeed at this process, we must have the business system in place, which parallels the MBNQA Criteria. If you invested in the winners of the MBNQA, you would have done better than the Dow. This should support the reasons to implement this business process. The tactical side is addressed by the quality system and Lean Six Sigma. Let's conclude with a flow of the process to successful implementation of the Twelve Pillars of Six Sigma. Figure 19.1 contains the major items to consider in the implementation process.

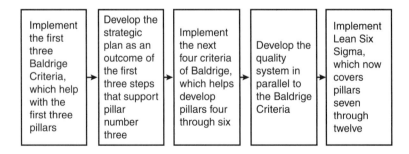

Figure 19.1   High-level process flow to successful implementation of Lean Six Sigma.

The knowledge worker becomes key to your organization's growth, process improvements, and measurement improvements. This knowledge worker position is the output of the Six Sigma program, which should create a permanent place for a process or development engineer who will provide knowledge and direction to drive the organization to address the current customer base needs. The future needs will still be derived through the marketing and sales functions.

The organization will gain a process-focused, customer-driven, measurable system to provide the products and services to current and future customers. Once you have implemented the MBNQA Criteria, lean, and Six Sigma, you should see the following indicator improvements develop:

- Profitability increases
- Capability increases
- Higher inventory turns
- Lower employee turnover rates
- Improved lead times
- Increased throughput
- Increased customer satisfaction
- Increased sales
- Improved responsiveness
- Increased market knowledge
- Increased competitiveness
- Increased capacity

As an alternative implementation approach, the organization may start the Baldrige Criteria and implement the Six Sigma approach in parallel to achieve early impact of savings. In the measure phase of Six Sigma, the lean approach will be applied to the activity flowchart. This approach does work for some organizations that have the people with the proper experience level to implement the parallel programs.

CHAPTER QUESTIONS

1. What will the knowledge worker position be able to do for the organization now and in the future?

2. How will the reduced costs realized from the Six Sigma process be documented and captured to demonstrate the savings of the project?

3. How will the process changes made in the Six Sigma process be documented to show improvement?

4. Will profitability be affected by the implementation of the Lean Six Sigma approach?

5. How will small companies be able to implement the Six Sigma approach?

6. What are some of the indicators that should improve as a result of the Six Sigma implementation?

7. How will full-time Black Belts affect the improvement process?

8. Will part-time Black Belts succeed in the implementation of the continuous improvement using the Six Sigma process?

9. How will the DMADVIC process fit with the success of the program?

10. What is the most important support you can provide to the Six Sigma process?

SUGGESTIONS FOR FURTHER READING

Bossidy, Larry, and Ram Charan. *Execution.* New York: Crown Publishing, 2002.

Breyfogle, Forest W., III. *Implementing Six Sigma,* 2nd ed. Hoboken, NJ: John Wiley & Sons, 2003.

Brue, Greg. *Design for Six Sigma.* New York: McGraw-Hill, 2003.

Drucker, Peter F. *Management Challenges for the 21st Century.* New York: HarperCollins, 1999.

———. *The New Realities.* New York: Harper & Row, 1989.

Eckes, George. *Making Six Sigma Last.* New York: John Wiley & Sons, 2001.

George, Michael L. *Lean Six Sigma.* New York: McGraw-Hill, 2002.

Harry, Mikel, and Richard Schroeder. *Six Sigma.* New York: Doubleday, 2000.

Marash, Stanley A. *Fusion Management.* Fairfax, VA: QSU Publishing, 2003.

Naumann, Earl, and Steve Hoisington. *Customer Centered Six Sigma.* Milwaukee, WI: ASQ Quality Press, 2001.

Schonberger, Richard J. *World Class Manufacturing.* New York: The Free Press, 1986.

Shingo, Shigeo. *Zero Quality Control: Source Inspection and the Poka-Yoke System.* Cambridge, MA: Productivity Press, 1986.

Spande, Peter S. *The Six Sigma Way.* New York: McGraw-Hill, 2000.

Welch, Jack. *Jack: Straight from the Gut.* New York: Warner Business Books, 2001.

20

Evaluating the Six Sigma Process

We audit many processes to ensure that they are still performing or complying with the standards of our operations. Therefore, it is practical to audit or evaluate the effectiveness of the Twelve Pillars of Six Sigma process.

REVIEWING THE TWELVE PILLARS
OF LEAN SIX SIGMA PROCESS

Many areas in the Twelve Pillars of Six Sigma process should be reviewed to ensure that the improvements are successful. Some of the important areas are:

- Number of successful projects
- Number of trained Black Belts
- Project selection process in place and operating
- Executive team involvement
- The dollar savings impact on the bottom line
- Effectiveness of the training
- Drop-out rate of the Black Belts
- Number of trained Green Belts
- Knowledge level about Six Sigma within the organization
- Project completion time lines
- Success of champions
- Effectiveness of strategic plan

It is the task of the Six Sigma coordinator and executive team to develop a method of measuring the level of Six Sigma knowledge and success for the projects selected in the Six Sigma process. George Eckes has addressed some of these measurement techniques in his book, *The Six Sigma Revolution.*[1]

A revolution is taking place in the Six Sigma process, and our task is to evaluate and try to predict whether the revolution is moving our organization in the right direction and whether the Six Sigma philosophy is taking hold for continuous improvement to take place. We are searching for a cultural change within the organization. The best measure of success is the knowledge level of the Lean Six Sigma concepts within the organization and process knowledge about variation within the process. The organization must see bottom-line profit results tied to the Black Belt projects.

TEAMWORK AND RELATIONSHIPS

Before we get too involved with all the measures to evaluate for success, we need to cover two important points that the organization must look at prior to implementation of the Lean Six Sigma program. These two areas are the use of teams and relationship building. The ability to work as a team is sometimes difficult in certain cultures. Now, when I am talking about teams I do not mean committees of people meeting or separate meetings to address issues. I am referring to two or more people working together on a common, agreed-upon goal who share the same concern for the outcome of the charter or task at hand. If the organization has not provided good training on facilitation of a team and how different people need to work together as a functioning group, I suggest that a separate training program be completed or the Lean Six Sigma training developed with this training included. For the organization to be successful, we must consider the art of negotiation, understanding the different ways people communicate, styles of management, how conflict is handled, and how to generally facilitate a diverse group. This will be required of the team leaders and facilitators. We are only touching the surface of the soft types of skills that are important to any implementation program.

For the implementation of the MBNQA Criteria, a quality system, and the Lean Six Sigma tactics, the organization needs to be able to work together using the skills just described. It has been my experience that if we work with the people of the organization to understand their needs, the customer's needs, and the key process people's needs, we usually are successful together in completing the necessary changes to improve. It is not always this simple. Being able to recognize others and focus on facts rather than feelings and being able to use the skills of compromise and consensus will help you progress through the difficult issues. Sometimes an evaluation of beliefs and values during the strategic planning process will bring to the surface issues that need to be addressed before you begin to implement change. My suggestion is that you need to determine how your personnel work together now. If you see a need for more teamwork skills, specify that this be provided as part of the Lean Six Sigma training provided to the Black Belts and Green Belts.

BLACK BELT PROJECTS

One indicator used to identify progress is the number of projects that a Black Belt can handle in one year and how successful each Black Belt is in resolving the problem and minimizing variation in the process under study. Successful programs should show three to four projects per year per Black Belt with $500,000 to $1 million in savings in total. This pace will occur until you reach a savings of roughly 10 percent of your gross sales. At this point you should be implementing the DFSS/DMADVIC process to release new products and processes at the 5 to 6 sigma level of capability. If this does not occur, you probably will continue with retrospective Six Sigma investments. The projects that the Black Belts are working on should have come from the executive council, using the project selection process they developed.

PROJECT SELECTION

Another good review is to analyze the types of projects selected and whether future projects are being selected when Black Belts become available. There should be a list of projects awaiting the Black Belts. The project selection process becomes critical in this evaluation. We need to ask: "Are projects being selected against some criteria that have been accepted by the executive team?" This part of the process is critical to the success of Lean Six Sigma. The projects held in limbo to be assigned to Black Belts should show the level of attention that is required to solve existing problems. Having a number of projects waiting for Black Belts will allow the selection process to match Black Belt skills to project needs more effectively. The other evaluation should focus on the type of projects selected and the success at achieving the bottom-line results expected from the projects. The selection criteria for project selection were covered in more detail in Chapter 5. This selection process must be evaluated for its success in selecting the proper projects for improvement.

TRAINING

The training and consulting effectiveness needs to be evaluated, too. Effective training will produce people who have learned a skill that can be applied to everyday use. If you think about it, the learning process exposes a person to an act or activity that can be used to make it easier to perform a job. We invest in the future using a new investment method, save costs on an existing process, or improve upon a situation with a new method. The learning process should be evaluated by testing the student and following up on the application of the skills learned. The application review might involve reviewing a project or observing a task to determine whether the method is understood and being used properly. The point here is that all Lean Six Sigma training should be evaluated by reviewing a set of test results during training and on-the-job evaluation of application of the new method or tool after training is completed. I have taught at several universities, including the Milwaukee School of Engineering, University of Dayton, and Loyola University of New Orleans. The courses that we taught in which a project could be given to test the application of the theory and apply the methods learned by the students yielded an improvement in the learning process. The process should be to teach, or lecture, on the concepts, apply the concepts to a project, and then apply the concepts to the student's job activities. The student can relate to the on-the-job activities and attempt to be successful at using them in an actual application. My advice is to look for training and facilitation that will provide the information, examples, and application methods to the students.

Now, back to the evaluation of training effectiveness. Each student should be capable of passing some tests for knowledge of the skills. A passing grade of 80 or above should indicate the knowledge level necessary for the tools. If more than one student fails the tests, you may want to check the training methods, examples used, or the facilitator. The next task is to test out the application of the knowledge by evaluating the results of projects selected to demonstrate the skills use in the project. If the projects are showing that the methods and tools are not being used properly, the training must be changed to accommodate the students.

The next evaluation should be on the knowledge level of the Lean Six Sigma process at all levels of the organization. Questionnaires, surveys, and walk-arounds will help determine whether the Lean Six Sigma culture is setting in place within the organization. We should not perform this evaluation until the program has been in place for one to two years and all the awareness training has been completed. The best approach for this evaluation is the use of a survey or questionnaire performed at the management level.

CONSULTING

Let's consider the evaluation of the consultation help that may be provided to the organization on Lean Six Sigma. The consultant working with the organization to implement the tactical approach for the organization might be evaluated against the following:

- The results of the training and projects supported by the Master Black Belt
- The responsiveness to the organization's needs
- The knowledge about the Lean Six Sigma process
- The relationships that are developed
- The support provided after the training
- The cooperation with the organization's personnel
- The availability of the consultant to the organization
- The attitude of the consultant
- The ability to help the Six Sigma coordinator
- The ability to relate to the organization

This subject was covered in more detail in Chapter 6.

RESULTS

Now we are left with the final implementation and financial evaluation process. If we have effective training, good Black Belt selection process and a good project selection process, the financial results and project implementation process will be successful. The accounting department should be in charge of the final financial review, and the executive council should review the success of the project improvement. If you are not receiving a 15 percent to 25 percent return on the investment in the training, consulting, and project resources, then the process may not be as effective or as efficient as it can be for the program. The projects should bring in a minimum of $50,000 in savings, on average, or something was wrong in the project selection process or the Black Belt application of the tools.

ROUTINE EVALUATION OF SIX SIGMA

With all the above in mind, the Six Sigma coordinator should be establishing a process for routine evaluation of Six Sigma knowledge, customer and process knowledge, and financial results realized from the projects. The executive council should evaluate the overall success of the program by asking questions about the skill levels of the Black Belts and the skills themselves chosen to be applied to the projects. They should also evaluate whether the Green Belts are being used to help the Black Belts and whether the Green Belts are taking on their own projects as they apply to their jobs directly.

The definition of a successful project must be bottom-line results of $50,000 or more. We can also consider the reduction in variation of a process as a success, but it should lead to increased capacity or reduced scrap or rework in the process. If the project was selected through a good process, reduced costs should not be a problem for the team. If we cannot achieve a savings, we are not on track with the project selection process. The problem definition and selection process by the Black Belts is not effective or the champions are not effective if the projects are not a success. The project charter development in the define phase should have been developed with the champion and the process owner. This process may not be working because of difficulties in the definition or the support provided to the Black Belt. The charter must define the problem and focus on the key processes and the customers. The champion must help the Black Belt through this process and agree with the charter. The project selection process must allow the organization to meet its goals.

NUMBER OF BLACK BELTS

The number of Black Belts required by an organization depends on the size of the organization, the complexity of the processes within it, and the capability and capacity of the processes to deliver to the customer's needs. My best answer is that about 1 percent of the total employees within the organization should be Black Belts. For every 1000 employees, we need a minimum of 10 Black Belts. The decision is yours, but full-time Black Belts at a reasonable rate will bring at least a 10 times improvement in process performance and will bring a million dollars per year, per Black Belt, to the bottom line. This progress should be achievable for the next two to three years and, if the organization starts using the prospective Six Sigma approach, new processes should begin to operate between the 5 and 6 sigma level at the start.

THE DESIGN PROCESS REVIEW

This evaluation process covers the most important part of the Six Sigma process review: the establishment and use of the DMADVIC process. The organization needs to begin developing new products and processes under the DMADVIC process to ensure that the customer's needs and expectations have been established. This also leads to the use of quality function deployment to develop the most critical design characteristics that must be met to achieve customer satisfaction and processes that will produce the output at the Six Sigma level of performance. The first six pillars of the Six Sigma approach are definitely required for the prospective Six Sigma approach to work and succeed. This is what most organizations are missing when they take on the retrospective Six Sigma DMAIC process only. Yes, they will have success for the next two to three years, but that will fade because the new products and processes will not be capable of meeting the customer's needs every time. My advice is to start with the DMAIC process and then, within one to two years, implement the DMADVIC process into new designs so the prospective approach starts to develop. In fact, the content of this book was changed to reflect the need to perform the DMADVIC process as the best improvement for the future of the organization.

As a quick review, we will cover the critical steps in the up-front DMADVIC process and then highlight the design improvements to be made with this approach. The first six pillars support the beginning of the design process. We must develop the marketplace concepts from the start of the project. The services and the products must perform within the requirements of the market, and we must determine whether segmentation of the market is important to consider for market needs. This will allow us to properly address the key customer base that we will want to distribute to. We need to understand the key segmentation of the market if we are to be successful. With Pillar One completed, we are ready to have the leadership team evaluate the present and future needs of the organization to enable it to address various market conditions. This will be accomplished by letting the listening posts of the organization gather data that will be turned into information about the conditions of the market, the political environment, and the future environmental conditions that may affect the output performance of the organization. Once the leadership has developed enough information to determine the strengths, weaknesses, opportunities, and threats for the organization, they are ready to tackle the Third Pillar of strategic planning. This must be performed with care and understanding. This process can take from three to four weeks to develop a valuable strategic plan. It will take several weeks to put the final touches on the strategic plan. The future projects of the organization will be determined through the objectives and goals that will be developed from the TOWS analysis. This was discussed in detail in Chapter 5.

THE DESIGN PROCESS DFSS AND DMADVIC

Now we are ready for the project selection alignment for the Black Belts that will be derived from Pillar Three. The Black Belt selection process and the training needs of Pillars Four and Five will be completed to support the new projects selected. This will lead to design projects that include the appropriate design personnel who will be trained in the DMADVIC process before beginning the design process. These two pillars are very important after the organization has selected the proper projects to work on. The proper personnel, the right training, and the proper application of the tools will lead to successful outcomes that will satisfy the marketplace and directly affect the customers of the products and services. The last major pillar in the preparation phase is the development of the voice of the customer needs and expectations. Therefore, Pillar Six will allow the team to select the proper customer base to study in regard to needs and expectations. With this completed, we are ready for Pillar Seven and the development of the key processes and their characteristics to fulfill the requirements of the customer.

During the design process, we are ready to design the product or service, using the key tools of the design process after the project objectives have been developed by the voice of the customer and the quality function deployment process. Some of the main tools used in the design process are in the following list for our review, and were discussed in more detail in Chapter 6 and Chapter 7. The main tools required in the design and development process are:

- New project management
- Advanced process control
- Pugh concepts
- Anticipatory failure determination
- Taguchi analysis
- Tolerance analysis

- Monte Carlo simulation

- Design for assembly

- Design for manufacturability

- Design for reliability

- Design for durability

- Design for testability

- Design for maintenance

- Design for the environment

- Implementing the design

- Design verification

Once the design principles are completed as listed above, the team needs to verify they have met the customer's needs and the design objectives by establishing a series of tests to perform during the verification process. The outcome of the verification process will lead to some improvements and final control for the implementation phase. The implementation phase is then covering the manufacturing sector or the service process for the customers. The improvement and control phases of DMADVIC are close to the ones used in the DMAIC process. The major differences might be in the addition of new processes using new equipment, methods, or materials to deliver the product or service to the existing or new customer base, or both. Now might be the time to revert back to the capability studies for existing or new processes to deliver to the needs that have been developed. In a way, the improvement or implementation process must verify that the new process will provide the key characteristics defined in the quality house of the quality function deployment process. The result of this phase will be a defined process that will be analyzed to verify that the output of the process(es) will meet or exceed the customer's needs. The control phase will then require a control plan for the new process. Realize that the design and improvement or implementation of a new process will also involve some verification during this design phase before implementation.

There is another subject that should be considered by the organization. I have used concurrent engineering to align the design of the product with the design of the process to produce the product. This concurrent effort allows the organization to develop the processes to manufacture the product or produce the service and create supplier requirements while it is developing the actual product or service. This process must be considered part of the DMADVIC process. Let's consider the concepts of concurrent engineering now.

CONCURRENT ENGINEERING REVIEW

The term *concurrent engineering* focuses your resources to develop new designs that will work the first time while doing many activities in parallel. Five major issues drove many organizations to reexamine the way products and processes are designed. They are:

- Producing products that are competitive in price, features, and quality level.

- Designing products that are not readily manufacturable to the requirements.

- Support issues are not considered during the design.

- The design is not readily assembled.

- Complex process difficulties.

The competitive pressures felt by most organizations have led them to consider the concurrent engineering approach to designing products. Using this process with the DFSS process will provide defect-free products at the lowest cost. Some Japanese companies used concurrent engineering in another format as early as 1972. Using QFD, design for manufacturability and assembly techniques, robust designs, and the loss function concepts of Taguchi, the Japanese have been designing products that have fewer errors and are easier to assemble and manufacture. Most of these concepts are available to us in the concurrent engineering approach and DFSS (DMADVIC) approach. Dr. Genichi Taguchi, in *Introduction to Quality Engineering,*[2] considers further design concepts to improving design robustness. The variability of a process will cause quality problems as we try to meet the tolerances set by the design and the customer. The design engineer must understand the variation in the process that makes the part and the needs of the customer who will use the part. Taguchi uses the example of a pane of glass being cut to fit a window. The window has a nominal dimension that will vary, and the glass-cutting process will cut the glass to a nominal value with some variances in dimension. Concurrent engineering allows the manufacturing personnel to work with the design and customer needs to arrive at the proper tolerances that will achieve the end-use needs. Sometimes the design personnel need to run experimental designs to determine the capability of the process and the design to meet the needs. These experiments will allow the personnel to achieve a robust design that will function under the process and customer variations. Phillip J. Rose also covers the Taguchi variation and loss function concepts in his book *Taguchi Techniques for Quality Engineering.*[3]

For the concurrent approach to work, we need to work the design and manufacturing activities in parallel with a lot of interaction and coordination between the support activities. This approach involves multifunctional teaming of several diverse people. The concepts of design for manufacturability and design for assembly are part of the concurrent engineering principles that must be performed on the design concepts during the design, not after the design function is completed.

Automotive organizations use a similar concept to concurrent engineering, but it is called advanced product quality planning principles.[4] A flow of the design process steps is shown in Figure 20.1, and an outline of the design process follows:

- Define the scope of the project.

- Plan and define the steps in the project.

- Design and develop the product or service.

- Perform a feasibility study to meet the needs of the customer.

- Perform a process design and development for the product or service.

- Validate product and process.

- Perform feedback, assessment, and corrective action.

- Install a control plan for the process.

The automotive business sector proscribes that these different steps are not performed in sequence but in parallel as much as possible and has developed the flow in Figure 20.1 to show the overlap that can exist to help with quicker turnaround for new designs.

Concept initiation	Program approval	Prototype	Pilot	Launch
Planning				Planning
	Product design			
	Process design and development			
Plan validation				
		Product and process validation		
			Production	
Feedback and assessment				

Figure 20.1   Typical plan for the new design process as identified by the automotive business.

Figure 20.1 shows the parallel flow of the steps and the interaction that may occur during the development process. This concept is the same as the concurrent engineering process we discussed previously.

CONSIDERATIONS DURING CONCURRENT ENGINEERING

Before concluding our review of the concurrent engineering process, we need to discuss some other points that are considered part of the design process. They fit into the steps of the design of the product or service and the design of the processes to fill the needs of the customer. During the design process, the team must consider the materials, technologies in mechanics, and electronics that may help improve the design and the use of different elements, chemicals, or materials that may affect the design performance. This requires the design and development departments to keep abreast of the state-of-the-art techniques in their respective fields to ensure that they are considering all aspects of new technologies. Once the concept design has been selected, the team evaluates the organization's ability to deliver the required results using the latest technologies and current or future processes.

The design and development function must consider the reliability requirements of the customers and how the design will be able to meet these requirements. This also leads to durability requirements in the hands of the customers and their use of the products or services. These requirements should have been developed during the voice of the customer phase and the development of the quality function deployment phase of the Twelve Pillars of Six Sigma. Sometimes prototypes need to be built and alpha or beta testing conducted to verify the durability and reliability capability of the design. Structured analysis of the design is required as part of the concurrent engineering process. There are many tools, such as computer-aided engineering, computer-aided design, design for manufacturability, and computer-integrated manufacturing, that will help with the design generation and review.

The next item the concurrent engineering team will consider is the demand flow manufacturing requirements. The goal is to create the shortest cycle time to produce the product or provide the service to the customer. This will be discussed in more detail in Chapter 21. Some questions that need to be answered are:

- What are the assembly steps?
- What activity is accomplished in each step?
- How many units need to be produced each day?
- How long will it take and how many people are needed to complete the units?

The flow of the concurrent engineering process is depicted in Figure 20.2.

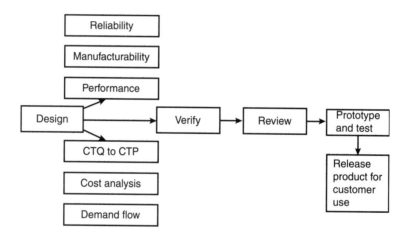

Figure 20.2 Flow of the parallel and sequential portions of the design in concurrent engineering.

CHAPTER QUESTIONS

1. Why do we need to evaluate the organization's commitment and understanding of the Six Sigma process?

2. If the evaluation of the Six Sigma process shows difficulty in succeeding, what course of action should the Six Sigma coordinator take?

3. What if executive involvement and commitment are found to be waning for the Six Sigma effort? What should be done to get the support back?

4. Why do we need to implement the DFSS process?

5. What is meant by a walk-around to determine the level of knowledge about the Six Sigma process?

6. How should the Twelve Pillars of Six Sigma be reviewed for support in this evaluation?

7. Who should perform the Six Sigma process evaluation and who should review the evaluation results?

8. How long should the executive team wait after the program begins before performing the Six Sigma evaluation?

9. Why should we evaluate the effectiveness of the Black Belt and Green Belt training? How can this be accomplished effectively?

10. Who should evaluate the financial results of the projects and the program and why?

SUGGESTIONS FOR FURTHER READING

Bossidy, Larry, and Ram Charan. *Execution.* New York: Crown Publishing, 2002.

Breyfogle, Forest W., III. *Implementing Six Sigma,* 2nd ed. Hoboken, NJ: John Wiley & Sons, 2003.

Brue, Greg. *Design for Six Sigma.* New York: McGraw-Hill, 2003.

Costanza, John R. *World Class Manufacturing: The Quantum Leap in Speed to Market.* Denver: J-I-T Institute of Technology, 1990.

Drucker, Peter F. *The New Realities.* New York: Harper & Row, 1989.

Eckes, George. *Making Six Sigma Last.* New York: John Wiley & Sons, 2001.

———. *The Six Sigma Revolution.* New York: John Wiley & Sons, 2001.

George, Michael L. *Lean Six Sigma.* New York: McGraw-Hill, 2002.

Naumann, Earl, and Steve Hoisington. *Customer Centered Six Sigma.* Milwaukee, WI: ASQ Quality Press, 2001.

Schonberger, Richard J. *World Class Manufacturing.* New York: The Free Press, 1986.

Spande, Peter S. *The Six Sigma Way.* New York: McGraw-Hill, 2000.

21

The Lean Involvement
with Six Sigma

T he lean systems of operation replace the old concepts of mass production. The goals
of lean are to improve throughput, eliminate waste, reduce costs, improve quality,
and reduce lead time for products. The lean production methods should help you
create business and manufacturing processes that will be agile and more efficient. Lean
also will concentrate on the quality issues and costs of the processes. Most of the quality
issues concentrate on errors or defects in the process. This concept does not seem to
address the variation in the processes that may be causing the defects and errors, but the
Six Sigma tools could be used at this point. The Shingo concepts of zero quality control
address the defects by error-proofing the processes after the errors or defects have been
determined. The tools of Six Sigma help with the identification of the defects and the variation that causes them, so the decision that management must make is how to integrate the
lean steps with the Six Sigma phases for process evaluation and defect determination. The
best way to consider this process is to use the lean concepts to reduce waste, focus on continuous flow, and use the 5S program to provide for clean, structured operations at the
workplace. With waste and process flow taken care of, we can concentrate on the defects
and errors in the process that were not addressed in using lean concepts.

WASTE

The waste concepts of lean focus on the process wait times, rework or unneeded process
steps, unneeded motion, transportation, and inventory builds in work in progress (WIP)
and final inventory. The defects are reviewed in the process flow analysis, but it is difficult
to resolve them by using only the lean tools. Sometimes the lean people call these the
seven sins of waste. This can be accomplished by simply observing the process and looking for muda (waste) in the eyes of lean theory. Because work is a series of process steps,
which starts with raw material and ends with the final product, the waste can come from
many areas within this process. Some items to consider when looking for waste are:

- Build-up of inventory wastes labor, time, utilities, storage space, transportation
  costs, and inventory dollars.

- Defects lead to scrap and rework, which wastes labor, may damage the processing equipment, and cause more paperwork to document the rejects.

Defects also lead to lost revenue, lost equipment time, reduced process cycle time, and overproduction of product.

- The waste of overproduction is caused by the reject or yield of the process. This wastes space of inventory when things go right and the rejects do not occur, more raw material is consumed, which causes some of the wastes of building to inventory and lost customer demand. Of all the wastes, or muda, the waste of overproduction is the most serious and costs the organization the most in time and dollars.

- The waste of motion is when the process has non-value-added steps or unproductive steps. The wasted effort generally adds labor costs to the manufacture of the product. Part of the waste of motion is the process, and part may be in the handling of the product.

- Types of waste include waiting for material, subassembly, or machine availability. This waste costs labor time and can lead to rejects if damage occurs to the product while waiting for the availability of the machine or activity.

- The waste of transportation costs cycle time and labor. Added transportation can also lead to damage, misplacement, and loss of product. It also adds to storage or work in process inventory if the transportation is associated with overproduction or waiting time.

- The last area of waste is processing waste, caused by inadequate machines that are not capable of producing the product or are not efficient enough in producing the product. Sometimes the process is made too complex and can be simplified to make the steps in the process easier and more foolproof or mistake-proof.

The lean organization needs to evaluate these areas of waste and eliminate them to become more efficient or productive in the manufacturing of the product or provision of the service. The approach to take is to eliminate muda first, then implement good housekeeping with the five S's, and finally standardize the process steps. This waste concept can lead to thinking of the waste of the facility or space, the waste of design and of employee talent. The start-up of production can cause waste if not planned and implemented properly. As you can see, many of the process activities within any organization can be evaluated for waste affecting time, costs, and materials. Some other points of muda considered by Masaaki Imai in his book on Gemba Kaizen are: waste of time in our daily activities; the mura of irregular operations, which wastes time because of interruptions in the operations work due to unbalanced flow in the process work; and finally the muri, which wastes time because of undue stress or the strenuous work that is part of the process, thus causing the work activities to slow down.[1]

Process value analysis is another concept that will help in the lean organization. Value analysis, value engineering, and value stream mapping all work to identify the non-value-added steps of processes in the total value chain. We will talk about some of these tools in this chapter after we complete the outline of the lean organization.

LEAD TIME

In reducing lead time we need to consider the concepts of batch and process delay, such as wait time, which affects cycle time, and in turn the lead time for the products that we are manufacturing. Lead time begins when we purchase our raw materials to meet the customer's demands and ends when we deliver the product or service to the customer. Sometimes we indicate that lead time does not end until the customer has paid us for the delivered product or service. Lead time is then the true measure of the organization's ability or capability to produce the product in the shortest time possible and then deliver it to the customer and be paid for it. If we simplify the processes, provide for quick line changeovers, and design the products and processes so variations of product or steps are controlled, we may be able to reduce cycle time. Work standardization, clean operations, and setting the process in order or arrangement will prevent motion and operational delays.

VALUE MAPPING

The value mapping process that helps us identify waste and added costs takes the flow of activities in production to build the product and flows the material and information within the process. When this flow is put together, the connections of all these factors are identified and used to spot non-value-added steps. The organization needs to understand the entire flow of material, product, information, and handling. This will allow the personnel performing the value mapping process to determine what is needed to produce the product and where opportunities exist to improve cycle time and to reduce waste. The value stream map uses different icons to display activities, information, changeover, kanban, and so forth.

Another output of the value stream mapping process is improvement of decision making in the process flow. If the team developing the map steps back and looks at the issues that have been documented and the flow of material, product, and decisions, they will start to see opportunities to reduce the non-value-added activities to the process. The opportunities to reduce waste will show up as the process is reviewed and observed. The reduction of waste will help improve cycle time and reduce costs of the process. In fact, good lean operators can stand in the middle of the production or processing operation and spot muda. Non-value-added time can also be in the eyes of the customers when they are waiting in line for a service that cannot be delivered in that line and they must start over again in another line. This, too, is part of the value stream mapping process.

KAIZEN

Kaizen means continuous improvement, which implies that everyone will be involved with little expense to consistently improve our situation in our work and life. This process focuses on incremental improvements of the process. Under kaizen, management must maintain the process and manage improvements of the process. Kaizen categorizes the improvements either as innovation to do things differently by using new methods or machinery or as improvement upon the present condition by step function improvements. Kaizen approaches the operation using process thinking rather than functional thinking. The process is what the customer sees at the end of the day. The improvement process of kaizen uses Deming's plan-do-check-act approach to problem solving. In other words, the process is reviewed for improvement and plans are put in place to improve it. These plans are then verified or checked, and we take steps to make the improvement a permanent part of the process. The kaizen approach also speaks with data.[1] It uses the data to analyze the process and the problems of the process. Does this sound familiar? (Six Sigma approach.)

The major systems of the kaizen strategy are:

- Just-in-time production system

- Total quality control

- Policy deployment

- Suggestion systems

- Total productive maintenance

- Small team activities

Because kaizen deals with improving the process, we need to determine what to focus on within the organization. Kaizen seems to indicate that the focus should be on quality, costs, and delivery. This is acceptable, but we need to drive these ideas lower into the organization and address specific processes that need to be consistent, performed at the lowest possible cost, and delivered on time to the customer's needs. This will be achieved only if we start with the customer, the marketplace, and the organization's needs. *Gemba Kaizen* refers to the real place where improvements are needed. This is usually where the work activity takes place. The work is within the process. The process can be any activity that adds value for the customer. So, kaizen takes its effort to the production area where work occurs.

LEAN ORGANIZATION

The lean organization will focus on the following activities in some fashion and not necessarily in any selected sequence but as outlined below:

- Customer value stream analysis

- Push system analysis

- Pull system implementation

- Waste analysis

- Production activities analysis

- Lead time analysis

- Takt time analysis

- Material flow analysis

- Motion study

- Transportation study

- Value stream and chain map

The value stream map is created in the same way as the as-is map in the DMAIC process. You use sticky notes to record activities, transportation, information into and out of the process, records produced, and material flow. The team takes a quick tour of the process from start to finish. We must make sure that all components of the process flow have been identified. Then we identify the representative customer of the output of the process to determine takt time for the customer. We begin mapping the process from the selected start to the finish, recording the current state of the flow of activities. In the value chain we sometimes need to include the suppliers as the start of the process. This helps evaluate the entire process from release of order at the supplier to the end customer we deliver the product to for use. The team will create a lead-time graph at the bottom or top of the value stream map showing the value added and the non-value-added production lead times. When completed, the team should display the final map and review it with all the personnel who work within the process. The map could be left alone for several weeks with missing steps added as needed when reviewed by the employees. Many of the referenced books on lean have the example symbols or icons to use for the flow mapping process. The takt time of the process is calculated using the following formula:

Takt time = available daily production time ÷ required daily quantity of output from customer demand

The example in Figure 21.1 shows how takt time applies and is calculated for a process.

If we produce ahead of the takt time, we are making product for inventory, or overproducing product. If the value stream is not producing to takt time, we need to investigate the causes. Applying the one-piece flow concepts will help define the possible causes.

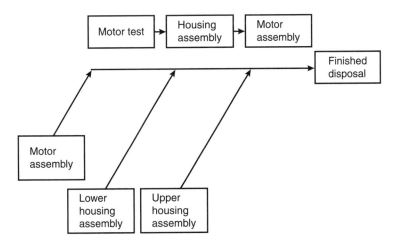

Takt = Daily minutes per shift × number of shifts ÷ by demand at capacity

Daily minutes per shift = 480
Number of shifts = 1
Demand at capacity = 25

480 × 1/25 = 19.2 minutes per operation

19.2	19.2	19.2	19.2
Motor assembly	Motor test	Housing assembly	Motor assembly

Figure 21.1 Takt time calculation and flowchart for construction of disposal unit.

The one-piece flow concepts will eliminate the batch flow where possible, which causes delays in the process. Although there are batch-processing companies, such as those that process chemicals that run in batches, some of these principles are still helpful in these industries. Another area to look at is the changeover and set-up times for product line changes. This can increase the cycle time to produce a single product.

5S

5S should have been applied to the process area as part of the lean process. The five S's are: *sort* the area so items are arranged in order to be identified and seen quickly; *shine* or clean the area of clutter for better efficiencies; *set* the tools and materials in order to be found quickly; *standardize* the process steps and materials where possible; and *sustain* the standards. The work standards can lead to load leveling, which will prevent the organization from overproducing product for inventory. The way we sequence the building of product could affect the leveling of the production. This is discussed in more detail under demand flow concepts. This might also be called the one-piece flow concept.

5S is sometimes referred to as the five steps of housecleaning. It is better to work in a clean house than a cluttered house. As we clean the house, we sort out the unnecessary items not needed for the process and eliminate them. We then organize the work tools into the proper order so we can locate them quickly when they are needed for the process activities. The process personnel then scrub their areas so the process shines and is free of debris. This process of cleaning and even performing some maintenance is made a permanent part of the process to keep it running smoothly. The last step is to standardize the steps of the process and maintain the consistency required for successful operation. Some people start out by tagging everything around the process that is not necessary to maintain for the process. The best approach is to prepare the personnel for the organization of the work by explaining the philosophy behind the program and the benefits of 5S before starting.

VISUAL MANAGEMENT

Lean organizations also concentrate on visual management as a way to have all employees see waste, understand the operational standards, and improve efficiency. The steps that allow us to accomplish this are: use the five S's, control all work with a control plan, and establish work standards that are displayed for the employees to see and make sure the employees understand them. Visual management means that when problems are detected, we show them to the team and help manage them. The results of the line or process should be displayed as well as the mistakes or errors. The standards should also be posted, and the targets for the operation and process should be visible for the operators. If the personnel know what they need to target, you will eventually be hitting the targets for the process and the operation.

ERROR-PROOFING

The next major area to address in lean is the practice of error-proofing the process when errors are noted or observed. Dr. Shigeo Shingo does this very well, and his book is referenced at the end of the chapter. Let's go through an overview of the concept of error-proofing or mistake-proofing. This approach will help us resolve certain errors so that we do not have to be concerned with their occurrence. The error-proofing process eliminates error by preventing it from occurring in the first place. In a lean operation, when a defect occurs, production must stop to fix the error immediately. Error-proofing looks at these areas to focus on: inspection at the source, 100 percent inspection, immediate feedback when the error occurs, and error-proofing devices. The inspection points will not allow defects to move forward, but we really want to prevent those defects from occurring in the first place. The common error-proofing devices that Shingo[2] talks about are: limit switches for indication, guide pins for location, counters to count parts, check sheets to verify tasks, and alarms to alert operators to faults. The concepts are generally thought of as zero quality control for zero defects and are intended to catch defects at the source through inspection. The prevention activities are usually called Poka-Yoke systems. Shingo also addresses the agents of production, which are the methods used, the space and flow for production, and the time it takes to produce the product. The process elements considered are the work involved, the inspection method used, delays, and transportation concerns, similar to the lean-based operation.

The use of inspection is good if all other alternatives fail. One hundred percent inspections detect defects but entail considerable time and trouble. Some statistical methods try to get around these inspection issues by cutting the task time by using sampling plans. This method tries to use Poka-Yoke measures aggressively to prevent the problems from occurring in the first place. To approach zero defects in the process, Shingo developed seven steps to follow. These steps are listed below for your review. These steps also help with the implementation of the lean organization.[2]

Step One: Application of statistical quality control using control charts based on theoretical inspection sampling plans.

Step Two: Use of Poka-Yoke methods to reduce errors and minimize inspections.

Step Three: Successful implementation of Poka-Yoke and self-check inspections.

Step Four: Reduce sampling inspections and use 100 percent inspections using Poka-Yoke and self-inspections to reduce errors.

Step Five: Develop source inspections to detect errors at their source and make changes immediately to reduce defects.

Step Six: The achievement of one month of production with zero defects.

Step Seven: The basic concepts of the zero defects QC systems are in place.

DEMAND FLOW

We need to consider the demand flow concepts to achieve the takt time we discussed earlier. Demand flow involves a series of steps that can be taken to sequence the production process so that it flows to the demand of the customer's needs and ensures the product is manufactured to meet the demands of the customers rather than for finished inventory. This will help us reduce the level of finished inventory of product. The steps for demand flow are as follows:

- The order of the assembly process must be defined.

- The activities for each step must be defined.

- The number of units to be produced each day needs to be determined.
- We need to determine how many minutes each operation in the assembly process should take.
- The number and skill level of employees required for the process need to be determined.
- The time it takes to finish a product needs to be determined.
- The process needs to be sequenced.
- The sequence of events needs to be analyzed for value-added time, set-up time, move time, machine time, and labor time.

ONE-PIECE FLOW

The demand flow concepts are similar to the one-piece flow mentioned earlier. One-piece flow is the movement of products through the manufacturing process one unit at a time. One-piece flow concepts have been introduced by many large organizations into each operation in the production process. One-piece flow also helps reduce the cycle time of the process and reduces waste in production delays and wait times. The defect rate of the process is reduced, and the organization has more flexibility. A requirement of the one-piece flow is fast changeover times for product changes, using SMED, which will be discussed next. The products should be designed to be able to be assembled simply and require fewer set-ups. The one-piece operation also requires the use of the demand flow or pull system of manufacturing. The demand flow or pull system only produces product when a customer demand exists. Usually the final operation in the pull system drives the order needs. All these systems of manufacture operate best with automated equipment.

This approach is the set-up of the process to be able to handle one piece of any item at a time and change over quickly to another one piece. I saw this displayed very well back in the 1980s by Allen Bradley in Milwaukee, WI, on an assembly line that was fully automated. This process is in contrast to the old batch mode and equipment utilization principles. Now, having said that, some industries need to run in batches because of the configuration of the operation and the product. Still, the batches could be made smaller and the changeover faster even in these industries. One-piece flow focuses on the manufacturing process rather than wait time, transportation of products, or material and storing inventory (WIP or finished inventory). It will make the production process flow smoothly. One piece at a time will be creating a steady workload for the employees involved. The advantages to one-piece flow are: the lapsed time between the customer order and the delivery to the customer is reduced; wait times are prevented; excess inventory is reduced; damaged product is reduced; defects are revealed earlier; operating cost is reduced; and more flexibility is obtained.

For the organization to be able to establish a one-piece flow operation, the following points need to be considered:

- Simplify the flow of materials.
- Make sure that the materials and product move in the same direction.
- Locate equipment for ease of maintenance.
- Eliminate non-value-added steps in the process.

- Use FIFO inventory stocking.
- Arrange the piece parts for ease of entry into production.
- Locate the steps in the process as close together as possible.
- Make sure all the work areas and walkways to the assembly areas are clear and easy to get around.
- Material input and output operations should be separated.
- All parts need to flow through the process in the processing sequence.
- Maximize the operator's and equipment's productivity by shaping the line for efficiency.
- Allow space in the production layout for full inspection of the materials and equipment that will be used to produce the product.
- Minimize work in process.
- Cross-train the operators to use equipment up and down the line from the piece of equipment they are presently running.

SMED

The quick exchange of the methods and equipment for the changeover of production will help improve the cycle time of the production process. With the ability to change over a process quickly, machine capacity is increased and manufacturing errors are reduced, which will also help with reduced inventory requirements. Improvements in cycle time of the process help shorten lead time of delivered products or services to the customers. The implementation of a SMED (single minute exchange of die) program requires that we evaluate the time it takes to change over to a new product or service using the present equipment. If the time is longer than three minutes, we may want to look for faster and better ways of changing over the line and tooling to increase throughput and reduce the cycle time of the process. The standardization of the tools or parts used for exchange of the dies will help improve the efficiency of die changeover. This leads to the topic of process standardization.

STANDARD OPERATIONS

In the lean organization, the standardization of operations develops the most efficient manner of performing the work activities that must be completed for the successful output of the process. The standard operation is usually documented and the tasks are performed in a set manner or sequence. The work standardization effort breaks down the process to activities that are defined and controlled to provide a more consistent process that services the customer's needs better and is more repeatable. To develop a standard operation, we will document the work activities and sequence that must be performed in a set way to provide the consistency required of the operation. This is accomplished by using Black Belt teams to determine the process takt time, the process cycle time, and the standard quantity of work. The standard workflow sequence is documented and the workflow process chart developed. The standard is reviewed continuously for ways of improving the operation even further. All the information on takt time calculations, process workflow charts, and cycle time calculations are discussed in more detail in Chapters 21 and 22.

THE KANBAN OPERATIONS SYSTEM

The kanban operation is a visual aid signal that triggers the pull of product flow through the manufacturing process. A kanban system synchronizes the work process by using a card that contains the information on what to produce, when to produce it, how much to produce, how to produce it, and how to transport and store the product. The kanban system is very effective when the customer base requests uneven demand flow of product. This system will help the organization limit its production to only what is required and not to overproduce a product. The outcome should be a production-smoothing effect that allows for the required quantity of product to be produced per day, using takt time to understand the capacity of the process. A kanban system will indicate priorities to the production personnel based on current conditions of the process without unnecessary paperwork. Kanban uses depend on the inventory system that is present. It is usually called a constant order quantity system or constant order cycle time system. The constant order quantity system uses a reorder point calculation to determine the number of kanbans to use. The constant order cycle time system uses a maximum inventory calculation to trigger the number of kanbans to use. The formulas and more information about kanban can be obtained from the sources at the end of this chapter and the resource list in the reference section of the book.

TOTAL PRODUCTIVE MAINTENANCE

Total productive maintenance (TPM) is a series of methods used to evaluate all the equipment that is used in the production process to ensure that the equipment will be ready to perform its tasks when asked to produce. The team-based activity enhances normal maintenance and involves every worker. Since the goal of the TPM program is improved performance and reliability of the production equipment, the metric used to evaluate performance is overall equipment effectiveness (OEE). This metric involves equipment breakdown, time needed for equipment set-up and adjustments, time lost to work stoppage, time lost to tooling changes, time lost to inefficient set-up, and idle time. Time spent producing defective product could also be included in this metric.

Next, we need to implement autonomous maintenance, in which operators are trained to perform routine maintenance. Before you implement this program, make sure that workplace contamination is eliminated, that proper lubrication is determined, that leaks are solved, and that routine inspections and maintenance can resolve machine down time and keep the area safer and cleaner. Some items to consider in this maintenance process are as follows:

- Preventive cleaning measures
- General inspection of equipment
- Cleaning and lubrication to the standards developed
- Initial equipment cleaning
- Process discipline to the standard
- Autonomous inspection
- Independent autonomous maintenance

The next areas to address are: the establishment of a maintenance program for reactive maintenance as items break; preventive maintenance to avoid equipment failure; predictive maintenance to determine when something is about to fail; and maintenance prevention by improving the design of the equipment to survive the present environment. A maintenance program is developed from the items listed.

LEAN MEASURES

Some lean measures to consider when a program is implemented are:

- Inventory turn level
- Overall equipment effectiveness
- Value-added to non-value-added steps of the processes
- On-time delivery rate
- Order fulfillment lead time
- Rolled throughput yield
- First time through or first time yield quality

CYCLE TIME OF PROCESS

The management of the cycle time within a process provides a different approach to traditional operating practices. The major focus is to eliminate non-value-added activities, which are distinguished in the terms of essential versus nonessential activities. The objective is to provide a true linear business flow from receipt of order to shipment of product. Statistics show that 90 percent of the activities of a flowed process add no value. This holds true for the processes that support manufacturing and sometimes take up 60 percent of the activities in the process from receipt of order to delivery of the product. You might think of it as the race car's pit crew versus the airplane mechanics' turnaround time. The pit crew uses its time to stop the car, raise the car, loosen and remove the tire nuts, replace the tires, replace and tighten the nuts, clean the windshield, refuel, and then lower the car and send it back out on the track. This all occurs within 10 to 15 seconds. The object is to keep the car on the track and the airplane in the air. Maybe the airline industry could learn something from the pit crew's approach to turnaround time. A tire change on an airplane takes 40 to 70 minutes depending on availability of a replacement and the mechanic.

The traditional operating procedures concerning material resource planning (MRP) for industry are obsolete because they accept operating practices that never expose waste. MRP ideas do help with time management for cycle time management but sometimes at the higher cost to the process. In the past, companies organized work around groups of machines and by functions. This leads to more work in process inventory and more movement of materials throughout the plant. This work in process inventory buries defects that we are trying to eliminate in the Six Sigma process. This process was traditionally called a push system of manufacturing. MRPII and optimized production technology have been released as software programs to control the material and machine flow. These programs usually discourage productivity improvements, and changes are very expensive. This same traditional approach lets marketing dictate new designs without consideration of the customer's needs analysis because of time constraints. A line operation has no influence on the development of designs or process development when this approach is used.

With cycle time management[3] we are looking at a total linear business flow of information, materials, and activities that support manufacturing. We evolve from a push system to a pull system of manufacturing. This requires good communication between all functions and departments of the true demand from the customers. To make this process work, we will concentrate on the following areas of the process of manufacturing, including ordering and activities that support manufacturing. Table 21.1 contains some of the areas to address for improvements in manufacturing and support.

Table 21.1 Areas to address for improved cycle time in manufacturing and manufacturing support processes.

For the manufacturing process	Manufacturing support services
• Tool changeovers	• Travel time to the operations
• Parts shortages	• Sales order changes
• Parts quality issues	• Engineering changes
• Poor manufacturing quality	• Computer down time
• Travel time caused by plant layout	• Clerical delays and errors
• Down time caused by poor maintenance	• Office equipment down time
• Poor design process that causes poor quality	• Distribution delays and errors
• Poor process designs that cause poor quality	• Unnecessary approvals

Some concepts that help drive us to the continuous flow cycle time management process are provided in the following list of tools in the lean organization that help overcome the problems listed in Table 21.1:

- Single minute exchange of die (SMED)
- Reduced travel time by providing continuous flow of information and materials and developing line balancing
- Elimination of rework
- Elimination of non-value-added or unnecessary steps in the process
- Use of concurrent engineering
- Providing preventive maintenance to operations and support equipment
- Development of a good training program for all operations and support activities that affect process activities
- The use of kanban to pull materials needs
- Measuring quality with the necessary precision, accuracy, and discrimination
- Development of suppliers through purchasing
- Production control of order entry with engineering and purchasing
- Shorter cycle time to order materials and manufacture products will help reduce inventory costs

Table 21.2 Some industries with cycle time reduction possibilities based on value-added steps versus non-value-added steps.

Organization	Steps	Value-added steps	Percentage
Textiles	100	10	10%
Electronics	250	25	10%
Food processing	35	9	25%
Hotel	45	35	60%

Cycle time becomes the measure of productivity for the operation. This eliminates buffers in the cycle, reducing defects in the process and control movement of product within the plant. The idea is to produce only what you can sell immediately and pull it through the process steps as fast as possible with zero defects. Another buzz phrase often used is computer-integrated manufacturing (CIM). It is used to find ways to reduce processing time with simplified systems that can be less expensive to operate and that automatically eliminate errors. These are the same concepts employed by the Twelve Pillars of Six Sigma.

The investment in MRP programs will become more effective once we have implemented computer-integrated manufacturing and reduced the cycle time of supply and the process to manufacture the product. Some examples of potential reduced cycle times are listed in Table 21.2.

The cycle time should be measured for each major process of the operation. The reduction of the time provided to meet the needs of the customer base in the industry that the organization is operating in and the market conditions noted will become important. The formula for cycle time is presented in Figure 21.2.

The following example provides an analysis of the cycle time to manufacture a stuffed, printed circuit board for an electronics firm over a 30-day period.

Bare board inventory	5000
Component inventory	35,000
Ending board inventory	1000
Ending component inventory	500
Boards in stock	5000
Boards started on line	2000

Base line cycle time: CT = average activities in the process / average speed of the line.

The average speed of the line = start rate + out rate / 2.

Cycle time for services = Activities in process / Activities completed per time period.

Figure 21.2 Formulas for calculating the initial cycle time of the process.

CT = average work in process ÷ line speed = (beginning inventory + ending inventory ÷ 2) ÷ (start rate + out rate ÷ 2).

CT = (5000 + 1000 ÷ 2) ÷ (5000 + 2000 ÷ 2) = 3000 ÷ 3500 = .85 month based on 30-day month.

.85 × 21 days per month = 18 days

The above data tells us that the typical board takes 18 working days to process through the line.

Note: The days of inventory for the components does not come into play unless we do not have enough components to stuff the board assembly.

The impact of the reduced cycle time will be to reduce operating costs, improve the balance sheet, and dramatically improve profits. This is exactly what computer maker Dell has done for itself and is the reason others cannot catch up to the system Dell uses. Inventory reduction reduces interest charges, makes money available for use in other capital needs, and provides better cash flow. Facility expenses usually decrease, quality improves with reduced rework and scrap, and administrative costs are lower. All this leads to improved productivity, increased efficiency, and improved operating profits. The typical flow of cycle time improvements is depicted in Figure 21.3.

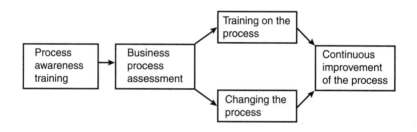

Figure 21.3   The flow of actions taken to improve the cycle time.

CHAPTER QUESTIONS

1. Name the major steps of a lean organization.

2. What are the areas of waste in a production process?

3. What is lead time to the customer, and how is it calculated?

4. What is the team looking for in value stream mapping?

5. What are the major systems of kaizen?

6. How is takt time calculated?

7. What does takt time provide to the operations personnel?

8. What are the five S's of the lean enterprise?

9. What is normally displayed in visual management for an operation?

10. What points must be considered in one-piece flow manufacturing?

SUGGESTIONS FOR FURTHER READING

Costanza, John R. *World Class Manufacturing: The Quantum Leap in Speed to Market.* Denver, CO: J-I-T Institute of Technology, 1990.

George, Michael L. *Lean Six Sigma.* New York: McGraw-Hill, 2002.

Imai, Masaaki. *Gemba Kaizen.* New York: McGraw-Hill, 1997.

Macinnes, Richard L. *The Lean Enterprise Memory Jogger.* Salem, NH: Goal QPC, 2002.

Schonberger, Richard J. *World Class Manufacturing.* New York: The Free Press, 1986.

Shingo, Shigeo. *Zero Quality Control: Source Inspection and the Poka-Yoke System.* Cambridge, MA: Productivity Press, 1986.

22

Integration of the Malcolm Baldrige National Quality Award, Lean, and Six Sigma

Now that we have a good idea of the detail of lean and Six Sigma processes, we need to tie these concepts together with the way to run our business, which is defined by the Malcolm Baldrige National Quality Award Criteria. How can we tie the processes and the criteria to the daily operations of the business?

The MBNQA Criteria have seven categories that can be used effectively to run the business. I have spent 10 years as a senior examiner with the Baldrige process, most recently as alumnus to the process. I have consulted for many organizations that use the criteria internally to improve the business. Use of the criteria helps the organization make plans and measure the current process for improvements that will support the business objectives. One way to look at the seven criteria is that the first three categories help the organization define what business it is in and what it is doing in the marketplace. The planning process in category 2 takes the market information and customer information from the leadership in categories 1 and 3 and integrates them into the organization's strategic plan. Category 2 covers the organization's planning process. The executive team will lead the organization in the proper direction if the concepts of the first three categories are followed. This integrates well with the first six pillars of the Twelve Pillars of Six Sigma process support. From categories 1, 2, and 3, the leadership team must develop the strategic plan for the organization. The output of these three categories provides the direction that the organization must take to succeed in the near and long-term future. The criteria are not as prescriptive a system as I seem to be explaining here, but the main point is that the company's goals, direction, and objectives come out of this process.

Category 4 provides the data collection and measurement for the organization, process, and methods of collection to determine how the organization is performing in relationship to the key processes and to evaluate the business driver's performance against the plan and operations results. Category 4 links the process effectiveness to the results that are monitored in category 7.

Categories 5 and 6 provide the methods and key processes by which the organization will design, produce, and improve its situation based on the key processes and key customer needs developed from the first three categories. If you follow the process, category 7, which provides the results, will show improvement in your key indicators and whether they are going in the right direction. It is hoped that you can see that the Baldrige Criteria are followed throughout this book as we progress from the market through the strategic planning process to project selection and improvements by the Six Sigma process. The key processes are improved to meet the customer needs, which are well defined when using the Baldrige Criteria. The list in Table 22.1 presents the seven criteria with their subcategories and the areas of concern for 2005. If you are interested in more information about the award process and the criteria, you may contact the American Society for Quality in Milwaukee, WI, or The National Institute of Standards and Technology (NIST) in Gaithersburg, MD.

LEAN

Now, how does lean complement the Six Sigma process and vice versa? Lean has some basic tools the practitioner can use to improve process throughput in the organization and reduce waste within the processes. Both lean and Six Sigma are the tactical tools that the organization can use to improve the business processes defined within the Baldrige Criteria. Lean uses the following concepts:

- The just-in-time process system
- SMED (single minute exchange of die)
- Total productive maintenance
- One-piece flow of product
- Kanban systems
- Pull systems
- Kaizan implementation
- Autonomation
- Safety
- Standardization
- Production leveling
- Value stream mapping

If you implement lean without Six Sigma, you will improve the flow to the point where the defects are stopping or creating a bottleneck in the process flow. Application of the Six Sigma principles will help resolve the defect or problems within the process by reducing the variation that is causing the delay, bottleneck, or stoppage. Lean concepts watch for muda (waste) in the process and apply the principles of the five S's and kaizen to align the process steps in sequence with the least amount of movement by hand, using mistake-proofed designs and assembly methods with no or minimum set-ups and delays. I know there is more to lean than that one sentence describes. Lean is discussed in more detail in the previous chapter. Lean allows the organization to manufacture one piece at a time in the most efficient way possible. As long as the process is defect-free, things will run smoothly. What generally happens is that we lower the inventory level by using lean until the defects start to surface in the process. This is when the war on waste meets its enemy, the variation of the process. This variation is caused by key input and process factors that affect the process output. The Six Sigma tools will allow us to determine which X factors affect the output the most. Some operations are applying lean and Six Sigma on the same processes simultaneously, while others implement lean first and then apply the Six Sigma tools to further

Table 22.1   2005 Malcolm Baldrige National Quality Award Criteria outline.

1.0 Leadership

    1.1 Senior Leadership System

        Vision and Values

        Communication and Organizational Performance

    1.2 Governance and Social Responsibility

        Organizational Governance

        Legal and Ethical Behavior

        Support of Key Communities

2.0 Strategic Planning

    2.1 Strategy Development

        Strategy Development Process

        Strategic Objectives

    2.2 Strategy Deployment

        Action Plan Development and Deployment

        Performance Projection

3.0 Customer and Market Focus

    3.1 Customer and Market Knowledge

        Customer and Market Knowledge

    3.2 Customer Relationships and Satisfaction

        Customer Relationships Building

        Customer Satisfaction Determination

4.0 Measurement Analysis and Knowledge Management

    4.1 Measurement Analysis and Review of Organizational Performance

        Performance Measurement

        Performance Analysis and Review

    4.2 Information and Knowledge Management

        Data Information and Availability

        Organizational Knowledge Management

        Data Information and Knowledge Quality

5.0 Human Resource Focus

    5.1 Work Systems

        Organization and Management of Work

        Employee Performance Management System

        Hiring and Career Progression

    5.2 Employee Learning and Motivation

        Employee Education, Training, and Development

        Motivation and Career Development

    5.3 Employee Well-Being and Satisfaction

        Work Environment

        Employee Support and Satisfaction

6.0 Process Management

    6.1 Value Creation Processes

        Value Creation Processes

    6.2 Support Processes and Operational Planning

        Support Processes

        Operational Planning

7.0 Business Results

    7.1 Product and Service Outcomes

        Product and Service Results

    7.2 Customer Focused Results

        Customer Focused Results

    7.3 Financial and Market Results

        Financial and Market Results

    7.4 Human Resource Results

        Human Resource Results

    7.5 Organizational Effectiveness Results

        Organizational Effectiveness Results

    7.6 Leadership and Social Responsibility Results

        Leadership and Social Responsibility Results

improve the process. My research has led to the conclusion that both complement each other and that applying lean first has its benefits.

Within the lean process, the total productive maintenance of equipment is used to keep the process equipment up to requirements of the process so performance of the process level meets the needs of the process under study. Preventive maintenance of the process is another way of identifying the potential problem areas and preventing down time of equipment, the same way you change your oil and lubricate your automobile to keep it performing properly. If maintenance is performed per the manufacturer's specifications within the recommended time frame and usage requirements are observed, the equipment will continue to perform to the specifications of the process needs. If we abuse the maintenance program, something will wear more, interact with other factors, and cause the performance of the process to change. Total productive maintenance uses some of the advanced techniques to monitor processes during routine maintenance to note changes that may lead to performance issues. The use of temperature and vibration profiles of the equipment can tell the maintenance crew if something is wearing, changing performance, or binding, thus varying the output performance.

The five S's of lean (sort, set in order, shine, standardize, and sustain for the process) help the organization establish more repeatable and efficient outputs. The kaizen events help reorganize the process flow to continuously flow product without delay or bottlenecks. The sequencing of product using a pull system produces only product that will sell and be delivered to the customers. The process has no or little work in progress and a minimum of finished goods inventory. When we are sequencing product, sometimes errors or mistakes occur because of process missteps or variation in materials, methods, machines, and management of the process; measurement of the process; or the environmental changes acting upon the process. This is when application of the Six Sigma problem-solving and process improvement tools will be used to reduce variation and eliminate the mistakes or errors.

It is my impression that a good total productive maintenance process should be established ahead of Six Sigma and lean. Lean is a good start for grasping the amount of waste the organization is running within the process. This will also help identify areas for the Six Sigma continuous improvement process.

LINKAGE OF MALCOLM BALDRIGE NATIONAL QUALITY AWARD TO LEAN AND SIX SIGMA

To provide some direction for an approach, we should line up the business process using the MBNQA Criteria. The criteria will help drive the business. Now the measurement systems results, category 4 of the criteria, will lead the organization to areas that require improvement. The strategic planning process and market-needs analysis will provide opportunities for the tactical tools of lean and Six Sigma. This is easily tied together with the first six pillars of my approach to the Twelve Pillars of Six Sigma. The first six pillars are part of the MBNQA Criteria. If we obtain information from the marketplace, have leadership involvement and commitment, and develop the strategic plan, the first three categories of the Baldrige Criteria correspond to my first three pillars of the process. The next three pillars help us choose the proper training and Lean Six Sigma approach for the projects chosen and the customer base we are addressing.

Once we have chosen the projects, training, and customer base, the foundation is in place to drive the charters for the Six Sigma projects and use the last six pillars to provide the tools and concepts of the Six Sigma DMAIC and DMADVIC processes. The lean portion of this implementation is captured at the beginning of the retrospective DMAIC process. Lean would not apply to DMADVIC because we would be designing a product or process to function within a continuous flow process.

We hope you can see how the three concepts link together to capture the essence of the business systems, areas to address, and the tactical tools to improve the systems, processes, and final product and service quality provided to the customers.

CHAPTER QUESTIONS

1. Why should we link lean with the Six Sigma process?

2. Do the Malcolm Baldrige National Quality Award Criteria help with the implementation of the Six Sigma process?

3. How can the Malcolm Baldrige National Quality Award Criteria help run the business processes?

4. Which of the lean concepts fit well with the Six Sigma approach of DMAIC?

5. What are the five S's of the lean concept?

6. How does TPM fit with the Six Sigma continuous improvement process?

7. Why do the lean concepts not apply to the DFSS/DMADVIC process?

8. Who should lead the Baldrige and Lean Six Sigma integration process?

9. Can we implement the concepts of lean, Six Sigma, and the Baldrige Criteria by themselves?

10. How will category 7 of the MBNQA Criteria on results tie to the Six Sigma efforts?

SUGGESTIONS FOR FURTHER READING

Bossidy, Larry, and Ram Charan. *Execution.* New York: Crown Publishing, 2002.

Breyfogle, Forest W., III. *Implementing Six Sigma,* 2nd ed. Hoboken, NJ: John Wiley & Sons, 2003.

George, Michael L. *Lean Six Sigma.* New York: McGraw-Hill, 2002.

Imai, Masaaki. *Gemba Kaizen.* New York: McGraw-Hill, 1997.

———. *Kaizen.* New York: McGraw-Hill, 1986.

Marash, Stanley A. *Fusion Management.* Fairfax, VA: QSU Publishing, 2003.

Naumann, Earl, and Steve Hoisington. *Customer Centered Six Sigma.* Milwaukee, WI: ASQ Quality Press, 2001.

23
Conclusions

The final story on the Lean Six Sigma efforts may not be seen for five to ten years. The possible outcomes may include some stagnation at companies that have not integrated the Twelve Pillars of Six Sigma approach into the organization. These companies will have captured the proverbial low-hanging fruit but will have found it difficult to reduce the variation and costs. This leaves fewer projects to complete with less and less attention from the executive team. Eventually the Black Belt projects stop coming and everyone is integrated back into the original organization. The full-time Black Belts are lost in the shuffle. This would not be bad if the process of continuous improvement, statistical thinking, and focus on customer and process have been integrated into the organization. Then process improvements will continue to grow.

WHERE IS THE ORGANIZATION NOW?

The Twelve Pillars help in implementing a Lean Six Sigma process, and the results depend on the present culture of the organization and what systems are already in place within the organization. In the best case, the organization has already been using the MBNQA Criteria to drive the business systems, has a minimal quality system that is capable of meeting the intent of the ISO 9001, and needs only to learn the lean and Six Sigma concepts and tools to start the implementation. It may take 6 to 12 months before results start to show up.

In the next case, the business system in place is minimal or nonexistent and the quality systems are not functional or not in place at all. In this case you should start to review the MBNQA Criteria and put a plan in place to implement business systems to support the first three criteria. This can take anywhere from one to three years. Somewhere in the process of implementing the criteria you should consider implementing the minimal quality system of ISO 9001 alongside categories 4 through 6 of the Baldrige Criteria. This, too, could take one to two years for a fully functional system to be in place. After two to four years you are ready for the proper implementation of Lean Six Sigma. This approach sounds like it will take a long time, but the rewards are outstanding. The organization will understand which are the key business drivers as well as quality system level of performance. Then the organization can plan for the improvements needed to meet the criteria of category 7 of the MBNQA. Of course, if you have the resources, you may speed up this time line by performing some of the implementations in parallel, because all these programs do tie together. Someone with good planning and leadership skills may be able to guide the process to completion within two to three years, with results occurring along the way.

CULTURAL CHANGES

Hopefully most organizations will continue to integrate the cultural changes to support customers' ever-changing needs. If the organization does not focus on the customer, key processes, business drivers, and measures of the dashboard, they will ultimately loose market share and reduce profits. The successful organizations of the future will be agile, stay in tune with the market and customer needs, and focus on the key processes to deliver consistent products and services. Service will become even more important as we lose our manufacturing base. Yes, we will continue to lose manufacturing of repetitive processes to other countries. Our next success will be to develop knowledge workers who support key priorities to support the plan.

PLANNING AND KNOWLEDGE WORKER CONCEPTS

The progressive organization will use strategic planning concepts, market analysis, and customer interviews to stay ahead. They will cultivate knowledge workers to focus on key processes that will satisfy the customer's needs. The ever-changing needs will be satisfied by process changes and improvements, technology changes, and keeping track of key measures to ensure that our direction is maintained. Tomorrow's needs will be reflected and met in today's knowledge worker. I believe that the Black Belts and Master Black Belts will become these knowledge workers if the organization adopts the Six Sigma way. It is hard to predict the future organization, but if you keep track of political, environmental, technological, and market changes, you will not miss the future needs. The organization will need to be agile enough to change to meet these needs as required. The future is yours to take.

THE APPROACH OF THIS BOOK

Now let's spend some time reviewing this book's approach to being successful at the Lean Six Sigma process. First, start with the understanding and implementation of the MBNQA criteria. A copy of the Baldrige Criteria may be obtained from the National Institute of Technology at Gaithersburg, MD, or the American Society for Quality in Milwaukee, WI. Then implement the quality systems around ISO 9001 to support the business systems. Once you have implemented the systems to run the organization to meet the criteria and elements, we can use the Lean Six Sigma approach to provide the tactics to reach the results in category 7. From the criteria, you will have implemented the first six pillars of the Twelve Pillars of Six Sigma. What remains is the Six Sigma DMAIC and DMADVIC processes.

CONCERNS AND SUGGESTIONS

The concerns that I have are that the executive staffs do not have the patience or the capability to practice teamwork to be able to link the MBNQA Criteria with lean processes and Six Sigma processes to become successful. My inclination is that the whole process can take three to five and even ten years. Some organizations do not have this amount of time, and those that do will not be willing to wait for the results.

I offer the following suggestion to small and large institutions: First, make sure your organization stresses the importance of building relationships inside and outside the organization. We must focus on people skills to be able to work together, work with our customers, and work with the community. These are also important aspects of the MBNQA process criteria. Once we have established the organization's values and beliefs, we need to see that all employees will support them. I cannot overemphasize the communication needs inside and outside the organization to support any process. The values, beliefs, and goals must be understood. This is a test! How many of your employees know your vision, mission, and objectives? This may let you know whether you are indeed communicating.

COMMUNICATIONS

The idea of good communications of the vision, mission, and objectives must be in place before we start the planning process and deciding how we will meet the vision and mission. This is where strategic planning will help the organization set the direction of the future.

The strategic plan will lead us to objectives and goals for the organization, each plant, and each department. If we plan well, we will succeed. The plans will allow us to understand where we need to improve. This is where the Lean Six Sigma process comes into play for the organization. The approach and the tool set will provide the way to tactfully accomplish the mission and, in turn, the vision. The Black Belt projects must align with the strategic plan and support the objectives that come from the plan. This means alignment of projects to departmental and the organization's plans for the future. This is sometimes hard to do. The organization must have the patience to go through the process.

Now with the plans, objectives, and goals in place, we need to have the measures to follow the implementation plan. This is not easy, but if you stay the course, the road will be rewarding along the way. We hope you can see that the Twelve Pillars of Six Sigma will help you achieve your mission and then your visions. Six Sigma and lean provide the tools, which help the MBNQA business process to achieve the results of category 7.

SMALL BUSINESS OPPORTUNITIES

At this point you have the outline to success for the organizations of the future. Now let me mention the opportunities to use these kinds of processes in small businesses and the home environment. Think about the idea that everything in life is a process. How we develop the process and implement it depends on our knowledge about the customer of the process, the process steps that add value to the customer, and how we measure the process. We need to focus the business on the market, customer, and key processes. Then we need to plan how we will satisfy the customer's ever-changing needs. The approaches used to meet those needs will allow us to succeed in the future.

The suggestion here is that we approach the future of our organization, whether it is a small business operation or large institution, by adopting the MBNQA Criteria to run our business, Lean Six Sigma approach to improve it, and the dashboard measures to monitor it. You can develop a plan for each of these phases you need to follow to improve your small business. This approach will allow the organization to define its customer base and determine the needs and expectations of these customers. With the customer needs determined, we can use the quality function deployment process to determine the CTQs for the process to maintain the output of the process.

The same approach could be used in your personal life. Everything we do is a process. How we define the process, what parameters to monitor, the results of the process, and the final output of the process is up to us. Even the process of cooking meals is a specific detail of measures and controls to ensure that the meal meets our tastes and fulfillment needs. This means that the same processes of DMAIC may apply to our personal endeavors at home or within our communities.

Appendix A

Answers to Chapter Questions

CHAPTER 1

1. The fundamentals of a good Six Sigma program begin with the need to improve the status quo. When the management team feels the need to improve key business processes, the process of Six Sigma will begin. The outcome of the strategic plan should be the development of key dashboard measures for the organization to succeed in the plan outcome. These indicators must be important to the key processes and business drivers of the Malcolm Baldrige National Quality Award Criteria. The indicators will ensure that the organization will improve the performance results with the improvements made. Therefore, the strategic planning process should occur before we plan the Six Sigma implementation process.

2. The knowledge worker concept we obtained from Dr. Drucker is what will become the future worker's capability to solve process variation problems. The Black Belts of the Six Sigma process will definitely have the capability to fill this position. In the next few years we will be faced with new cultural issues that the knowledge worker will encounter, using process know-how, knowledge of problem solving, and statistical knowledge of how to handle the data obtained from the process to solve problems and improve the capability of the process. This new culture will require that we focus on the customer's needs, the process measures, and the dedication to improving the process. This is exactly what the Six Sigma Black Belt will be doing.

3. PDCA for strategic planning is not a cycle but a Sigmoid curve, which allows for the continual improvement of the planning process to lead the organization. This process will affect the continual improvement of the strategic plan as the organization evolves.

4. Leadership involvement in the strategic planning process is the number one requirement. Sometimes this causes change to occur in the organization or requires a change in the organization's structure. The leadership is the main point in this change process and will participate in the change process to support the new needs.

5. The development of a project selection process will be key to the success of the Six Sigma program. Not only should there be a project selection process but also a selection process for selecting the Black Belts and Green Belts for training to ensure that we will be successful. After the implementation of the selection processes for Black Belts and Green Belts, we need a review process to monitor the projects. These are the fundamentals of the building blocks covered in the first Six Pillars of Six Sigma. We will also need to prepare for the training and consulting and the customer and market information needs for the first six pillars.

6. The new paradigm of Six Sigma is the use of data and statistics to identify the differences, distinctions, and commonality of processes using the different methods, materials, people, machines, environments, and measurements. The other concerns or paradigms are the focus on the customer, the key processes of the business, and the measures of the processes.

7. Drivers of change in the organization are:

   • We pay the price for failing to take advantage of an opportunity.

   • We will miss a key element in moving from/to "first class" or "leader."

   • We will miss the cornerstone to the overall business strategy.

   • We will miss a major competitive distinction we can gain.

   • We will miss a powerful tactical advantage to overcome a weakness.

   • We will miss something interesting and enjoyable.

   • We will miss our chance to grow the organization.

8. PDCA for strategic planning is not a cycle but a Sigmoid curve, which means that we will have cycles of improvement as we move up the growth curve for the market we are addressing with the strategy.

9. The pillars are: market and customer knowledge, leadership commitment, strategic planning, training and consulting, voice of the customer, quality function deployment, customer and process measures, process capability, process improvement, maintain the improvements, and recognition (see figure on page 255).

10. A lean organization uses lean concepts and the lean enterprise approach to simplify the production process, eliminate waste, and improve cycle time to produce the product.

CHAPTER 2

1. If the management team is not supportive of the Lean Six Sigma process, the program may die in the next two to three years. The management group may have to embark on some type of team building exercise to ensure that they will be able to function as a team. Most management teams, if diversified, will have varying viewpoints and approaches to achieving the vision and

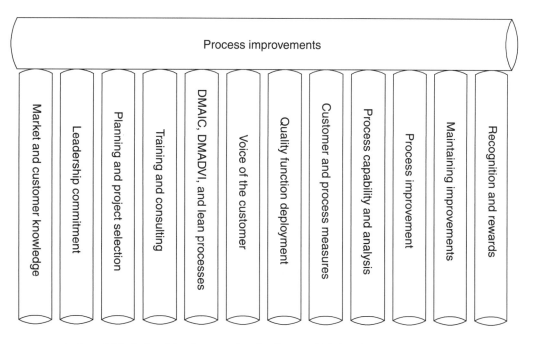

mission. This is healthy but can be detrimental if the viewpoints and approaches disrupt the mission. If this step is not completed, the future projects and goals of the organization will be in jeopardy. We do not want a team that is totally in agreement, but we need a team that sees the mission and goals as needed to fulfill the organization's destiny or vision and to ensure that the stakeholders will be properly rewarded for their investments in the organization or processes.

2. The Green Belts should have two weeks of Six Sigma training. The Black Belts have four weeks of training, and the depth of the training on Six Sigma tools is greater. The Black Belts receive more advanced statistical tools and leadership skills training.

3. The project champions need to go through a training program that will cover the Six Sigma philosophy, the meaning of variation within the process, voice of the customer, quality function deployment, measurement systems analysis, use of control charts, process capability, the strategic planning process, and a quick overview of the advanced tools of hypothesis development, designed experiments, regression analysis, and other needs. This training, along with their commitment to support improvements and projects, will help maintain the Six Sigma process.

4. The Six Sigma process will not receive all the benefits that are possible to achieve, and, depending on what pillar or item is missed, the process may not be successful. All 25 items discussed in this chapter are fundamental to the improvement process.

5. Once the projects are in place with Black Belts and Green Belts assigned for completion, we need to consider a project review process to verify progress and determine whether help is needed. This approach should allow for the

stages of DMAIC to be reviewed as the project progresses through each stage. We must keep in touch with the project and process owners at least once per month to ensure that the projects stay on course.

6. The process flow for the Six Sigma process and the concepts or steps do not have to be performed in the exact sequence presented, but all the concepts should be completed to achieve the results that will provide the reduction in process variation and the reduction in throughput to deliver the output to the customers. The results will then be tied to the financial improvement of the organization.

7. All the points in this chapter do support the Six Sigma process and will help in the success of projects. Missing some of these points may not jeopardize the Six Sigma process but could affect specific projects.

8. The use of Master Black Belts will help with the maintenance of multiple projects when you have 20 or more Black Belts. Master Black Belts need to take two more weeks of Design for Six Sigma training and pass a test on the DFSS process.

9. There is no difference in the Twelve Pillars and the flow of the process, but the sequence is not important once the strategic plan is in place.

10. The champion covers three levels of the organization. There usually is an executive champion, who understands the Six Sigma process and supports the implementation within the organization. The next level of champion is the Six Sigma coordinator, who helps in the Black Belt and Green Belt selection process and the project selection process. The last champion is the individual, who supports the specific project and provides direct help to the Black Belt.

CHAPTER 3

1. The strategy must consider cultural issues first and then the strategies versus the organization's capabilities to deliver. Based on the strategies chosen after the importance matrix is analyzed, the organization will prioritize the issues. Sometimes we need to ensure that we have addressed the proper market segment of the organization's products and services.

2. Listening-post information will become the input into the strategic plan, using an importance matrix or other planning processes. The organization will need to develop a market needs and expectation analysis that is derived from the listening posts or other sources of data and information input. If the organization develops this analysis from a broader marketplace approach, the processes that deliver the product and services will be evaluated against the organization's ability to deliver to those needs and expectations. This information will then ensure that we address the market and customer needs.

3. The following items need to be considered in the market analysis in order to select the market and segmentation that we will be addressing and before we address the customer's needs based on regional or global markets:

   • Determine which market the organization wants to be in and evaluate it, using the sources available to the organization that determine the market needs.

- Develop listening posts for the market chosen to gather knowledge about the differences, regionally and globally, in the marketplace.

- Determine whether there are any governmental or political effects on the market chosen for the product or services offered. Evaluate the risk in this area.

- Determine the different economic and environmental conditions that will affect the marketplace.

- If the market is a niche market, determine the special needs being fulfilled in the area.

4. The areas that may concern the organization for future projects or products are:

- The global market differences that may require different products or services. This will help determine differences that must be met by the processes developed. If we can develop one process to fill all market and customer needs, the organization can become the economic producer or service provider to the market.

- The regional and regulatory differences in the country(ies) where the product or service is delivered.

- The costs to produce or provide the service for the different and varying market needs.

- The potential environmental effects on the market, including product or service effects on the natural environment, customer alternatives that are less damaging to the environment, and the laws and regulations that control the environmental effects.

- The value that the product or service provides to the customer.

5. Windows of opportunities for the organization that may be considered are:

- The organization's own unexpected success and unexpected failures, and the unexpected success and failures of the organization's competitors.

- Incongruities. Especially incongruities in the process, whether of production or distribution, or incongruities in customer behavior.

- Process needs.

- Changes in the industry and market structures.

- Changes in demographics.

- Changes in meaning and perception.

- New knowledge.

6. The data we obtain from the market analysis and the customers has to be turned into information that will help the organization focus on the market and customer needs internally and drive all cross-functional departments to keep the same market and customer focus. This is accomplished by using tools such as the tree diagram or the house of quality, defined in the quality function deployment process. We will focus on the deployment process for quality function deployment. The Malcolm Baldrige Criteria also cover the need to focus on the customer and the marketplace and sometimes offer some guidance by suggesting items to review in this area.

7. The market analysis provides that all aspects of the business unit, the market and customer effects based on needs, the changing environment, laws and regulations, and technological advances must be considered when developing and updating the strategic plan.

8. The organization needs to maintain a focus on the market and the customer to ensure that the changing environment, customer needs, and market needs will be addressed by the future service or products that the organization will be delivering. This will require good channels of communication with the front-line scouts of the organization to the executive staff. This communication will help with existing service and product performance issues as well as help drive the new development process. Most organizations have the marketing and sales departments focus on these issues. In the Design for Six Sigma process, as a proactive activity and in the reactive activity of process improvements, the Black Belt and improvement team need to be involved in the transfer of knowledge about customer and market needs to the organization's departments that meet those needs.

9. Porter's generic strategies are: competitive strategy, cost leadership, differentiation, cost focus, and focused differentiation. The organization must select one or more of these strategies when considering the approach that will be taken to address specific product or service markets.

10. The organization obtains the customer's needs in several ways. They include interviews, focus groups, surveys, and observation of the customer. The purpose of determining customer requirements is to establish a comprehensive list of all the important quality characteristics that describe the service or product. This list will help us focus on customer's measures and determine what will help us develop customer loyalty.

CHAPTER 4

1. The executive staff and the quality council are created because of the need to ensure that the organization's vision and mission are in place and that they support the leadership's vision and mission. This will help in choosing the proper projects and the Black Belts who will help in the continuous improvement process under the Six Sigma umbrella.

2. There are three types or levels of champions in most organizations. The executive champion supports the Six Sigma improvement process and is knowledgeable about DMAIC and DMADVIC process. The next level of champion is the organization's Six Sigma coordinator, who understands the Six Sigma concepts, all statistical tools used, and the problem-solving process and who supports the Black Belts by overseeing their projects and helping with the project reports to management. The last level is the project champion, who is usually the sponsor of the project and desires to see the project succeed. This person will select and directly support the Black Belt and help obtain the resources, prepare reports, and select Green Belts to help with the project as necessary.

3. The management team must focus on the customers, the market, the regulatory environment, the competition, and the economic conditions that will affect the plan. The strategic planning process must be led by the management team and use the input from the market and customer information developed from the first pillar. These inputs into the strategic planning process will help the team to recognize which improvement projects need the attention and support to drive the organization in the appropriate direction.

4. The project selection should start with inputs from the management team and their direct reports based on current indicators and problem areas. A decision matrix should be created to help with the selection process. This decision matrix needs to consider most of the following:

   • Improvement in plant and/or customer quality levels.

   • Lower costs and/or prices to the customer.

   • Improved delivery.

   • A champion who supports the project.

   • The process owner approves the project.

   • The resources are available to perform the project.

   • The project affects more than one department.

   • The project requires Black Belt skills to be applied.

   • The project will have a financial return of at least $50,000.

   • The results of the project will support the key business indicators.

5. The people skills of the executive team must be brought forth to allow for promotion and use of the methods and statistics, along with new technologies that will support the improvements. Most of the changes will affect the way people work. This will require that management and the work teams consider the actions necessary to allow the changes to work. As with any change process, resistance to change needs to be overcome. The management team can help during the implementation phase by providing support for the changes and understanding the cultural changes that must go along with the physical changes.

6. The dashboard of indicators that the executive team uses to measure the performance of the business is usually in place already. The team needs to review the indicators and determine whether any new indicators or changes to existing ones are required for following the progress of the operations, customer satisfaction, and the market. Some indicators to consider are:

   • Delivery rating

   • Plant inventory dollars

   • Inventory turns

   • Daily contribution margin

- Customer quality
- Supplier quality
- Safety rating
- Linearity
- Number of changeovers
- Productivity
- Accidents per worked hour
- Parts per person per day
- Delivery performance
- Scrap
- Outbound premium freight
- Customer delivery performance
- Six Sigma savings
- Plant income
- Closing days
- Employee turnover
- Volume to plan
- Profitability

7. The high-level process map will start with the inputs required for the operation and include the key processes that will change the inputs to the outputs for the customers. This map will allow the staff to point out the critical processes for the organization that must be maintained through measurement. This high-level map will ensure that we understand the key processes that we must perform well on for success.

8. The Six Sigma coordinator for the organization is the person who understands the Six Sigma concepts, all statistical tools used, and the problem-solving process and who supports the Black Belts by overseeing their projects and helping with the project reports to management. This person also keeps management apprised of the status of the Black Belt and Green Belt projects.

9. Commitment is knowledge and action based upon that knowledge. The management team does not obtain the knowledge by delegating the planning, project selection, Black Belt and Green Belt selection, and project reviews and support. This means that the management team must see a need to improve the business processes and then take the time to draw up a strategic plan and align it with the selected project.

10. Management commitment means that the project activities must support the goals and objectives of the planning process outcomes. Then, to ensure that

the projects will succeed, the management team must review each project's status and support the continuous improvement process with the necessary resources. The leadership of the organization transforms and motivates followers by making others aware of the importance of the Six Sigma process. A leader can relate to the vision, and followers trust him or her. The style of leadership, such as charisma and intellectual stimulation, is important.

CHAPTER 5

1. We need to develop, change, or improve the strategic plan, vision, mission, values, and critical success factors of the organization in light of the change to be made. This is usually performed annually and updated as needed when internal and external changes affect the plan.

2. If you are losing market share in an area, the organization should use forward integration while addressing intensive forward-looking market development and penetration.

3. A good mission statement takes the following into consideration:

   • Customers

   • Products or services

   • Markets

   • Technology and materials

   • Concern for survival, growth, and profitability

   • Philosophy of the organization

   • Self-concept of the organization

   • Concern for public image

   • Concern for employees

4. Company beliefs and values are the culture of the organization and usually consider the following items:

   • A set of ideals and sense of purpose.

   • The organization's essential and enduring tenants.

   • Guiding principles are not to be compromised.

   • Not to be confused with specific cultural or operating practices.

   • Purpose is the reason for existing.

   • Value is simply our worth in usefulness or importance to the people in the organization.

The values and beliefs are important because this can be the reason some people will resist change to the culture. If the change goes against these values, the personnel may resist the change.

5. In a value map, tradeoffs are made between benefits of a product. The scales on the perceptual map are the level of the benefit per dollar of each price. Each brand is placed on the map according to the level of benefit it offers, relative to the other brands, divided by its unit cost.

6. The external forces are:

   • Economic conditions, both current and expected in the near future, such as social, cultural, demographic, world market, and environmental conditions.

   • Political, governmental, and legal actions that have occurred or will occur.

   • The effects of wars on the market.

   • Anticipated technological advances.

   • Competitive market and results.

   • International regulations and standards.

7. SWOT analysis examines the strengths, weaknesses, opportunities, and threats affecting the organization. This metric analyzes strengths against weaknesses and opportunities against threats in each quadrant. The TOWS analysis uses a threats-opportunities-weaknesses-strengths matrix. This metric compares threats against opportunities and weaknesses against opportunities. The major differences are the approach to the issues in the matrix body and then the strategy selected.

8. Key internal and external factors strengths and weaknesses are:

   • Corporate structure

   • Corporate resources

   • Marketing

   • Finance

   • R&D

   • Manufacturing and service

   • Human resources

   • Management information systems

   • Opportunities and threats

   • Societal environment

   • Task environment

9. The areas to concentrate on for external forces that may affect the organization are:

   • Economic conditions, both current and expected in the near future, such as social, cultural, demographic, world market, and environmental conditions.

   • Political, governmental, and legal actions that have occurred or will occur.

   • The effects of wars on the market.

- Anticipated technological advances.
- Competitive market and results.
- International regulations and standards.

10. The top five competitors in four industries should be identified. An important part of an exceptional review is to identify rival firms and to determine their strengths, weaknesses, capabilities, opportunities, threats, objectives, and strategies. Key questions are:

- Who are the major competitors?
- What are the competitors' strengths?
- What are the competitors' weaknesses?
- What are the competitors' objectives and strategies?
- How do the competitors respond to economic, social, cultural, demographic, geographic, political, governmental, technological, and competitive trends affecting our industry?
- How vulnerable are the competitors to our alternative strategies?
- How vulnerable are our alternative strategies to responsive counterattack by our major competitors?
- To what extent are new firms entering and old firms leaving this industry?
- What key factors influence our competitive position?
- How have the sales and profit rankings of major competitors changed over recent years? What has caused these rankings to change?
- What is the nature of supplier and distributor relationships in this industry?
- To what extent could substitute products or services be a threat to compliance in this industry?
- How easy is it to enter our industry?

CHAPTER 6

1. Champion, Green Belt, Yellow Belt, and Black Belt training differ only in the amount and level of training devoted to team skills, management skills, negotiation skills, statistical thinking, and the problem-solving process. The Green Belt will have training in these items:

- Teams and teamwork requirements
- The art of negotiation
- The ability to audit or evaluate differences in processes and the ability to act accordingly
- Change management

- The Six Sigma philosophy
- The Twelve Pillars of Six Sigma
- The DMAIC process
- The DMADVIC process
- Obtaining the voice of the customer
- Using the quality function deployment process to change the customer's voice to the process needs or CTQs to CTPs
- Understanding process controls
- Understanding process variation
- The difference between variables and attributes (continuous and discrete)
- Measurement system analysis
- Projects planning
- Problem definition
- Project charter development
- Process and quality costing
- Shewart charts
- Value stream mapping and process mapping
- Process capability analysis
- Project management
- Hypothesis analysis and comparison testing

The champion training will contain the following subjects:

- Strategic planning process
- Key organization success factors
- Coaching skills
- Project selection
- The DMAIC process
- Six Sigma philosophy
- Operations measures development
- The Twelve Pillars of Six Sigma
- Process improvement analysis
- Change management
- Leadership skills
- Training on the tools of Six Sigma DMAIC process

- Obtaining the voice of the customer
- Using the quality function deployment process to change the customer's voice to the process needs or CTQs to CTPs
- Understanding process controls
- Understanding process variation
- The difference between variables and attributes
- Measurement system analysis
- Projects planning
- Problem definition
- Project charter development
- Process and quality costing
- Shewart charts
- Value stream mapping and process mapping
- Process capability analysis
- Project management
- Hypothesis analysis and comparison testing
- Regression analysis
- Designed experiments
- Chi-square analysis
- Multi-vari analysis
- Multiple regression analysis
- Response surface analysis
- Failure modes and effects analysis
- Control plans
- Benchmarking process
- Problem-solving process
- Design for manufacturability
- Sampling plans
- Mistake-proofing
- Project selection process
- Lessons learned process
- Black Belt selection process

2. Design for Six Sigma will contain the following subjects:

- Obtaining the voice of the customer and market knowledge
- Advanced quality function deployment
- The Six Sigma philosophy
- Statistical thinking
- Process focus
- The DMADVIC process
- New project planning
- New project management
- Advanced process control
- Completing Black Belt DMAIC training
- Pugh concepts
- Anticipatory failure determination
- Taguchi analysis
- Tolerance analysis
- Monte Carlo simulation
- Design for assembly
- Design for manufacturability
- Design for reliability
- Design for durability
- Design for testability
- Design for maintenance
- Design for the environment
- Implementing the design
- Design verification

3. The design and development needs required for achieving the Six Sigma level of performance on future products and processes will use Design for Six Sigma (DFSS). These products will be developed with the needs of new markets, existing markets, and new customers in mind.

4. It is important that Black Belts also become good negotiators, understand change management strategies, and be skilled at obtaining consensus. It is crucial that the trainer consider the organization's culture and emphasize teamwork, leadership, and facilitation skills. This means that the training must be developed in modular form so that the trainees will receive the important aspects of the people skills required for leading and for

implementing changes. Black Belts must learn several skills in order to become leaders: leadership, open-mindedness, statistical thinking, problem solving, process thinking, customer focus, and project management.

5. Master Black Belts are the most experienced with the tools, project management, and implementation of successful projects. Their training must continue in order for them to become leaders of the process and the most skilled users of the tools that are crucial to the continuous improvement of process and customer focused measures. For the Six Sigma improvement process to succeed, the "people issue" needs to be considered during training. Most organizations are continually training employees to become team members and team leaders.

6. Master Black Belt training adds the ability to teach these subjects and advanced tools and skills to lead several projects at one time while maintaining open communication with executives. These skills are learned through a training process that will expose the students to the theory, accompanied by the immediate application of the skills to theoretical processes and then to actual organization experiences with the company's processes.

7. It is also beneficial for the Master Black Belt to have training in the Design for Six Sigma (DMADVIC) skills and the Malcolm Baldrige National Quality Award Criteria.

8. The detailed amount of training required depends on the organization's present culture and problem-solving process effectiveness. This can vary tremendously, but all the topics and tools should be mastered by the Black Belt and Master Black Belt.

9. You should base the organization's training needs on the present knowledge base and the needs of the future Master Black Belts, Black Belts, and Green Belts. The training must be performed by an experienced Master Black Belt and must be evaluated to ensure the success of the training. The evaluation of the training will be in the form of a formal test on the subject matter and then a hands-on application of the theory on a practical project that the organization has picked for the Black Belt.

10. The challenge for the trainer is to monitor and evaluate the project application properly to verify that the material learning process took place. Consulting on the projects and processes improvement required achieves the target for the project. We must link the tools usage to the problem-solving process for the project and ensure the specific goals can be meet. It would be beneficial if the trainer for your organization had the following characteristics:

- Leadership skills

- Good facilitating skills

- Broad engineering background unless you are working only with transactional processes

- Ability to question the status of the organization

- Good analogy skills
- Mechanical and electrical aptitude
- Process analysis ability
- Good materials understanding
- Practical application of skills in your type of business
- Process flow technology knowledge
- Situational skills
- Builds confidence in the process being taught
- Good process mapping skills
- Works well with the executive council and the staff

CHAPTER 7

1. DMADVIC is the proactive Six Sigma program, and DMAIC is the reactive Six Sigma program. The major differences are in the level of advanced tools that are used in the DMADVIC process.

2. The lean process considers the seven areas of waste, lead time of the process, value stream mapping of the process, SMED, TPM, the five S's, and error-proofing the process. The seven areas of waste are:

   - Overproduction caused by poor planning, forecasting, and response to errors as well as the lack of understanding the customer's needs.

   - Waiting to be able to produce an activity because of downstream process problems.

   - Transportation within the process that is considered wasted effort and sometimes causes more errors and problems to occur because of process queuing.

   - Extra processing to compensate for errors that have occurred in some of the processes within the operation.

   - Poor inventory management resulting from inaccurate forecasts, errors in processes, and overproduction caused by problems within the processes. Excess levels of inventory occur when problems in delivery, manufacturing, and supply are anticipated.

   - Motion within activities that are unnecessary and do not add value to the process or product. These may be in the form of extra steps, improper handling of materials, or back-and-forth movement of parts.

   - Defects in the product caused by errors within the process, including supplier or previous processes.

3. The DMAIC process should follow the set sequence, but you may need to return to the previous phases if the project does not reveal the expected results.

4. The DMADVIC process will establish good designs that will be released at the Six Sigma level of performance. This will ensure that the retrospective DMAIC process will not be required of these designs.

5. The lean process attacks waste, and the DMAIC process attacks variation of the processes.

6. SMED (single minute exchange of die) is part of the lean process, which improves the changeover time for tooling and methods. This will reduce waste and improve cycle time of the process.

7. We error-proof a process to eliminate the error and prevent it from returning.

8. The prospective improvements are implemented during the design and before release to manufacturing. Thus, the problems are resolved before release. The retrospective approach solves the problems after the product is released.

9. Total productive maintenance is a team effort to reduce down time of the equipment that is used to produce the equipment. Use of TPM (total productive maintenance) as part of the process is to ensure that every piece of equipment in use during production will be able to perform to its requirements when needed. This will allow the organization to focus on improvement of equipment in order to maintain consistency in the production environment.

10. The control phase of DMAIC establishes the control plan and reaction plan to use if the process variation returns. It controls the improved process so it will stay in place.

CHAPTER 8

1. *Attributes* are the physical or abstract characteristics of the service or product. *Consequences* are the results of using the service or product. Attributes are generally objective and measurable.

2. The affinity diagram sorts the consequences desired by the customer into logical groupings. The groupings allow us to define the major categories the customer wants addressed.

3. The Kano model helps us understand why consumers do not recognize all the consequences that are important to them. The graphical depiction of the Kano model uses two axes, the degree of providing desired consequences and the level of customer satisfaction, ranging from dissatisfaction to loyalty.

4. The itemized rating scale asks the consumers to rate each consequence on a specified scale of importance. It is easy for the consumers to understand and answer. This ranking allows us to enter them into the QFD matrix, which allows for the rating of the technical hows in the process.

5. The only way to determine consequences is to ask the consumer, obtaining the voice of the customer. Two primary ways to obtain the voice of the customer are through interviews or focus groups. In both cases, we ask the customers what is important to them when selecting a service.

6. The interviewer leads the discussion through questions, which have been prepared to collect the desired information. To elicit consequences from consumers, we use a technique called probing. The interviewer takes each attribute mentioned by the consumer and asks "why."

7. The anchored scale provides a ratio measurement; we may use the mean as the measure of average, and we may multiply the results times the brand ratings.

8. The voice of the customer data allows us to prioritize the consequences to develop the quality house in quality function deployment. The prioritization allows us to determine the importance of the key process parameters that must be monitored and controlled in the process.

9. We use focus groups to gain the same information that interviews do, but we are dealing with a group of people instead of individuals. This is the next best approach to the interview. The biggest advantage of a focus group is that the members of the group tend to stimulate ideas from one another, much like brainstorming. A trained moderator usually runs the focus groups because working with groups is more difficult than working with individuals. Someone who has training as a facilitator probably has the skills necessary to run a focus group for purposes of acquiring the voice of the customer. The reason that we bring similar people together is that they tend to communicate with each other more readily than people who vary from each other significantly. In addition, the similarity in the consequences they desire helps them stimulate additional ideas from other members of the group.

10. The rank order scale provides a list of consequences and asks the consumer to rate them in order of importance from one to the number of consequences listed. The anchored scale provides a ratio measurement; we may use the mean as the measure of average, and we may multiply the results times the brand ratings.

CHAPTER 9

1. We set a goal of creating one to three technical requirements for each consequence (the hows). More requirements gives us too many technical requirements to handle; fewer will not adequately provide for satisfying customers. We use a creative process to organize the technical information that helps ensure that we properly develop and define the technical requirements. We use the tree diagram to create requirements in a way similar to the use of the cause-and-effect diagram to generate root causes.

2. We compare all relationships between the voices of the customer (needs) to the technical requirements (hows). Once we have completed this relationship matrix, we evaluate it for technical hows with no relationship to any of the wants (needs) of the customer. We need to question and eliminate these, if possible. This matrix will also point out if we created too many requirements, or hows, during brainstorming. We should have filled in no more than 50 percent of the blocks and should have created a random pattern of filled-in

blocks.[1] If this pattern occurs, we will have computed the matrix property and can select the best choice of requirements to meet the customer needs.

3. The roof of the quality house (this may be why we call this matrix a house) quickly becomes the groups' design control method to ensure that we consider the interactions between the technical process parameters. These interactions will affect the customers' needs if we are not careful.

4. The tree diagram links the want or consequence to the technical requirements while performing the analysis. We compare all relationships between the voices of the customer (needs) to the technical requirements (hows). Once we have completed this relationship matrix, we evaluate it for technical hows with no relationship to any of the wants (needs) of the customer. We need to question and eliminate these, if possible. This matrix will also point out if we created too many requirements, or hows, during brainstorming. We should have filled in no more than 50 percent of the blocks and should have created a random pattern of filled-in blocks. If this occurs, we will have to select the best choice of requirements to meet the customer needs.

5. Each technical requirement is a way that we can use (process or design) to meet the corresponding consequence desired by our customers. Each needs to be within our control and to contain an attribute we can vary within our service or process. Each also needs to be measurable so we can set objectives and determine whether we are meeting them.

6. The how measurement ensures that the process can perform to the engineering requirements.

7. The middle of the customer needs-to-hows matrix of the quality house should be about 50 percent full with random patterns of levels of correlation. If this does not occur, we are not developing the right number of technical hows to meet the customer's needs.

8. If the customer does not rank the needs or consequences, the final rating of the relative importance of the hows will not be calculated and we will not determine the relative importance of the technical requirements to the customer.

9. The consequences from the customer are a better input to the needs of the customer for the quality house.

10. The cause-and-effect diagram is one of the tools that help us develop the hows or technical requirements for the customer wants.

CHAPTER 10

1. The as-is process map is the existing process as the actual activities are occurring in flowchart form. It specifically addresses the current process as seen by the players.

2. The CTQ is the customer's critical to quality characteristic as developed through the voice of the customer.

3. The CTQs are transformed to CTPs by using the quality house from quality function deployment. If we use the QFD process for transferring the key customer needs to key processes and the process characteristics needs, the customer measures will be met.

4. The voice of the customer, documented in Chapter 8, should lead us to the key CTQs for the customer base and market segments we decided to address. Each CTQ should have its own measure. The CTQ is then the function of Y for the process output. The main task at hand is to establish the key process characteristics that will affect the process so that the output Y factor will be affected. The next step is to determine the optimum level of the X factor in the process that will maintain the output consistency. Remember, $Y = f(X_1 + X_2 + . . .)$. The QFD process, DOE, or multiple regressions can determine the X's.

5. The quality house in quality function deployment should lead us to the key processes and measures that are important to the process input or controls that must be maintained to achieve the output requirements. The main task is to establish the key process characteristics that will affect the process so that the output Y factor will be affected. The next step is to determine the optimum level of the X factor in the process that will maintain the output consistency. Remember, $Y = f(X_1 + X_2 + . . .)$. The measure for the how is usually determined by engineering.

6. Current process measures are developed to understand the present stage of development of the process and to look for actions required to improve the processes. Now we need to verify that we have all the measurements that are required to deliver the customer the product or service they expect. The measurement systems analysis will verify that we can accurately measure the characteristics.

7. The quality house in QFD is used to develop the key processes and the key measures that are required for meeting the customer's needs.

8. The as-is process maps for the process will provide the current conditions of the process and help us develop an issues list to improve upon the current conditions.

9. The difference between the SIPOC and the lower-level activity map is the level of detail in the activities within the process.

10. The process map of the process will provide the cycle time of entire process, each activity cycle time, the defect rate of specific activities, the difference between the lowest and highest cycle time of the activities, the current process issues, and the non-value-added activities.

CHAPTER 11

1. The C_p value provides the overall design capability, using the specification spread and the six standard deviation spread of the process. The C_{pk} value takes into consideration the centering of the process by looking at the mean

of the process to the target of the specification and the three standard deviation spread of the process for each side of the normal curve.

2. The C_{pk} indicator is better when evaluating the process capability for the customer or engineering specification needs. We are comparing the mean of the process and the spread to the engineering or customer specification target and tolerances. The higher the capability number, the better you are in meeting the customer specifications. For Six Sigma capability, C_{pk} should be at 2.0.

3. Yes, the Six Sigma capability is equal to C_{pk} of 2.0.

4. The causes of poor process capability are the variations within the process from special and common causes.

5. The process spread needs to be reduced by reducing the variation within the process, and the mean of the process needs to be centered to be closer to the target of the specification.

6. In a capability study, the voice of the process is being compared to the voice of the customer. Another way of saying this is that the specification with its tolerances is compared to the process variation and mean.

7. This capability of .67 means that we are not capable of meeting the specification of the customer or engineering.

8. Process capability will tell the planners which parts or products they will have problems delivering to the customer.

9. The Black Belt must reduce the process variation and control the mean of the process to the target of the specification to improve capability of the process. The DMAIC process will help the Black Belt achieve these results.

10. In short-term capability, the process may not have seen all the natural variation or common cause variation to determine the long-run effects of these variances.

CHAPTER 12

1. The results of the project would not develop, as we would have estimated if the team did not complete the implementation process properly. This could be caused by a poor implementation plan, a lack of implementation, or an analysis phase that was not completed properly.

2. The Pugh analysis will help select the best design by using a formalized approach to evaluate the solutions developed by the team.

3. All the process and results stakeholders need to be involved in the selection of the best solution and implementation plan for the improvement phase.

4. The implementation success rate is verified by the financial and process characteristics improvements from the original measurement phase.

5. If the implementation phase is not successful, the team should verify that the implementation plan was followed. If it is successful, return to the

measurement or analyze phase to review the measurements and the root cause analysis.

6. The design block diagram used in the DMAIC and the DMADVIC process provides a detail of the design concepts so the solutions can be compared to the original design and to develop the FMEA for the new designed product or process.

7. The improvements result of the project should use the same indicators used in the define and measure phases of the project. Sometimes new indicators are developed in these phases, but the comparison still goes back to the define and measure phases.

8. The implementation plan can be developed by using Gantt charts, Pert charts, or Microsoft Project.

9. The implementation phase must contend with possible resistance to change in the process or product. The resistance to change or change management is an important subject that must be covered in the Black Belt training and considered for the changes that will take place. The cultural issues of the organization need to be considered when we are implementing Six Sigma and when the changes for the project are implemented in the process. We need to convince the people involved in the process to implement the remedy to the problem. The practical issues that affect implementation of the changes will need to be considered. The best way to prevent resistance is to include the people who need to support the change to help in the selection and implementation of the best solutions to the problem.

10. The changes can be implemented more efficiently and effectively by considering some of the following items when determining why there is resistance.

The current beliefs of the organization and employees.

The current habits of the employees.

The current practices of the organization and the employees.

Traditions of the organization shared by the group and taught to new members.

Experiences of the employees.

Defense of vested rights in the organization.

Intrusion by outsiders is felt by the organization as a negative.

Resentment of exclusion from the planning or implementation.

Embarrassment at the magnitude of change not seen before.

Past failures with similar initiatives.

Uncertainty of the change taking place.

Comfort with status quo and habits of the past.

Conflicting messages from management on change.

Not being part of the process change.

CHAPTER 13

1. Process controls need to be put in place to maintain the improvements made by the DMAIC process. We need to consider the type of controls that will be used to control the process and the measures. We can also configure the new step or different methods that are used in the process. The use of control charts and control plans can ensure that we monitor the new process. If changes occur, we will have a reaction plan to maintain the original gains made by the initial changes.

2. If we are not using the control chart to control the process because it has a very high capability, the control chart is not beneficial.

3. If the control phase of the DMAIC process is not used, we have a high chance of the implemented changes reverting back to the original steps. Then the level of performance will not be maintained and we have lost all the process gains.

4. The control plan must outline the steps to take to perform the measurement, how to take the measurement, and what should be controlled to maintain the process output to the requirements. The documentation of the control plan must be simple so that the operator easily understands how to use the control. During the controls phase, we can use the list of actions. The first item requires the team to put an action in place that will eliminate, or mistake-proof (Poka-Yoke), the process so the error will not occur in the first place. This level of action allows for a change that will eliminate the errors or the reason for the process variation. If we cannot eliminate the step in the process, or redesign the product to eliminate the material or component variance effects, the next approach is for the team to focus on a means of automating the process. If the technology or costs prohibit the automation of the process with automatic feedback, then we must at least notify the operator of the machine that the error has occurred and we will not process any more goods or services until it is corrected.

5. To maintain the improvements made by the DMAIC process, we need to consider the type of controls to use for the process and measures. We can also configure the new step or different methods that are used in the process. The Black Belt, as the change manager, needs to understand the project focus and work with the team, using team skills. This same Black Belt will need to know how to handle conflicts and how to resolve outstanding issues with the team. The art of negotiation and team facilitation will be required.

6. The control of implemented changes will require that we understand the process dominance factor for the effectiveness of the changes to be felt by the output. The dominance factor is what affects the output most. This dominance factor will be derived from the material used, the set-up of the process or the equipment, and the tooling within the equipment. Sometimes the operation will be dominated by the operator and his/her skills.

7. The Black Belt, as the change manager, needs to understand that the project focuses on teams and team skills. This Black Belt will also need to know how to handle conflicts and how to resolve outstanding issues with the team.

8. Self-control of the process occurs when the operator receives a message from an indicator about changes in the process condition and adjusts the process to maintain the controlled condition.

9. The Black Belts need good listening skills when implementing change to understand what resistance may exist. Critical to the communication process is the need for the Black Belts to become good listeners to ensure that they hear the facts from the resistors and the people who will help in the change process. This gives the Black Belts time to address the concerns and to counter the resistance with facts and information that will, we hope, overcome the resistance.

10. Poka-Yoke is the same as mistake-proofing a process. This will help eliminate the mistake or at least alert the operator when an error occurs.

CHAPTER 14

1. The financial returns must be greater than the time spent on the project, resources used, and capital investment put into the project. The best way to do this analysis is to perform an ROI on the project. The Black Belts must become familiar with the questions to ask when researching the sources of savings for the cost analysis. The accounting department will usually help in the cost analysis process. The management staff needs to know the financial as well as the process improvements that are being made during the project. Most financial departments should be satisfied with an ROI analysis based on incurred costs versus the annual savings realized from the project. Returns of 20 percent to 30 percent are not unheard of, and they can be greater once the Black Belts are running more projects.

2. The best way to show the results in the project is through the return on investment analysis. This analysis is best performed with the help of the professional financial personnel within the organization. The Black Belts should take counsel with the controller of the plant, or division, to arrive at the methods and the target numbers, which will prove out the gains of the project.

3. The Black Belt must take the lead in the project definition to provide the savings projection. The importance of the results must be stressed with the team. The Black Belt should take the lead in presenting this information.

4. The cost of quality consists of the following:

Cost to maintain customer needs

• Conformance

—Appraisal/audit

—Prevention

- Nonconformance

  —Redoing

  —Failure

5. The organization must not forget to address the recognition of and rewards for the projects completed by the Black Belts and Green Belts. This is required as part of this financial analysis pillar. The recognition will provide the needed motivation to continue the continuous improvement process. The organization now has the tough job of recognizing the successful efforts of the Black Belts and Green Belts. In the recognition process, we need to focus on teamwork success as well as the project success. The return on investment for the organization as a whole must be in the range of 15 to 25 percent or we are not using the skill level of the Black Belts and Green Belts properly.

6. The typical cost analysis approach will consider the total investment in the project and savings from the project. The savings must be verified by reducing the cost of producing the product, increased capacity to produce more products, or a reduction in overhead costs. All the savings must show up on the bottom line. Some economics to consider in the analysis of the project are: Black Belt, Green Belt, champion, and executive training costs; project time for the team; capital equipment needs; process change costs; project expenses and the personnel costs for the project. The savings in materials, reduced rework, or increased processing should offset the costs.

7. When first starting out, it should not be a problem for your Black Belts to provide a savings of $100,000 to $250,000 on the average project. So with 10 Black Belts, the total savings to the bottom line can be anywhere from $1 million to $2.5 million on an annual basis. If Black Belts can complete two to three projects per year, they can return millions of dollars to that bottom line.

8. The typical cost analysis approach will consider the total investment in the project and savings from the project. The savings must be verified by reducing the cost of producing the product, increased capacity to produce more products, or a reduction in overhead costs. All the savings must show up on the bottom line. Some economics to consider in the analysis of the project are: Black Belt, Green Belt, champion, and executive training costs; project time for the team; capital equipment needs; process change costs; project expenses; and the personnel costs for the project. Some areas to consider for the cost of quality are: The conformance costs will be audits, quality education, prevention methods, tests, verification, reviews, checking and inspection. The nonconformance cost areas will be: rework, reprocessing, retesting, retyping, expediting, inventory, down time, and warranty costs. The savings must offset the costs.

9. The cost areas to consider are given in the figure on page 278.

10. The gains of most projects consist of reduced rejects, increased throughput, increased capacity and, sometimes, increased market share. These process successes must be discussed but, let's face it, the project must save the

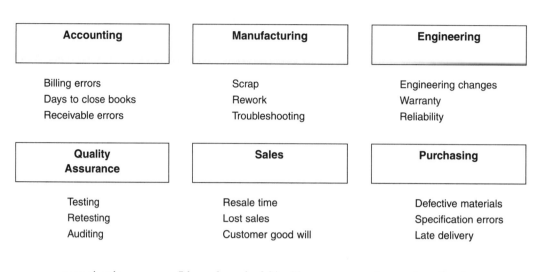

Accounting	Manufacturing	Engineering
Billing errors	Scrap	Engineering changes
Days to close books	Rework	Warranty
Receivable errors	Troubleshooting	Reliability

Quality Assurance	Sales	Purchasing
Testing	Resale time	Defective materials
Retesting	Lost sales	Specification errors
Auditing	Customer good will	Late delivery

organization money. I have heard of Six Sigma companies saying that they might have gone out of business if they had not followed this improvement process. This is a testimonial for Lean Six Sigma.

CHAPTER 15

1. The paradigms for Six Sigma that the management team must overcome are: process focused, strategic planning, customer focus, data and information focus, improvement focus, problem-solving process, cultural change, project selection process, data analysis, development of the knowledge worker, and teamwork environment.

2. The Black Belt will fill the knowledge worker position because of the knowledge base developed and the freedom that will come with this position. The people being trained within the organization become more familiar with the organization's processes and key business drivers, thus more valuable to the organization and knowledgeable about the organization. The Black Belts also become experts in problem-solving methods and understand the use of statistics in data analysis that is required to determine the direction to take to improve the process. This knowledge worker will help the organization improve the key processes, which will link to the key process measures and the operation's dashboard metrics. When this occurs, the industry, customer, and company knowledge will be used to meet or exceed customer expectations.

3. The move to a process-focused organization is a difficult change for some organizations. Two reasons for this difficulty are that the various departments are developed in a silo fashion and that we tend to focus on the discipline of the function such as materials, quality, and engineering rather than the process that needs to be accomplished. The discipline of the function gets lost in the process and is hard to maintain. My experience with this functional-to-process shift has been that the organization becomes more efficient and

customer focused, but the needs of the discipline are lost. The way we overcame the discipline loss was to create task groups that shared the movements and ideas of the discipline in a committee or association format.

4. The establishment of measures for the organization's dashboard and the key processes is critical to the success of the Six Sigma improvement process. Most organizations have measures, but we must make sure that they are the right measures to achieve the organization's strategic goals and the goals of the Black Belt projects. Some organizations find that keeping and tracking these measures is a new paradigm. Measuring key indicators for success means that the dashboards must align with the goals of the organization from the strategic plan and with the process measures and departmental measures.

5. We do not need to create committees for all the functions, but a corporate-level quality or materials function might keep up with the discipline and involve all of the other process personnel to keep them in tune with the functional disciplines and the changes occurring within them. Then the process-focused team will become part of the process and not lose the concepts of the functional disciplines.

6. The knowledge worker will become the logical and analytical thinker who will help improve operations and customer satisfaction. To fulfill this position, data will be required from the customers, marketplace, and key processes. We must be patient enough to allow this person to grow and learn the proper tool set and the right characteristics to control the key processes and business drivers.

7. If we are not selecting the right projects, we will be improving the wrong processes, and the bottom-line results or ROI we expected will not be obtained. The right projects will align with the strategic plan, and this requires that the Black Belt have access to the plan.

8. The organization does need to change from function focused to process focused to implement the Lean Six Sigma process.

9. Key processes must be improved, and success will depend on the amount of improvement that will be made. These processes will align with the business goals.

10. Some other paradigms to consider for Lean Six Sigma implementation are results orientation, skilled team players, and business process knowledge.

11. The cultural issues will probably be in the areas of process focus, measurements, and their evaluation with the focus on results. The organization must consider its present culture and the culture required to implement and support the continuous improvement Six Sigma process. This means that the present culture must be recognized and the new culture required to support the process.

12. The executive team needs to take the lead in ensuring that the cultural change shifts to these new paradigms.

13. The key business drivers and key processes are addressed when the Malcolm Baldrige National Quality Award Criteria are implemented and the key processes will be derived from the customer and quality house.

14. The awareness training and changing the reward system within the organization will help overcome the paradigm shifts.

15. Most problems and issues with the improvement process will require the use of cross-functional teams, which require facilitation and guidance.

CHAPTER 16

1. Black Belts become very knowledgeable about the key processes of the organization. They learn how the processes are measured and how the inputs to the process must be controlled. Having the problem-solving skills, the knowledge of statistics, and the data requirements to gain information and key measures, Black Belts will become the new knowledge workers for that particular process, product, or service. The communication process of a Black Belt becomes critical for the success of the projects. The knowledge gained about the marketplace and customers as well as the processes of the business leads to success.

2. The Black Belt soon becomes the expert on a process used for specific products or services. Using the lessons learned from Black Belt training, the Black Belt can improve the process and put the proper controls in place to maintain consistent output. The organizations that implement the Six Sigma approaches must be sure that the Black Belt selection process will support the knowledge worker concept.

3. The more process, business, and market information that the Black Belts gain, the more dependent the organization will become on them to use the information to improve operations and customer satisfaction. The best data I can find on this subject say that most Black Belts are in demand by various service and manufacturing industries to support their operations. The best approach for an organization is to grow their own knowledge workers. The need for knowledge workers is even broadening into the healthcare and education fields. This knowledge is required for the Six Sigma process and is the reason for the successful projects.

4. If the organization keeps improving processes using the Black Belt's projects, they will become the process experts for all processes across the organization. The selection process for the Black Belt becomes critical for project success. They will become the knowledge workers of the organization and must have the skills and abilities of leadership and management as well as technical capability.

5. If the Black Belt has the proper attitude and aptitude, the projects taken on will succeed, the Black Belt will learn, and soon the individual becomes the subject matter expert to the organization. The challenge to the organization is

how to keep this person happy and challenged. The career path becomes a necessity.

6. The knowledge worker is a natural tie to the Six Sigma Black Belt concepts. The Black Belt who works full time as the problem locator, problem solver, and change agent will be an asset to the organization and himself or herself. If the Black Belt has the proper attitude and aptitude, the projects taken on will succeed and the Black Belt will soon become the subject matter expert to the organization. The Black Belt criteria must be developed to select the leadership and manager skills for the projects.

7. The Black Belt who becomes the knowledge worker of the next century will require certain skills, abilities, and the drive to succeed. This person will have to want to learn and apply different skills required of the key processes of the business. The desire to learn, improve the operations, and serve the customer will help the person succeed in Six Sigma and at the organization. There may be many avenues to success within the organization, and the Black Belt will have the knowledge to succeed in any of them. Choosing the Black Belt becomes a challenge for the organization.

8. The knowledge worker concepts should be started at the start of the Lean Six Sigma program.

9. The knowledge worker requires knowledge of business systems, the market for the products, the customer's needs, the processes, and the people skills.

10. The knowledge worker position can be filled by comparing the list of requirements to the person's skills. They are:

- Logical thinker

- Computer literate

- Good statistical thinker and analyzer

- Desire to improve the status quo

- Leadership skills

- Stay-with-it attitude

- Lots of energy

- Open-minded individual

- Good communicator

- Good listener

- Team player

- Respected by peers

- Company loyalty

- Desire to learn

- Good engineering fundamentals
- Good negotiator
- Knowledge about the business

CHAPTER 17

1. We find that manufacturing organizations spend most of their time looking at internal process variation, using statistical tools to find, understand, and control variation. The service industry can also improve processes, using measurement systems analysis, run charts, frequency plots, Pareto analysis, as-is and should-be mapping, capability analysis, and solutions matrixes. The selection of tools to use differs, based on complexity of the industry. If you review the listing of subjects in Chapter 7, you will note that many of the tools are used in a sequential problem-solving process. Therefore, more tools will be used as the processes become more complex. The transactional situations for most services will use less of the tool set than complex manufacturing, development, and testing processes. The service industry is usually working with the discrete data of several transactions. The tools used will move toward the discrete side, such as P and C charts for defectives and defects. The measurement systems analysis will require that we use the Kappa or attribute method of analysis.

2. The cost of quality will show areas of opportunity for project selections and help with the financial justification of the project.

3. The selection of tools to use differs, based on complexity of the process in any industry. More tools will be used as the processes become more complex. Transactional situations for most services will use less of the tool set than complex manufacturing, development, and testing processes.

4. The tools that could be used for not-for-profit organizations are:
   - Voice of the customers
   - Cost of quality
   - Quality function deployment
   - Affinity diagrams
   - Process as-is map
   - Run charts or time charts of data over time
   - Histograms or frequency charts for the picture of variation for continuous data
   - Measurement systems analysis
   - Control charts for discrete and continuous data
   - Lean waste concepts
   - Tree diagram
   - Sampling plans

- Cause-and-effect analysis
- Chi-square tests
- Lean demand flow concepts
- Measuring results
- The should-be process map
- Lean five S's and SMED concepts
- Documentation and change process
- Training
- New methods to the process

5. The government would also be able to use this set of tools from the Lean Six Sigma approach. Most of the processes would be transactional, so they would align with the service industries.

6. Because these tools are generic, they may fit any industry. They would be used only to resolve the problems of cycle time reduction and variation reduction.

7. The service industry uses mostly discrete data because most of the processes are transactional.

8. The tool set has been established for Six Sigma and lean because they provide discipline to resolving problems.

9. The lean tool set considers the seven areas of waste, lead time of the process, value stream mapping of the process, SMED, TPM, the five S's, and error-proofing the process.

10. The Black Belt determines which tool to use by evaluating the data needs, the problem definition, the customers needs, the current issues with the process, and the analysis of the data.

CHAPTER 18

1. The first obvious potential failure to any program is lack of the executive management team's support and understanding of the process. This also applies to Six Sigma and its concepts for improvement. The executive team must be fluent in the Six Sigma process and its technical tools to be able to support the tasks in the process. Knowledge of the Six Sigma process and its implementation requirements will help produce successful teams and projects. The executive team must support this process to succeed in the improvement of key processes. All executives should participate in at least a one-day overview training and should strongly consider the three- to four-day champion training. Another area for potential failure is the definition of the project problem based on the project selection during the define stage. The Black Belt needs to articulate the project scope and problem definition to be able to set the direction for the data collection phase of the project. Sometimes this articulation is not

completed well and we need to redefine the project later as we collect more data.

2. The understanding of the Six Sigma process by the executive team is required, as well as support and commitment. The benefit is improved operation results and thus rewards. The continuous improvement and problem-solving process must be integrated into the organization, and this can be accomplished only by executive involvement in the process and commitment to support the process. Some organizations are starting to see some dropoff of the support because of a lack of patience and understanding of the improvement process.

3. Sometimes the Black Belt is not able to readily obtain the necessary data for the project. The data is not available or is difficult for the Black Belt to retrieve. Some projects drag on because of the lack of accurate and reliable data. Most information systems and metrology personnel can help in this area. The data collection processes becomes important in the define, measure, and analyze phases of the DMAIC process.

4. Without alignment of the objectives and goals of the organization to the strategic plan, these projects are given low priority by middle managers who want to see improvement in their specific areas. This sometimes leads to projects being selected in order to please an individual or department need. This can lead to poor alignment of projects and low return on investments. The executive team must be involved with the decision process for the Six Sigma process improvements to occur.

5. Another area for potential failure is the definition of the problem based on the project selection during the define stage. The Black Belt needs to articulate the project scope and problem definition to be able to set the direction for the data collection phase of the project. Sometimes this articulation is not completed well and we need to redefine the project later as we collect more data. The availability of resources is usually the reason for data issues. The project charter should contain a one-sentence problem definition, the goals and objectives that will be achieved, the measures required, the resources needed, and an outline of the plan.

6. When the executive team changes for any reason, the Six Sigma commitment should be revisited to check for any lack of support. This is when more executive involvement is required. The executive team needs to follow projects for execution and required help. The biggest challenge is to obtain the executive team involvement with the planning, selection of projects and Black Belts, and the training required for them.

7. The Black Belt may also fail to apply the proper tools in any phase, but especially in the analysis phase. This means that the causes of the problem are not really resolved. This is especially true if special causes are present for the process under study by the team. The application of the Black Belt tools must be reviewed on specific projects to ensure that Six Sigma tools are properly applied. The data also may not be displayed properly, failing to show patterns that will lead to potential causes. This may require using several tools until we can learn something from the data.

8. One of the biggest problems that may be experienced is the amount of time that the Black Belt needs to uncover the potential problem areas to provide for a successful project completion. If the resources and time are not made available to the Black Belt team, the project will take longer than anticipated to complete the results and the return on investment anticipated will be lower. This can cause some project teams to lose enthusiasm for the improvements, and the Six Sigma effort can ebb. To succeed, we need to spend enough time on the problem analysis to quickly identify areas of opportunity, find the root causes, and select the best solutions to resolve the issues in the problem statement.

9. All successful project completions should be provided with a celebration of some kind. Without some form of recognition we will have morale problems within the organization. We need to provide the recognition discussed in detail in Chapters 4 and 5. Recognition is important to the success of any effort, and especially to Six Sigma efforts because of the financial visibility that is brought into the picture during and at the end of the project. Without rewards, the effort might lose its effectiveness. Recognition does not have to be all financial, although that is nice. We can provide storyboards of projects in an open area for all the employees to observe.

10. If the organization does not select the knowledge workers of tomorrow as Black Belts, they will be looking at potential failures in the Lean Six Sigma implementation. A set of criteria that was discussed in Chapters 5 and 6 must be provided, and the candidates must be interviewed by the Six Sigma coordinator and some members of the executive council. If we fail to select the right Black Belt candidates, we will jeopardize the strategic plan and the success of the program.

CHAPTER 19

1. The knowledge worker will maintain customer focus, improve the key processes, improve the business processes, and find the future needs of the organization.

2. The financial costs and savings of the Six Sigma process will be captured and presented by the cost accounting department. The cost accounting department will work closely with the Black Belt to capture these costs.

3. The improvements for the projects will probably be documented by using the storyboard process for the executives. The financial review will take some of the following results. A small, $2 million to $10 million company would have savings opportunities of $100,000 to $1,000,000 if two or more Black Belts work on several projects during the start-up years. What this means is that two or three Black Belts working with five to ten Green Belts will allow the team to capture $100,000 to $1 million the first year and the next three years in a row. The problem for the small company is to support the use of full-time or part-time Black Belts devoted to the improvement of the process when they are needed to keep the present processes flowing. Project results should be

positive, and Green Belts should be supporting Black Belt projects and even taking on some of their own projects in their specific process areas. The executive team should observe that key indicators of the dashboard are continuously improving. The employees should see fewer process hassles and more process consistency. People should start asking to learn more about the Six Sigma way and show signs of concern for the processes and meeting customer's needs. The operations personnel should recognize how the process measurements affect customer needs and, in turn, customer satisfaction.

4. If the alignment of the projects to the objectives and goals is achieved, the reduction in waste, increased capacity, and improved planning will lead to better bottom-line profitability.

5. Sometimes smaller organizations will have the benefit of seeing the savings hit the bottom line sooner and can easily justify two to three full-time Black Belts from the start. The major difficulty for these smaller organizations is the implementation of the Malcolm Baldrige National Quality Award Criteria to run the business. The part-time Black Belt position should work for small companies. It is usually seen that the use of full-time Black Belts will return five to ten times their salary in a year.

6. The best improvement occurs when full-time Black Belts have taken projects that provide savings of $100,000 to $250,000 for medium to large organizations with somewhat complex processes. My definition of "medium to large" is more than 500 employees. The organization can be a low-cost, high-quality producer in your market. If you can maintain this new level of performance, you will have the edge to fend off new competition and prevent it from eroding your market share. The improvement indicators that should be seen are:

- Profitability increases

- Capability increases

- Higher inventory turns

- Lower employee turnover rates

- Improved lead times

- Increased throughput

- Increased customer satisfaction

- Increased sales

- Improved responsiveness

- Increased market knowledge

- Increased competitiveness

- Increased capacity

7. A $2 million to $10 million company would have savings opportunities of $100,000 to $1 million if two or more Black Belts work full time on several

projects during the start-up years. What this means is that two or three Black Belts working with five to ten Green Belts will allow the team to capture $100,000 to $1 million the first year and possibly the next three years in a row. The problem for the small company is to support the use of full-time or part-time Black Belts devoted to the improvement of the process when they are needed to keep the present processes flowing.

8. It is usually seen that the use of full-time Black Belts will return five to ten times their salary in a year. This may be hard to support at first for the small organization. The key is to obtain the Black Belt training at a public course or to find the training at one of your key suppliers. The part-time process will provide slower results from the process improvements made. We can save millions of dollars for an organization that has a billion dollars in gross sales. General Electric started to save as much as $1 billion after operating in the Six Sigma mode for five to seven years.

9. The DMADVIC process will start the proactive Six Sigma process by designing new products that are robust and at the Six Sigma level of performance.

10. The executive team must provide support by focusing on the processes that need to be improved and the level of the dashboard indicators that must be achieved. The dashboard indicators should be visited during the champion training. Remember, the opportunity for most organizations is 10 percent to 20 percent savings from gross sales. This savings will come from manufacturing, support processes, and eventually from suppliers. The dashboard indicators will also improve based on the project selection process. The integration of the Twelve Pillars into the organization will provide for the foundation and processes to continually improve and maintain improvements for the long haul. If your organization realizes a billion dollars in gross sales, you have the potential to save $100 million to $200 million with the Twelve Pillars to support the Six Sigma philosophy. The executive team needs to work with the Six Sigma coordinator to ensure that the project selections will allow these savings to occur.

CHAPTER 20

1. Our task is to evaluate and try to predict whether the revolution of Six Sigma is moving our organization in the right direction and whether the Six Sigma philosophy is taking hold for continuous improvement to take place. We are searching for a cultural change within the organization. The best measure of success is the knowledge level of the Lean Six Sigma concepts within the organization and process variation within the process. The organization must see bottom-line profit results tied to the Black Belt projects.

2. The Six Sigma coordinator should be establishing a process for routine evaluation of Six Sigma knowledge, customer and process knowledge, and financial results realized from the projects. The executive council should be evaluating the overall success of the program by asking questions about the

skill levels of the Black Belts and the skills themselves chosen to be applied to the projects. They should also be evaluating whether the Green Belts are being used to help the Black Belts and whether the Green Belts are taking on their own projects as they apply to their jobs directly. If we cannot achieve a savings from these projects, we are not on track with the project selection process. The problem definition and selection process by the Black Belts is not effective or the champions are not effective if the projects are not a success at the end. The project charter development in the define phase should have been developed with the champion and the process owner. This process may not be working because of difficulties in the definition or the support provided to the Black Belt.

3. The executive champion may not be providing the support and reviewing the results of the process. The organization may need to find another champion for the process. The Six Sigma coordinator needs to obtain management's attention by reviewing the evaluation of the program with them.

4. The DFSS process will allow for proactive action to take place for the Six Sigma program. This will ensure that new releases will be at or near the Six Sigma level.

5. Management reviews the process of Six Sigma by walking around the organization, observing the process, questioning the employees to determine the knowledge level, and listening to the understanding of the Six Sigma process. This walk-through will allow management to see whether the Six Sigma philosophy is understood and whether process improvements are occurring.

6. The Twelve Pillars concepts should be evaluated by the Six Sigma coordinator. We are searching for a cultural change within the organization. The best measure of success is the knowledge level of the Lean Six Sigma concepts within the organization and process variation within the process. The organization must see bottom-line profit results tied to the Black Belt projects.

7. The Six Sigma coordinator, along with the executive champion of the process, should evaluate the process. The executive team or council should review the evaluation.

8. We should not perform this Six Sigma evaluation until the program has been in place for about one to two years and all the awareness training has been completed. The best approach for this evaluation is the use of a survey or questionnaire performed at the management level.

9. The training and consulting effectiveness needs to be evaluated. Effective training will produce people who have learned a skill that can be applied to everyday use. If you think about it, the learning process exposes a person to an act or activity that can be used to make it easier to perform a job. We invest in the future by using a new investment method, save costs on an existing process, or improve upon a situation with a new method. The learning process should be evaluated by testing the student and following up on the application of the skills learned. The application review might involve

reviewing a project or observing a task to determine if the method is understood and being used properly. The point here is that all Lean Six Sigma training should be evaluated by reviewing a set of test results during training and on-the-job evaluation of application of the new methods or tools after training is completed.

10. The accounting department should be in charge of the final financial review and the executive council should review the success of the project improvement. If you are not receiving 20 percent to 30 percent return on the investment in the training, consulting, and project resources, then the process may not be as effective or as efficient as it can be for the program. The financial department must support the results and be able to defend the results.

CHAPTER 21

1. The lean organization will focus on the following activities or steps in some fashion and not necessarily in any given sequence:

   - Customer value analysis

   - Push system analysis

   - Pull system implementation

   - Waste analysis

   - Production activities analysis

   - Lead time analysis

   - Takt time analysis

   - Material flow analysis

   - Motion study

   - Transportation study

2. The waste concepts of lean focus on the process wait times, rework or unneeded process steps, unneeded motion, transportation, and inventory builds in work in progress (WIP) and final inventory. The areas of waste are generally in a production facility. Sometimes the lean people call these the seven sins of waste.

3. Lead time begins when we purchase raw materials to meet the customer's demands and ends when we deliver the product or service to the customer. Sometimes we indicate that lead time does not end until the customer has paid us for the delivered product or service. Lead time, then, is the true measure of the organization's ability or capability to produce the product in the shortest time possible and then deliver it to the customer and be paid for it.

4. When a value stream flow is put together, the connections of all the factors are identified and used to spot non-value-added steps. The organization needs

to understand the entire flow of material, product, information, and handling. This will allow the personnel performing the value mapping process to determine what is needed to produce the product and where opportunities exist to improve cycle time and to reduce waste that affects the costs of producing the product.

5. The Kaizen approach considers the following major items:

    • Just-in-time production system

    • Total quality control

    • Policy deployment

    • Suggestion systems

    • Total productive maintenance

    • Small team activities

6. Takt time = available daily production time (required daily quantity of output from customer demand).

7. If we produce ahead of the takt time, we are making product for inventory or we are overproducing product. If the value stream is not producing to takt time, we need to investigate the causes.

8. The five S's are: *sort* the area so items are arranged in order to be identified and seen quickly, *shine* or clean the area of clutter for better efficiencies, *set* the tools and materials in order to be found quickly, *standardize* the process steps and materials where possible, and *sustain* the standards.

9. Visual management means that when problems are detected, we need to show them to the team and help manage them. The results of the line or process should be displayed as well as the mistakes or errors. The standards should also be posted, and the targets for the operation and process should be visible for the operators. If the personnel know what the targets are, you will eventually hit the targets for the process and the operation.

10. The points to consider when implementing a one-piece flow system for manufacturing are:

    • Simplify the flow of materials.

    • Make sure that the materials and product move in the same direction.

    • Locate equipment for ease of maintenance.

    • Eliminate non-value-added steps in the process.

    • Use FIFO inventory stocking.

    • Arrange the piece parts for ease of entry into production.

    • Locate the steps in the process as close together as possible.

    • Make sure all the work areas and walkways to the assembly areas are clear and easy to get around.

- Material input and output operations should be separated.

- All parts need to flow through the process in the processing sequence.

- Maximize the operator's and equipment's productivity by shaping the line for efficiency.

- Allow space in the production layout for full inspection of the materials and equipment that will be used to produce the product.

- Minimize work in process.

- Cross-train the operators to use equipment up and down the line from the piece of equipment they are presently running.

CHAPTER 22

1. Lean has some basic tools the practitioner can use to improve process throughput in the organization and reduce waste within the processes. Both lean and Six Sigma are the tactical tools that the organization can use to improve the business processes defined within the Baldrige Criteria. So if you implement lean without Six Sigma, you will improve the flow to the point where the defects stop the process flow or create a bottleneck. Application of the Six Sigma principles will help resolve the defect or problems within the process by reducing variation that is causing the delay, bottleneck, or stoppage. Lean concepts watch for muda (waste) in the process and apply the principles of the five S's and Kaizen to align the process steps in sequence with the least amount of movement by hand, using mistake-proofed designs and assembly methods with no or minimum set-ups and delays.

2. One way to look at the seven criteria of the MBNQA is that the first three categories help the organization define what business it is in and what it is doing in the marketplace. The planning process in category 2 takes the market information and customer information from the leadership in categories 1 and 3 and integrates them into the organization's strategic plan. Category 2 covers the organization's planning process. The executive team will lead the organization in the proper direction if the concepts of the first three categories are followed. This integrates well with the first seven pillars of the Twelve Pillars to Six Sigma process support. If you follow the process, category 7, which provides the results, will show improvement in your key indicators and proof they are going in the right direction. The key processes are improved to meet the customer needs, which are well defined when using the Baldrige Criteria.

3. The executive team will lead the organization in the proper direction if the concepts of the first three categories are followed. This integrates well with the first six pillars of the Twelve Pillars to Six Sigma process support. From categories 1, 2, and 3, the leadership team must develop the strategic plan for the organization. Input for the strategic plan is derived from category 1, which examines the leadership system that monitors the organization, the

market, and most external sources of information. Category 3 provides customer input into the planning process when category 2 is used to develop the strategic plan. The output of these three categories provides the direction that the organization must take to succeed in the near-term and long-term future.

4. Lean uses the following concepts, which integrate well with the Six Sigma approach:

   • The just-in-time process system

   • SMED (single minute exchange of die)

   • Total productive maintenance

   • One-piece flow of product

   • Kanban systems

   • Pull systems

   • Kaizan implementation

   • Autonomation

   • Safety

   • Standardization

   • Production leveling

   • Value stream mapping

5. The five S's of lean (sort, set in order, shine, standardize, and sustain for the process) help the organization establish more repeatable and efficient outputs.

6. Preventive maintenance of the process is another way of identifying the potential problem areas and preventing downtime of equipment the same way you change your oil and lubricate your automobile to keep it performing properly. If maintenance is performed per the manufacturer's specifications within the recommended time frame and usage requirements are observed, the equipment will continue to perform to the specifications of the process needs. If we abuse the maintenance program, something will wear more, interact with other factors, and cause the performance of the process to change. Total productive maintenance uses some of the advanced techniques to monitor processes during routine maintenance to note any changes that may lead to performance issues. It is my impression that a good TPM process should be established ahead of Six Sigma, and lean is part of the design team's responsibility.

7. Lean would not apply to DMADVIC because we would be designing a product or process to function within a continuous flow process from the start.

8. The Malcolm Baldrige National Quality Award and Lean Six Sigma processes should be implemented and guided by the champions of the executive staff.

9. Any one of the lean, Six Sigma, or Malcolm Baldrige National Quality Award Criteria can be implemented separately and still show benefit to the organization, but they are limited until we see the total plan, determine the key processes, and apply the tactical tools to improve them.

10. Category 7 of the Malcolm Baldrige National Quality Award will show the results of improvements on product performance and the financial improvements for the projects that are implemented.

Appendix B

Minimum Level of Tools for Phases in the Twelve Pillars of Six Sigma

STEP	Definition	Tools
Define	Define the problem, charter for the project, and the gains to be obtained by the project.	Five whys data collection process, macro flowcharting, brainstorming and negotiation skills, critical to quality characteristics, voice of the customer, quality function deployment, affinity diagram
Measure	Obtain the present information about the process under study. Determine the process stability.	Check sheets, data collection methods, activity flowcharting, measurement systems analysis, run charts of data, frequency plots, Pareto charts, process sigma level, Shewart charts, DPMO level, process yield, rolled throughput yield, tree diagram, five whys, capability analysis
Analyze	Develop the statistical data to understand the variation in the process and which contributes the most to the output variation. Determine the process capability.	Frequency distribution chart, Pareto, flowchart analysis, cause-and-effect analysis, sampling techniques, normality test, run chart, control chart, capability analysis, scatter plot, multi-vari charts, correlation, regression, cross-tabulation, chi-square, z-test, t-test, ANOVA, DOE, response surface analysis, Taguchi analysis
Evaluate	Root cause verification.	t-test, regression analysis, ANOVA, Pareto analysis, scatter plots
Compare	Evaluate the changes made to the original data to ensure the cause selected will improve the process.	t-test, regression analysis, ANOVA, Pareto analysis, scatter plots
Improve	Select one solution and implement it.	DOE, surface response, EVOP, t-test, ANOVA, multiple regression, solution matrixes, implementation plan, mistake-proofing, FMEA
Control	Ensure that the new improvements to the process will be maintained.	Control charts, new methods, new equipment, training, new procedures
Evaluate	Compare the original measures with the new process improvements to verify the success of the changes made during the improvement process.	t-test, regression analysis, ANOVA, Pareto analysis, scatter plots, control charts, new methods, new equipment, training, new procedures

Endnotes

CHAPTER 1

1. Peter F. Drucker. *Management Challenges for the 21st Century.* New York: HarperCollins, 1999.

2. Fred R. David. *Strategic Management,* 6th ed. Upper Saddle River, NJ: Prentice Hall, 1997.

CHAPTER 3

1. Robert Ricci. *Quality Progress.* November 2003.

2. Fred R. David. *Strategic Management,* 6th ed. Upper Saddle River, NJ: Prentice Hall, 1997.

3. Peter F. Drucker. *Management Challenges for the 21st Century.* New York: HarperCollins, 1999.

4. Caroline Fisher and James T. Schutta. *Developing New Services: Incorporating the Voice of the Customer into Strategic Service Development.* Milwaukee, WI: ASQ Quality Press, 2003.

CHAPTER 4

1. Peter F. Drucker. *Management Challenges for the 21st Century.* New York: HarperCollins, 1999.

CHAPTER 5

1. Fred R. David. *Strategic Management,* 6th ed. Upper Saddle River, NJ: Prentice Hall, 1997.

2. Robert S. Kaplan and David P. Norton. *Strategy Maps.* Boston: Harvard Business School Press, 2004.

3. Robert C. Camp. *Benchmarking.* Milwaukee, WI: ASQ Quality Press, 1989.

4. Douglas P. Mader. "The DFSS Project Selection Process." *Quality Progress,* July 2004.

CHAPTER 7

1. Caroline Fisher and James T. Schutta. *Developing New Services: Incorporating the Voice of the Customer into Strategic Service Development.* Milwaukee, WI: ASQ Quality Press, 2003.

2. Dr. Shigeo Shingo. *Zero Quality Control: Source Inspection and the Poka-Yoke System.* Cambridge, MA: Productivity Press, 1986.

CHAPTER 8

1. Caroline Fisher and James T. Schutta. *Developing New Services: Incorporating the Voice of the Customer into Strategic Service Development.* Milwaukee, WI: ASQ Quality Press, 2003.

2. R. B. Woodruff and S. F. Gardial. *Know Your Customer: New Approaches to Understanding Customer Value and Satisfaction.* Cambridge, MA: Blackwell Publishers, 1996.

3. Griffin A. Hauser and J. R. Hauser. "The Voice of the Customer." Marketing Science Institute, Working Paper Report 92-106, 1992.

CHAPTER 9

1. Caroline Fisher and James T. Schutta. *Developing New Services: Incorporating the Voice of the Customer into Strategic Service Development.* Milwaukee, WI: ASQ Quality Press, 2003.

2. Ronald G. Day. *Quality Function Deployment: Linking a Company with Its Customers.* Milwaukee, WI: ASQ Quality Press, 1993.

CHAPTER 12

1. R. B. Woodruff and S. F. Gardial. *Know Your Customer: New Approaches to Understanding Customer Value and Satisfaction.* Cambridge, MA: Blackwell Publishers, 1996.

CHAPTER 13

1. Dr. Shigeo Shingo. *Zero Quality Control: Source Inspection and the Poka-Yoke System.* Cambridge, MA: Productivity Press, 1986.

2. Rosabeth Moss Kanter. *Confidence.* New York: Crown Business, 2004.

CHAPTER 16

1. Peter F. Drucker. *Management Challenges for the 21st Century.* New York: HarperCollins, 1999.

CHAPTER 20

1. George Eckes. *The Six Sigma Revolution.* New York: John Wiley & Sons, 2001.

2. Dr. Genichi Taguchi. *Introduction to Quality Engineering.* White Plains, NY: UNIPUB/Quality Resources, 1986.

3. Phillip J. Ross. *Taguchi Techniques for Quality Engineering.* New York: McGraw-Hill, 1988.

4. Patrick Northey and Nigel Southway. *Cycle Time Management.* Portland, OR: Productivity Press, 1993.

CHAPTER 21

1. Masaaki Imai. *Gemba Kaizen.* New York: McGraw-Hill, 1997.

2. Dr. Shigeo Shingo. *Zero Quality Control: Source Inspection and the Poka-Yoke System.* Cambridge, MA: Productivity Press, 1986.

3. Patrick Northey and Nigel Southway. *Cycle Time Management.* Portland, OR: Productivity Press, 1993.

APPENDIX A

1. Ronald G. Day. *Quality Function Deployment: Linking a Company with its Customers.* Milwaukee, WI: ASQ Quality Press, 1993.

Index